A Turbulent Life ? ? ?

Grace Boykin

Copyright © 2023 Grace Boykin
All rights reserved
First Edition

PAGE PUBLISHING
Conneaut Lake, PA

First originally published by Page Publishing 2023

ISBN 979-8-88793-394-8 (pbk)
ISBN 979-8-88793-411-2 (digital)

Printed in the United States of America

This book is dedicated to: My loved ones and those who are in heaven, family and friends.

Robby Boykin (heavenly brother who died at age thirty-nine) was a graduate of languages in Tulane University, a photographer for *American Horseman* and *American Dog* magazine, had a high IQ, and was smart and giving.

Weslee Sheaffer (heavenly son who died at age thirty-two) was a graduate of public relations in University of Florida. Brave! He fought medulloblastoma, meningioma, and glioblastoma brain cancers at age sixteen, was a paraprofessional, and became a teacher in public high school. He taught physical education and swimming with his wife, taught girls in the jail system, and was loved by all who knew him.

Jason Sheaffer is a graduate with a BS degree in business from the University of Phoenix, family man, dedicated father to a son and daughter, hard worker since age sixteen, disciplined, handyman, giving, and has had many hardships that he took in stride with love of the Lord.

Valerie Sheaffer is a smart, giving, and solid worker and Christian, and it shows in all she does.

Boykin Sheaffer is an intuitive grandson, candlemaker, rock polisher, and sculpture. He likes U2 videos and playing interactive video games. He is a good listener and tries to please all.

Veda Sheaffer is a horse-loving granddaughter, who is brave beyond belief from a life-threatening dog attack. She is timid and loves her daddy, brother, and Valerie.

Anna Olson (Hannah) is a helper in lending a hand to all in need and diligent at her work and her family, Nick and Rick. Hannah is the newest member of the family born in December of 2022.

Frank Boykin was a hardworking, heavenly grandfather.

James Robert Boykin was a bighearted, loving, dedicated, and honorable man in fulfilling all his obligations to others. He loved leaving tips with $2 bills as his father did with silver dollars.

Cora Lynn Boykin is a wise, smart, caring woman, who could tell a joke like no other.

Browder Rives had a refined, eloquent handwriting, who decorated for holidays, and had learned and taught the social graces to those open-minded and willing to learn. He also loved to dance.

Honorable Howard Rives was a loving, giving-till-it-hurt man, who was wise beyond his years. He respected and followed the law to a tee as a lawyer and in later years as a circuit court judge.

Riley Smith is a hunter, fisherman, and prosperous businessman, who continues making the family business successful for future generations and standing up for family in all surroundings.

Will Norton is wise beyond his years, successful in all works of life, trustworthy, and loving and giving to his family.

Dede, Jeep, and the entire Treft family are my childhood through adulthood friends. They are world travelers, successful in business, dedicated to their families, and would help anyone in need.

Helen Bivens is a sister in Christ, who is loyal and loving to her family to the point of jeopardizing her own health in life.

Ellen Davis is a caretaker to one with Alzheimer's and dementia, who provides nourishing, delicious food to neighbors and friends and heartfelt kindness to all in need.

A special thanks to all that purchase this book and have read it. Feedback would be very much appreciated, especially to those that can answer the questions in the introduction and throughout the book. You could be helping others face the turbulent tifmes and losses they have lived with and never shared and still living in the cobwebs throughout their brain and memories.

2022

Words of Wisdom

This autobiographical book of earth-shattering history opens the gates to memories that have never been realized, recognized, or open to the depths of the soul. Recalling memories with a traveling buddy and no finer of a friend and listening as one speaks and had begun to open the doors to unknown places enabled me to recall tragic memories. My listening and asking questions began to change my life in a positive way of learning my true inner self. Total recall was forgotten and behind the closed doors of my mental file cabinet that was slowly opening entries to my entire life. Until I was abducted!

This book can help the reader to cope, face, and forget the turbulent times throughout one's life and family in all levels of society. The cliché "mind over matter" is true when faced directly on, recognized, and dealt with by departmentalizing lifetime moments in your subconscious. Use your brain in effective ways of dealing with drama in one's life, sort them like a file cabinet mentally, never knowing when total recall will surface, and have the words shared to others who will listen or read about it.

Turbulence can affect your childhood and adulthood life at any given time. How does one learn to deal with those times? Learning when to keep emotions within and when you must let them out to someone is for your own safety, sanity, and good mental health. Recalling memories can help without holding them within, as this author has learned through personal experiences. I have found them to dissipate as I share with one or more people who listen with an open mind and may have had the same experiences in rendering me helpful advice. Voicing your opinion, good or bad, can help one communicate!

Elaborating on one's problems clearly and distinctly may help by wiping the slate clean of drama from their memory, as well as help another human to move on to the next chapter in one's life. A sounding board often responds with meaningful advice, which can be applied to the critical matter at hand. Helping one with a *turbulent life* can experience life to its fullest by traveling and facing failure and learning how to land on one's feet, but moving into the future is up to the individual. Deciphering good advice from unusable advice is learned by an individual in their own way and within their own time.

As the author, I have learned from my individual experiences what would help in deciphering good advice to apply to my own life. With insight, I have implemented ways to move forward with wisdom and unwavering clarity to know my true self. I am able to walk tall, feel good, and truly know who I am and to love myself, and help another to understand the pitfalls of one's life, whom you can immediately tell by their facial expressions, body language, and tone and affliction in their voices if they understood you or not. With responses, I was able to recognize people who felt sorry for me. Wallowing in self-pity is no way to live!

I don't know anyone who has not had turbulent times throughout their lives, and perhaps that is why they have been placed in my life. Learning, listening, writing, and maintaining an open and receptive mind when associating with friends has helped me as a writer recall and deal with some of the most turbulent and tragic days throughout my life and memories to dissipate from my subconscious mind.

As the author, I have found through writing, or rather it is shared with others through radio waves, TV, movie, e-book, audio, or print or just for therapeutic reasons, helps in dealing with one's crucial moments throughout adult life. To live my life with goals I have set for myself. I have realized life holds adventures and experiences at the least expected times during my life and to use my own judgment! In the past, others made decisions for me from childhood to adulthood, never letting me live my own life.

A TURBULENT LIFE ? ? ?

Live life to the fullest by making new goals and memories of what splendor one can experience. Enjoy, learn, laugh, and fulfill one's goals and wishes, which can be achieved in their current lifetime. With time, when I moved forward from isolation and lived in an apartment away from the life I once knew, I was living to the fullest! As an elderly adult, I finally set my achievable goals for myself. I was traumatized when taken from a life I had known of traveling to living alone in an apartment. I was encouraged by my traveling friend to write my autobiography, which I have found to be therapeutic. Tarasee involved my son, Bevo, to get his mother from where she was. He rented an apartment in his name on the lease without any knowledge to me. He took me to where I knew no one and away from a life I was living in harmony with God!

In order to know and be true to myself, I had to look from when my life began to know who I truly am in my senior years. Oneself can communicate by looking on the inside and outside oneself. Editing stories at age seventy about early childhood and past relatives history in learning my true self, I recaptured my character, mind, thoughts, and feelings of why I am this way and if I should change my ways. Past and present memories, I recaptured it into a computer with my keyboard once again. As I communicate and express myself through my writings, good or bad, I always know that it is through the eyes of the beholder to know one's true self. God helped me learn and communicate by looking into the depths for the discovery of my soul.

Abducted by the oldest in chronological years of the nicknamed "three stooges," I see my son and his family frequently. Bevo would visit almost daily as I was expecting furniture deliveries and other large items he had bought for me. I was able to exchange furniture I didn't care for and purchase what I liked. It was fun, and he was paid back from my funds. I, among others, question how long Tarasee, the controlling stooge, was planning to carry out the most devious act of one's abduction!

Many, many, questions… Will they ever be answered? One of the questions is what their motives were and why. Was money the root of all evil and the reason to change another person's life? The execution of abducting me was the lowest criminal and hurtful experience in my life to date! How and why would family members step so low and be so devious in planning one's abduction? The oldest stooge of a father and his second wife who I called Mimi. Tarasee has arrived, and it was often heard from cousins, friends, and family members when she played outside or would enter a room. Adults were heard saying, "The oldest controller of the three stooges has arrived!"

Who has the right to change one's life and vicariously live through another person's life? How devious is it for lying in a board meeting of Tarasee's trust to obtain money for herself and spread the lie written in the minutes that I was diagnosed with mental issues. Tarasee would come to destroy two joyful lives and believers of God in hopes to have an unsuspecting family member commit to a mental institution by way of abducting her. As the author, I still question the motive and real reason why she had to tell a documented lie and affect two people's lives forever. What reasonable answer does one have by saying, "It was to help you," when a person with all their mental faculties about them did not ask for help? The motion of uprooting me from a joyful life of seeing countryside through the states and the animals that roamed was an experience I will never forget. Animals I had never seen before (such as a wolverine that stopped on the road) and birds of many varieties were beautiful creatures, giving me a greater understanding, compassion, and knowledge in the differences of people's accents, customs, housing, modes of transportation, farming, weather, and terrains in the south, north, eastern, and western states. Was it God or the devil? The reader will need to decide the answers to these questions for themselves. This author passionately believes, as the saying goes, "Money and one's obsession to have power influencing other people's lives is the root of all evil!"

How sad it is to have one turbulent and tragic day throughout two lives to dissipate. Being so vindictive, vengeful, and hurtful to plot and destroy lives. Was it out of envy and jealousy? In one long-distance phone call to Gracie Lu, she said, "I want your life!" With her tone and affliction in her voice, I knew she meant what she said.

She needs to "learn to love as the Lord as he displayed it to us in his life on earth!" Then perhaps she will truly be happy and move forward in living her own joyful life in whatever way she chooses without getting into and ruining other lives. As the author of this book, I was able to recognize the behavior displayed by Tarasee. My mother lived vicariously through my life as her daughter and treated me as a best friend instead of an offspring, always sharing her thoughts and feelings to me as a young child, teenager, and adult. In praying to the Lord, she is in my prayers, hoping she will be able to move forward and not dwell on the past with her old photographs and videos of those family members entering her office at the family-owned company. She uses them in calendars and whatever other way to display the earlier years of her family's life. I hope one day, Tarasee's eyes and ears open to the willingness of understanding her own feelings, having the wisdom to know the qualities and interest that she chooses for herself and to pursue them. To make her leap of faith in living her own life in the future, she must leave her pain and past behind to move into the impending years.

The author poses the questions to all people who have purchased and read the book (in print or audio or heard about it from word of mouth, book signings, or at book clubs reviewing it) to get positive or negative feedback from the readers, especially from those who can answer all the questions asked throughout the book. It would be greatly appreciated, as you may be helping others who have experienced turbulence, horrors, and losses of loved ones throughout their years on earth to forgive and forget excruciating painful events and moments in their lifetime that could often prevent them from moving forward with one's own life and experiencing what all of life must hold.

Were memories of turbulent, tragic, painful, hurtful, sad, having losses of loved ones cause one to grieve and cause horror of making it too hard to recall? Or was it because of sharing the turbulent times throughout life with others and their witnessing it remind you of what you went through that made you stronger, with forgiveness to all that caused upheaval in your life to have a more fulfilled and joyful life with others?

2022

Training One's Mind to Forget the Tumultuous Lifetime of One's Horrors

Life may move at a snail pace or in a fast-paced environment. No matter what situation you are in, one learns to adapt by training your mind of what can or cannot be changed. Dealing with only the matters at hand! As the expression goes, "Let bygone be bygones." Always remember that in your adult years, family members, people near and far, are the ones who cannot live for themselves nor can ever be trusted. Helping one bury life's *turbulent life memories* in their subconscious mind and never to remember again is hard, but people can do it! If a tragedy occurs, recall a moment that your subliminal mind can remember and share it to your daughter, son, mother, father, clergy, psychologist, psychiatrist, friend or sisters in Christ, mentor to others, or readers. Turbulent life memories or drama can evaporate and never surface again with intense training and patience. Or is it the same with me, the author—finding myself alone and withdrawn, communicating through a keyboard and computer, and writing it down, as I never learned to express my thoughts from my informative years to adulthood and unable to orally express myself?

As the author, I have found that in helping others and sharing my turbulent life memories in return has helped me deal with a recollection of sad movies or recalling death situations. Learning to control one's sentiments can take a lifetime! I have found that memories can diminish, which I would recall or extrapolate from my subconscious mind and share it with others in order to help them. It could

A TURBULENT LIFE ? ? ?

out getting into and ruining other lives. As the author of this book, I was able to recognize the behavior displayed by Tarasee. My mother lived vicariously through my life as her daughter and treated me as a best friend instead of an offspring, always sharing her thoughts and feelings to me as a young child, teenager, and adult. In praying to the Lord, she is in my prayers, hoping she will be able to move forward and not dwell on the past with her old photographs and videos of those family members entering her office at the family-owned company. She uses them in calendars and whatever other way to display the earlier years of her family's life. I hope one day, Tarasee's eyes and ears open to the willingness of understanding her own feelings, having the wisdom to know the qualities and interest that she chooses for herself and to pursue them. To make her leap of faith in living her own life in the future, she must leave her pain and past behind to move into the impending years.

The author poses the questions to all people who have purchased and read the book (in print or audio or heard about it from word of mouth, book signings, or at book clubs reviewing it) to get positive or negative feedback from the readers, especially from those who can answer all the questions asked throughout the book. It would be greatly appreciated, as you may be helping others who have experienced turbulence, horrors, and losses of loved ones throughout their years on earth to forgive and forget excruciating painful events and moments in their lifetime that could often prevent them from moving forward with one's own life and experiencing what all of life must hold.

Were memories of turbulent, tragic, painful, hurtful, sad, having losses of loved ones cause one to grieve and cause horror of making it too hard to recall? Or was it because of sharing the turbulent times throughout life with others and their witnessing it remind you of what you went through that made you stronger, with forgiveness to all that caused upheaval in your life to have a more fulfilled and joyful life with others?

2022

Training One's Mind to Forget the Tumultuous Lifetime of One's Horrors

Life may move at a snail pace or in a fast-paced environment. No matter what situation you are in, one learns to adapt by training your mind of what can or cannot be changed. Dealing with only the matters at hand! As the expression goes, "Let bygone be bygones." Always remember that in your adult years, family members, people near and far, are the ones who cannot live for themselves nor can ever be trusted. Helping one bury life's *turbulent life memories* in their subconscious mind and never to remember again is hard, but people can do it! If a tragedy occurs, recall a moment that your subliminal mind can remember and share it to your daughter, son, mother, father, clergy, psychologist, psychiatrist, friend or sisters in Christ, mentor to others, or readers. Turbulent life memories or drama can evaporate and never surface again with intense training and patience. Or is it the same with me, the author—finding myself alone and withdrawn, communicating through a keyboard and computer, and writing it down, as I never learned to express my thoughts from my informative years to adulthood and unable to orally express myself?

As the author, I have found that in helping others and sharing my turbulent life memories in return has helped me deal with a recollection of sad movies or recalling death situations. Learning to control one's sentiments can take a lifetime! I have found that memories can diminish, which I would recall or extrapolate from my subconscious mind and share it with others in order to help them. It could be done with great concentration and extrapolating remembrances from my subconscious in a peaceful, quiet area, with no distractions, and in reoccurring dreams to enter my darkest memories. It was hard to deduce the turbulent memories I had shared with others and lost in my file cabinet deep within my mind. It is quite hard to move on with life with many of my memories that were unable to be shared with others for many years.

Unable to recall them readily, yet weeks later, I recalled a heartfelt event that presented itself and accepted the tragic, turbulent, and harmful effects to my health from the formidable years to adulthood. There are memories which I am unable to recall readily. Was it because I had already shared them to good listeners who offered meaningful and helpful advice? If anyone can answer the questions asked throughout the book, it would be greatly appreciated. Remember you may be helping yourself and others by responding to the questions. Your replies may also help you through the turbulent, tragic losses of loved ones, and situations you have faced or will face that are destructive to one wanting to carry on with life or those that live in the past.

2022

Illusions Can Often Be Truths

As I look up at the stars on a clear night, I realize it is not an illusion. Viewing with my eyes wide open and seemingly in focus is the vast magnificence of the universe that we are in the middle of and living in on earth.

Problems of the moment are often overwhelming and may last longer than a moment. As we speak and analyze ourselves, we see the visions that exist. One will experience a new thought or emotion as our moods change on a daily basis with some having never been named. With changes, one's emotions run high and low throughout a day.

One struggles with the challenges that can wake us up and often are insurmountable in one's thinking of them. It often feels as though my point of view on life is restricted as I focus on the ideas and reflections before me. Like the universe and the elements of weather and nature as the reactions, one faces and challenges on a daily basis. Considering as I look to understand the big picture of my life in its entirety, I find it impossible to do. At age seventy, it is hard to recall all the events of one's life.

Through courage, energy, and inspiration, I try to understand and move through the complexity of the problems. Thoughts are often cloudy as I get older but seemingly an important part of life in understanding and learning how to deal with my feelings. Families can be bitterly cold and icy toward their loved ones. I have witnessed stormy tirades where one loses all their emotions with raised voices (screaming, hollering obscenities) and out-of-control reactions of verbal and physical abuses. I find it hard to comprehend how I and numerous others can lose power over mind to not control their reactions. Emotions are hard to manage as a stormy weather on any given day. I can feel gloomy and weary, and tears can fall to the ground as if it is raining inside and outside with turbulent weather. Whirlwinds and turbulences cannot be ignored as if it is the calm before the storm. When a hurricane or fire hits with full force and all that is tangible is destroyed like memories in photographs, it is a part of myself. Yet strength to carry on comes from friends, sons and daughter, psychologists, doctors, neighbors, or as simple as a happy expression of a past loved one and a simple saying remembered as an understood statement. You rebuild your prospective on life as a tidal wave wipes one out. Then a turbulent tornado knocks the final blow and seemingly destroy one from the outside in.

I pick myself up and find the inner strength to carry on but lost in one's thoughts and struggles to see the brightness, living to help another as the best way through God. I was once a happy-go-lucky person, solemn in stature, and find the summers long, hot, and boring as life moves about.

The winter and cold have me chomping at the bit to walk fast and more energetic at a fast pace as I think positive thoughts of what to do today. With spring moving forward, I have less energy but able to see the beauty of nature all around us. In the fall, I seem to reflect on sights I have seen, making it harder to move on with my future. With God's blessings, we are in control of our own destiny. My thoughts can change at a whim as daily life upheavals have emotional moments such as a fall, a sickness, a loved one dying, or a reign of terror in the way of sickness and pain or from deceptions of one you come to know as a con. Once upon us, we can choose to have our eyes open or our eyes closed and continue through life with blinders on as I have done. I don't have the answer of why I was ignoring them till I can't anymore.

When the damage is done to one emotionally, it is often an up-and-down battle to repair. I cannot do it by myself, and the remedy for me is turning to God with my needs and in helping me to move forward. There is no rule as to how life affects everyone in different ways emotionally like twists and turns along the way, reading a book and turning the pages, or climbing mountains in an unseen pathway. It can affect families in all areas of life. As the universe moves on so must the family unit with love and understanding of all as the ultimate goal. Yet when broken, as mine had been, it is awfully hard to pick up the pieces and to trust one ever again. Now I am suspicious, not trusting, and can't ignore the sights and sounds of those who hurt me. Families come and go as it is destroyed by deceptions, lies, disbeliefs, sorrows, and unexplainable emotions that have no name, and one must learn to deal with. As each year passes, I find myself describing family interactions as tides in a sea, as each family member is different in looks, temperaments, and attitudes. Anger can reach points as the seas rise and fall as minutes pass in a given day. As the expression goes, blood is thicker than water, especially with ones you have birthed as sons and a daughter.

The successes of tomorrow are striving for that perfect fit, whether it be tangible or intangible. Having the intelligence, intuitiveness, stick-to-itiveness, and drive to carry on as one learns from their ancestors, even if one cannot understand what life has presented before them and not always followed or understand why an event took place, I move on with the fortunes I have learned from the knowledge of the Bible, books, and wisdom of others smarter than me.

My thoughts can be compared to a roller coaster as I have felt like I am on the edge of my seat, unable to operate on the straight and narrow, but dwelling in my past at times. With negative thoughts trying to interrupt my daily life, not always understanding the present and focusing on what's wrong rather than the future, perhaps this is the only way for the once a happy-go-lucky individual to learn every emotion there is, and some have probably no name to them, as the way to recognize myself.

One cannot go through life with the illusion of everything being right in the family or with life. The true meaning of the words *like* and *love* must become an intricate part of coming to like myself, therefore, being able to love others, knowing where I once came from and where I am going. One's success is often measured by accomplishments, goals, beliefs, and steadfastness. As my goal late in life, it is to become a best-selling author and help those in need!

2022

Eyes Wide Open and Blind

I have my eyes wide open, but they are closed and oblivious to the wrongs surrounding me. How can that be? Can it be that we are blinded by our past with people and events? Are our eyes controlled by our sentiments? Are tears of passion the way to answer the deep, darkest, depths of my soul? Perhaps with my trust and believing in God, the lights and colors will shine brightly in my eyes, allowing the intensity of sight in all actions of past, present, and future to see the outward and eternal devastation around me clearly with compassion and understanding. With clearness of mind and resolve to settle all the battles Satan has thrown at me, I must be in touch with my soul, heart, thoughts, and brain in bright, open conditions to uncap the most painful visions and eternal hurts in my life. Are these patterns ever in sync when turmoil is in our thoughts and surroundings? Does anyone have the answer? Who knows? Please answer.

    You can have purity of thoughts and happiness for years, but when something turns on the light in my mind that would trigger unresolved memories of my heart and soul, it would allow me to know just the destruction a Satan replica has caused in my life and within the family unit. Why do the innocent put so many barriers up before they can reach and understand the truth? Why does one inflict physical pain to themselves, leaving a permanent outward scar as well as the eternal scar? A mother's instinct is to protect all her children, and how could it happen that I didn't?

    How does one deal with an evil, dark heart that is consumed and entered the pure heart and soul, instilling havoc upon the innocent and lives of their family? Those that have opened their eyes partly, getting into focus on a daily basis, with eyes clear, do they ever try to communicate with the evil sinner, who does not know how to love or trust? They lie, they have no conscience, and they are deceitful. They are instilling hate in others, controlling, antagonizing, fighting, dominating, critiquing, and belittling others who did not come to their way of doing things or thinking. They are sinning on a daily basis by not coming in reality with one's sexual orientation, trying to manipulate those around them. One believes they are always right and never wrong by never saying the words out loud that they are sorry. With one possessing such behaviors, can you ever reason with them to admit they were wrong, having never said or believed within their soul or conscience that they were sorry? Do you turn to God to give you the strength to control your reactions, blood pressure, and walk away until you know those wicked qualities have completely disappeared from the premises, or do you confront your aggression?

How do I, as one who thought they were a loving, caring, and giving parent and later in life came to know they didn't have all the answers in parenting children, admit I was blind inside and outwardly acted as a puppet for much of my adult life. Perhaps I never faced reality until I had the courage to leave the one with devil-like characteristics as read from Bible verses.

As a parent, how do I help the victim who has been so traumatized? The parent, wishing they could turn back the hands of time, realized they could only go forward, but how? One day when the victim is ready, do you encourage them to prosecute the one who disguised themselves as a father but whose actions are evil? How do I prevent him from inflicting pain upon future grandchildren or others? How far did the abuse go, and will I ever know?

When's the right time to confront others who were possibly abused within the family? Being subtle and roundabout through the back door, should one open the path to knowing if one abused others in the family? Especially witnessing the eldest sibling being physically hit and bruised and thrown against walls not once but twice and maybe more, and when he slapped me in the face in my workplace, how and why did I not call the police? Why would one be so scared and afraid and not know the right thing to do, which was to call the police! Now knowing the youngest child was sexually abused, conned, and traumatized, the youngest child and mother got into counseling with a psychologist for years. Could the middle child have escaped the abuse, or did he? A mom must know to get him the counseling he needs. Face-to-face we must get into a truthful discussion. Can this be done? Who can do it other than the mother? Will the right words and time present themselves? I, with a heavy heart, come before God, who is the only way to righteousness, and I promise to help all involved with the abuse and to come to terms as well as to accept the truth that their father had done eternal damage. Their mother failed them in not having the strength to do what was right, with her eyes wide open, witnessing the physical abuse to her eldest son, by not calling the police? Not divorcing their father during the first or second time I visited an attorney, it was only on the third time that I had courage to proceed. I probably would have had all my children as they were young at that time.

The guilt is immense. How does one truly come to understand and learn how they could be so weak, always trying to avoid conflict? Now I am learning to face problems head on, yet asking unresolved questions. Will all come to terms with reality? Does the mother in certainty have the inner strength to face the issues before them? Please let the answers come as fluently as the questions came. So many questions, will they ever be answered with eyes and ears clear and open to understand all the answers? From a very confused, loving mother, who asks all involved to please forgive her for all her shortfalls and weaknesses, which is late in life, but now has the courage and strength to battle whatever forces the survivors see fit, with eyes more open than ever before. Just give us the wisdom to deal with it on a daily basis from those in heaven and those remaining on earth to truly follow the Lord with all his wisdom and guidance.

I knew that in order to write my autobiography, I had to step back in time and start with my grandparents on my mother Browder's side and aunts and uncles as well as on my father James's side and then to write of my parents, my brother Robby, my marriage, divorce, children, friends, and family-owned land company left as a legacy from my grandfather and grandmother Frank and others. My love of history seems to be the way for me to move forward in my older years, as looking back is the way of my future to move forward toward my final years on earth.

My Great-Grandparent and Grandparents on My Mother's Side

1800s and 1900s

My mother's side of the family didn't lead an exciting a life as my father's parents. They had a few dramatic adventures and turbulences in their lives. They were similar in backgrounds as my dad's parents were. My grandfather, who I would call Papa, had his own import-export lumber business to different countries. He had judges and lawyers in his family as well.

My great-grandfather on my mother's side was educated at Cumberland College in Missouri and was admitted to the bar in 1842. He served as Missouri Secretary of State from 1849 to 1853 and was elected as a Democrat from Ray County, Missouri. In 1857, he became Missouri attorney general.

He sat on the St. Louis Circuit Court in the election of 1870 and returned to the bench when he was elected as a judge of the St. Louis Circuit Court in the election of 1872. He was considered a liberal candidate to the court. He assumed office in 1872, but he died suddenly in June of that year. During his tenure as a judge, he delivered several noted opinions. He was a judge of the supreme court of Missouri from August 1859 to March of 1861. He was removed from the bench in 1861 along with others who refused to sign a loyalty oath, swearing allegiance to the Union in the American Civil War. They were replaced by three appointees who were elected to their seats in 1863, pledging allegiance to the Union.

Judge Ephraim Ewing was the tallest man in his family, and women were attracted to him and his congenial personality. The southern railways and Southern Railroad Company were key to the distribution of the minerals being mined near Iron Mountain and was prominent during the development of Iron Mountain Community in the nineteenth century. The judge and his family lived in the unincorporated community of St. Francois County, Missouri, near Iron Mountain, which is a mining site for iron and founded in 1836. Judge Ewing was appointed Secretary of State of Missouri, which he was in office for four years.

In 1848, his death from his disease was pronounced to be cerebrospinal meningitis, and at that time, it was known to shorten one's life. It was a turbulent time in his life trying to beat the disease. Judge Ewing at the age of fifty-four on June 21, 1848, his death took place suddenly near Iron Mountain and was buried in a cemetery in St. Louis, Missouri.

My mother enjoyed sharing the history of her grandmother, whom neither of us met but would come to see her portrait in the DAR (Daughters of the American Revolution) building. Alice Brevard Ewing was born in Richmond Ray, Missouri, on May of 1849 to Judge Ephraim Brevard Ewing and Elizabeth Ann Allen. Alice found love at first sight with John Read Samuel Walker of Kansas City. Mrs. Alice Brevard Ewing was bold and a strong-willed woman who introduced herself to Mr. Walker. They started talking idle chat, and after an hour or so, he asked her for a date, and that was the start of a wonderful romance. They had four children together. Ephraim Brevard Walker (my grandfather) was their oldest son. He had an older sister and two younger brothers, and he outlived them. He was called Brevard. His mother was the first vice president general and a distinguished woman, whose portrait hangs prominently on the walls of the Continental Hall in the DAR building in Washington DC.

The organization was founded in 1890 with Alice Brevard Ewing as an original founding member. Her portrait was painted by an unknown artist in Missouri. The large DAR building is on a city block and across the street from the White House. She was descended from General William Lee Davidson of North Carolina. She died at age sixty-five on January 10, 1914, in Kansas City, Jackson County, Missouri. It is a nonprofit organization that promotes historic preservation, education, and patriotism and supports veterans of wars. To join DAR, any woman, eighteen years or older, who can prove lineal bloodline descent from an ancestor who aided in achieving American independence can join. The documentation can be statement of birth, marriage, and death, as well as of the revolutionary service of her patriot ancestor.

The DAR Genealogical Research System (GRS) is a combination of several database created to organize the quantity of information collected since its inception in 1890. Their motto is "God, home, and country." Mama, Gaga, my mother, and I all became members of the DAR. Browder became a member and was a regent of her chapter in Clearwater, Florida. She gathered the papers for my children to join the National Service of the Children of the American Revolution (NSCAR), the oldest patriotic youth organization, whose membership is offered to anyone under the age of twenty-two, boy or girl, with lineal descended from those who rendered material aid to the cause of the American independence such as a soldier, sailor, civil officer, or patriot in one of the several colonies or states. Their activities focus on patriotism, service, and education about our American heritage. Once they turned twenty-two, my two boys, Weslee and Bevo, as members of the CAR, could join the Sons of the American Revolution (SAR), and my daughter was eligible to become a member of DAR, but like her brothers, their lives became so busy they decided not to.

Ephraim Brevard Walker (my grandfather who I called Papa) the first was born on November 17, 1893, in Boonville, Cooper County, Missouri. His father was John Read Samuel Walker. John was forty-seven, and his mother Alice was forty-three when she gave birth to him. He was of English and Scottish descent as his family tree was traced to the 1600s.

Grace Pruitt (my grandmother Gaga) was born in Clayton, Barbour County, Alabama, on October 7, 1897. Barbour County is in the southeastern part of the state of Alabama. The county seat is Clayton, and largest city is Eufaula. Its name is in honor of James

Barbour, who served as governor of Virginia. Her father was Oscar Browder Pruett; her mother was Ella Hill Parish.

Brevard left his hometown, Kansas City, Missouri, at the turn of the century in 1900. He followed in his father's footsteps when he had the lumber business before going into law. His younger brother stayed behind and continued the lumber business. Papa left to pursue a lumber business that he would call EB Walker initially and later added the name EB Walker and Son Lumber Company. The office is held in Mobile, Alabama. The company imported and exported lumber to other countries and is no longer in existence. He made a comfortable, sustainable business and was able to retire at a young age, living with his wife and family.

Shared Memories of Grandfather Frank

1885

Some of the untold stories and history you will read about in this book is about my grandfather Frank as he was a man who never lived a childhood and worked as soon as he was walking, doing family chores. As this author was one of his grandchildren, I was able to bond with him before he died. I was in awe of my grandfather Frank who had such energy and drive. His good deeds live on to many. As his favorite words spoken, you still see today, "Everything is made for love." You can see those words erected in a statue in his honor at his gravesite, in a game hanging rack at the hunting lodge, in songs, and throughout the state of Alabama.

I learned throughout the years from my father, mother, and other family members and friends, as well as a book written about him by his cousin, Edward Boykin, and later by going through hard cardboard file cabinets.

The scars of war were still deep in Alabama's countryside when Frank was born into a poor cotton-farming family. The blue invaders of the 1860s had left the backcountry poverty-stricken even twenty years later. The Boykin family immigrated to America from Kent, England, in 1685.

Frank belonged to the ninth generation of Boykin's, who imprinted their own unique stamp on the land with his hardworking housewife. Frank was eleven days old on March 4, 1885, when Grover Cleveland entered the White House, the first Democratic president since the civil war. Dixie Democrats felt they had at last found a friend.

World War I had set education back almost a half a century, and school was hard to come by in Alabama during Frank's youth. There were a few "blab schools where the pupils studied aloud in a drowning chorus outside not unlike the cries of a cloud of locusts. He learned his ABCs, but his spelling over the years was atrocious as he only attended school to the equivalent of two terms of four months each. He received his degree from the school of hard knocks."

Frank eagerly earned his first money bouncing out of bed at 4:00 a.m., milking the cows, and carrying milk to the kitchen in time for breakfast. As a sideline, he started a business selling the leftover milk at ten cents a gallon. He was a bell ringer of the church bell on Sunday, earning twenty-five cents a month and tolling for an occasional funeral. He did many odd jobs running errands, splitting kindling, lugging water, digging potatoes, whitewashing fences and outdoor toilets, and doing anything that would fetch a few pennies to help his family. My grandfather "carried the weight of the world and his family on his shoulders."

He was known as a "self-made man from early childhood to adulthood." He never experienced life as a child. His father who would be considered my great-grandfather was ill, and his last gift to Frank was a sleepy bluetick hound he named Jim. Frank shared his story with his children visiting the doctor one day, and Frank said, "This is the best rabbit dog in the country." The doctor was dubious as he watched the dog sleeping at the heels of Frank's feet. The doctor offered Frank a dime for every rabbit that dog catches in the next ten days. Frank fled, and the next day, he appeared at the doctor's doorstep with an old mule attached to a small flatbed wagon with forty dead rabbits. The doctor reached in his pocket and pulled out four crisp one-dollar bills. Frank felt he was rich.

Soon after the rabbit transactions, Frank's father died in 1893 when he was age eight. His mother was deaf and unable to work. Frank was the middle child and had more drive than his two brothers and his sister, working on a trestle for the railroad tracks being built for trains to travel.

A TURBULENT LIFE ? ? ?

Not being shy, he asked the foreman after introducing himself, "I am looking for work, sir. Can you use a water boy to serve your workers? It's getting hot."

Foreman replied, "You got something there, young man, but you are young. How old are you?"

Frank responded, "Eight, but I am strong, and I don't mind working."

Foreman said, "I will take you on as a water boy at thirty-five cents a day, and you can start tomorrow at 6:00 a.m. to 6:00 p.m."

Frank was so excited he ran home and gave some money to his mother, who was my great-grandmother who died before I could meet her. The spring was a half a mile up the tracks as he toted a full bucket with his seven trips a day. After several weeks, the foreman felt he needed to hire another water boy as the weather was hot with the sun being bright, and you could wring the sweat from the shirts off the railroad workers.

Frank said, "If I can find a way to carry twice as much water, can I have the thirty-five cents and then paying me a total of seventy cents a day?"

The foreman replied, "I will give you two days to devise a way to do that."

Frank rushed home from work, and immediately with his great-grandfather's drawknife, saw, and piece of seasoned oak board, in two hours, he whittled a shoulder yoke that he attached two short chains with a hook at each end. Strapped securely into the clever device, he was able to carry about three gallons of spring water to each hook. He carried two buckets at a time, walking faster with his hands free. The foreman was impressed with Frank being such a hard worker at such an early age. The seventy cents he earned was mostly given to his family to live on. When his job was completed as a water boy, he was promoted to the station house at $15 a month. He ran errands, waved flags, threw switches, kept books, dispatched the logging trains, engineered, and his favorite—which he told me—was conducting, and he met many people. He knew the railroad inside and out, meeting a lot of people along the line.

Traveling down the railroad, he saw vast acreage of timberland that could be bought at a pittance. When he got money, he vowed to himself to buy land and acreage. He yearned for money. The sawmill shutdown the railroad, and Frank had his first break from working but not for long. He continued to work and support his family. He was hired on a log raft to Mobile as if he were Tom Sawyer at age twelve. He began his quest of opportunities of making money. Zigzagging up and down the railroad, he saw vast acreage of timberland that could be bought at a pittance. When he got money, he vowed to himself to buy land and acreage. He yearned for money and took a job in a commissary, which he was born to be a salesperson, customers flocked to him with his jolly, effervescent personality, and the ladies loved him!

At age fourteen in 1899, Frank became a troubleshooter for the AT&N Railroad. Frank, wanting more money, took an extra job in commissary. He was a great salesperson, a store manager, and made $30 a month. With that job, he opened up his first bank account with fifteen dollars. At age sixteen, it was perhaps his most defining year. He ventured out on his own and got a contract from AT&N railroad to furnish crossties and bridge timber for widening the road. Frank had his headquarters in Calvert, Alabama. He supported his deaf mother, his two brothers, and his sister as he displayed his keen mind, stamina, due diligence, and ingenuity to those who knew him.

He built the largest brick general store in Washington County, Alabama, with a partner. He ventured out on his own and got a contract from AT&N railroad to furnish crossties for bridge and timber for widening the road. Papa had his headquarters in Calvert, Alabama. He worked to support his deaf mother, his two brothers, and his sister as he displayed his keen mind, stamina, due diligence, and ingenuity to those who knew him.

He had purchased a general store with a partner, who he later bought out. He built the largest general store in Washington County. They sold everything, even coffins, and employed a carpenter to fit the occupants. He took on various sidelines of hogs and gamecocks. He earned more money from the gamecocks than a hundred-pound hog. To supplement the general store, he built a dormitory and rented rooms to the unmarried workmen he employed cutting crossties and bridge timber. He sold ice-cold Coca-Cola from the spring in the back of the store to keep them cold. Also, from guns to coffins, you name it, he had it and anything that would make him money. His most profitable sidelines during his store days were the buying and selling of Texas mustang horses. He bought them in droves at $15.00 a head in Texas. He would break them in with a saddle and harness three a day, then sold them for $100.00 a piece, giving the purchaser up to two days to pay. Along with that was his livery stable enterprise. It was considered the taxi business of the day, picking up drummers (salespeople). He kept two double buggies waiting at the train station, picking up drummers day and night. Frank had friends up and down the Tombigbee River from McIntosh to Mobile, Alabama. He was small and robust in stature; he carried a sizable shooting arm and was a veteran of successful duels.

One day a Black man entered his store and asked to see a new-fangled gun he had displayed on the shelf.

"How much is it?"

Frank replied, "It's $40."

The man said, "I ain't got no $40."

Frank asked, "What do you have worth money? Maybe we can trade."

The man replied, "I have eighty acres of no-good land along the railroad near McIntosh. I've been trying to sell it for years, but nobody wants it."

The bartering system was widely used in the twenties to sixties in the rural areas of Alabama. You may find it still used in certain areas today.

Frank said, "Let's go look at the land."

It was eighty acres along railroad tracks near McIntosh and had trees and everything he liked on the land, and he knew it would turn a profit in the future. They went to the shop, and Frank gave the man the newfangled gun, and he got the deed for the eighty acres of land. A decade or so ago, he leased that land for mineral exploration, and a company found one of the world's largest salt domes on his property. Enough salt to supply mankind for four thousand years, an estimated two hundred and fifty-five billion tons. Clustered today on a fraction of the eighty acres of "no-good land" along the Tombigbee River and twelve or more industrial plants producing over fourteen thousand products from the salt underneath. It was considered the largest in the US and perhaps in the nation. As the years went on, Frank harvested a fortune in timber, real estate, livestock and naval stores, as well as investments in land.

Generations continue to receive royalty payments that range from 2 percent to 15 percent for five cavity storage areas that were negotiated through attorneys, past presidents, and current president of the family business. The family's third and fourth generations continue to benefit from it today and should continue to fifth and generations to come. It wasn't long before Frank began picking up modest-size pieces of land.

He expanded his crosstie business as it was successful with the biggest buyer in the east, the Southern Railroad, along to the end of the railroad tracks north of Mobile. Running along the AT&N tracts north of Mobile was ninety-two thousand acres that he leased the tract and later purchased it outright. Property values soared, and through good times and bad, he was suddenly worth millions. He bought land when no one else would buy it. He had the tenacity to hold on. It established the cycle for his timber operations: buy land, cut the timber, hold on to the land, replant the timber, and cut again in a few years. At age eighteen, in 1904, he was becoming known as a tycoon.

As word of mouth spread quickly, President Herbert Hoover's prospector noticed and was observing Frank. He called him over; Frank walked over to his table and sat down.

"I've watched you for a while. The oilmen play cards and drink half the night, while you purchased leases, and you are a hard worker. I am Charles Wood, a geologist prospecting for future President Herbert Hoover," he said. "Son, if you really want to find oil, go to the forks of Alabama and the Tombigbee River where the two rivers flow together as oil flows the same direction as water and why the convergence of two rivers was the surefire spot to drill for the nation."

A TURBULENT LIFE ? ? ?

Bright and early, he rode his horse "Old Faithful" to the site of purchasing leases on the Tombigbee River.

Years appeared to go by fast for Frank as he harvested a fortune in timber, real estate, livestock and naval stores as well as investments in land. In three years, Frank built the largest turpentine distillery in the south and perhaps the nation. The outlay for the finished turpentine plant was close to the million-dollar mark. It staggered the imagination of people in the small-town community. Frank was ingenious and helped the dynamite industry to soar by using dynamite for stump removal. Frank's stills were turning out 1,500 barrels a day, and they figured their profits daily at $1,000 per twenty-four hours. He sold out the turpentine business leased for his crosstie and turpentine operations at the top, lot stock, and barrel to a group of bankers in New York City.

The land Frank bought or projected he and his partner into promoting new communities, real estate, and other advancements. The partnership dissolved selling off their assets, divided what they had, and went their separate ways. Their assets consisted of timber, sawmills, lumber, crossties, cattle, crop financing, pinelands by the thousands of acres, and sixteen turpentine stills with one being the world's largest. They had commissary stores doing a rushing business.

Frank was propelled into having a real estate office. His slogan was "enjoy the thrill of selling land by the square mile." As the years went on, Frank harvested a fortune in livestock, timber, real estate, and naval stores, as well as investments in land. Everything he bought like King Midas turned to riches, but he also had a heart of gold. He gained the reputation of being a good Samaritan, as well as a tycoon. Along the way to fame and fortune, he found the time and money to educate his brothers and sisters, picking up the bill for their college educations.

He set up six beehives in the woods near the swamps, and the bees moved in shortly after. Within several years, the original six hives had multiplied to 3,600, which didn't surprise him at all. Bees require plenty of wildflowers and water close by, and his land was the perfect environment for them to flourish. The other bees he sold by the pound but made it a point to never sell the honey the hives produced. The sweet golden reward he left for the bees that gathered it, making sure they had the nourishment that nature intended. Frank eventually sold his bee business, which was by then became the biggest in the south with customers from all over the United States and Canada. He hired and trained a young man to oversee the bee business.

Everything Frank held onto, he had the vision to make what he could to succeed and turned it into a substantial profit, or you can say even into gold, and people would be heard, saying, "There's the man with King Midas's touch."

Shared Memories of Frank and Other

Early 1900s

In 1912, at age twenty-seven, he purchased an additional thousand acres that rounded out his holdings in the river, giving him thirteen miles of river front at the mouth of the rivers. In recent times, eighteen drilling sites have struck oil on property adjacent to his, thus vindicating what Herbert Hoover's prospector prophesized more than a century ago.

Frank always told his children growing up, "Land is a wonderful thing to own. It never changes. Life comes and goes—storms, sunshine, rainy weather, moonlight, and roses—and everything else, comes and goes, but land, day and night, continues growing its timber. I know nothing that is better than land, not even a government bond."

Land was his livelihood and made him wealthy beyond his family's expectations.

In 1912, he also bought an eight thousand and six hundred tract of land at $25 an acre in Chickasaw, Alabama, on the Mobile River. The tract had twenty-three miles of frontage on two rivers. He convinced the owner to sell him the property, and Frank didn't have the money to cover the check he wrote. Within twenty-four hours, he was able to get money from his turpentine business and the bank to cover the check. He knew if the check bounced, the deal would be off. The deal went through, and later sold the site to United States Steel Corporation and profited $750,000, which was far more than he paid for the land.

Frank settled in Mobile, Alabama, in 1913, at the age of thirty. My dad explained to me his dad was a gentleman who followed tradition and etiquette as he was known to love women. He had met a beautiful young lady one day, and he asked her to go out several times, and she would reply no. He strolled up to who you call Other at school one day as she had attended college and became a teacher. He asked her to go out again, and she finally said yes. He knew at that moment she was who he would marry. She grew up in a Methodist family, as her father was the minister of the small church they attended on Sundays and holidays. It was customary too ask Other's father for her hand in marriage, and he did so.

Her father replied, "It is okay, but up to my daughter."

Frank asked, "Where is she?"

Her father replied, "On a train after her exhausting day of teaching her students at school and going to the city of Macomb."

Frank gathered his brown Texas mustang horse Old Faithful and galloped to catch up to the moving train to find the girl he loved, as the train had just left the station, riding as close to the locomotive as possible without spooking his horse. He looked in every car window till he saw who he felt was the most beautiful girl he had ever seen with her big heart on the inside and her beauty on the outside. He saw her in a passenger car and galloped his stallion close enough to jump from Old Faithful onto the train. Frank walked to Other in her seat and got on one knee, opening a beautiful engagement ring, and asked her to marry him. Stunned as she covered her mouth at the boldness of her suitor and surprised in disbelief as it was so unexpected, she said yes. He put the beautiful engagement ring on her finger. All the passengers and spectators began clapping and were in awe of the young couple. Frank kissed her goodbye, gathered Old Faithful, and galloped to his home to tell his family he was getting married.

The engineer horrified as he heard screaming from passengers all the way to the engine car, and he stopped the train. The abrupt, unscheduled stop had passengers on the edge of their seats in the other cars, nervous, and scared as they believed robbers were boarding the train to steal jewels and money from them. When he saw Frank, who he knew, he congratulated him and then got the train on the move again.

The Wedding of Frank and Other

It took place in 1913 in a Baptist church with friends and family. Among the wedding gifts Frank gave his bride was Diamond Shore, a gorgeous black horse she came to love and ride.

The newlyweds moved to Mobile, Alabama, in 1913 and settled immediately into a comfortable large house with sizable rooms, a broad porch, a lovely yard, and a front lawn lined with azaleas and a cast-iron deer. Inside, Other embellished it with elegant furnishings and rare pieces that were often conversation pieces for friend and family that visited. It was a wonderful home to raise their active children. They were to own the home for as long as they were married.

My dad taught us all, including my sister, how to shoot and kill the different game living on the plantation fifty miles north of Mobile. We loved tagging through the woods with Dad on the hunting preserve, where he taught us to shoot straight and tell the truth. He took us coon-hunting with his dogs as soon as it was dark. We would bring back at least five of the furry little fellows with the feathery tails. He would allow us kids to collect forty cents apiece for the coonskins.

Frank became a member of the Methodist church with Other, a member of the optimist club, and was involved with many charitable organizations. When Frank was elected to US Congress from the Southern District of Alabama, Dad said, "In fact, my father always gave my mother credit for her help with his letter writing, her editing and teaching him some of his learning skills." I was happy to hear my father recalling life's moments of his past that he had long forgotten. It was intriguing to me. Listening to his recollections of his childhood, I began departmentalizing mental notes about the memories he shared with me at the early age of seven in 1959, and I would often write them in my diary I kept with a lock and key.

James said, "My father became a millionaire three times in his early years." He was unable to buy the boat he and his wife wanted to call the Carlotta for his family to enjoy fishing and leisure time on the Gulf of Mexico. He had to rebuild his businesses throughout his life. He had total of over eighteen different businesses. The partnership business entered every business they believed would make money. They went into the Satsuma orange business and began shipping oranges by trainloads. Three years later, a bitter frost killed thousands of trees, which put them out of the orange business. It was a traumatic time as it almost broke them, but they survived. In 1906, at age twenty-one, he could retire with millions of dollars in assets. His real estate office in Mobile soared to land office proportion.

World War I

1914 to 1918

World War I began with the assassination of Archduke Franz Ferdinand of Austria-Hungry. Before the war, Mobile, Alabama, was a sleepy southern town of around 112,000, whose main industry was shipbuilding. Frank served as an official in Alabama production of shipbuilding companies that were responsible for 52 percent of all vessels produced on the Gulf Coast during the conflict. Alabama Dry Dock and Shipbuilding Company (ADDSCO) was important to Mobile's economy.

He was proud of the sacrifices people made in World War I, especially with the shipbuilding enterprise. The United States entered into the war in helping the navy during the war by escorting and transporting two million US soldiers to France. Frank had told me at his hunting lodge one day that the few soldiers left from that war told him stories of feeling like the earth booms from the heavy artillery and how they would crouch into corners huddled close together. The steel helmets offered little protection from the machine guns. It was the most horrifying battle to those that served and fought in it. Many never seeing such likes of devastation, and some had everlasting battle scars and nightmares of the war.

A defense contract transformed the Mobile municipal airport into Brookley field that became an Army Air Force supply depot and bomber modification center. Frank's naval stores supplied materials for ships, clothing, and necessities people needed during that hard time in Mobile.

Frank maintained his timber, crosstie, real estate business, and others as well. Around eighty-six thousand Alabamians, Black and White, fought in the war. Approximately 2,500 men died in the attempt of winning the war. After World War I, there were serious problems with Mobile's Port Authority. In 1917, Mobile had a labor shortage, and the majority of its shipbuilding facilities were not sufficient. John Barnett Waterman moved from New Orleans, where he was born in 1865 and moved to Mobile, Alabama, in 1902. He started Waterman Steamship Company in 1919 with $2,000.00 in capital and one ship called the *Eastern Sun*. Waterman helped expand Mobile to become a booming city. The steamship company became a major employer for jobs in Mobile. It played an active part in developing ships during World War II. John Waterman changed the steamship industry and had many patents. Frank felt honored to know him and to help with his successes through the years.

Malcolm McClean acquired Waterman Steamship Corporation of Mobile, Alabama, as a base of operations. McClean by the ICC was told he could not be in the trucking business and shipping business at the same time, so he got out of trucking. I came to know one of Malcolm McClean's employees, John McCown from Mobile. One might say John came to be his right-hand man and learned containerization and shipping from McClean who changed the cargo-shipping industry. McClean was instrumental in making the containerization industry what it is today. McClean and McCown obtained several patents in the ship-container business. McClean bought many jobs and enhancements to the city of Mobile. My grandfather Frank had negotiations with McClean and considered him a treasure to the shipping industry and in helping the Port of Mobile to survive through some tough times.

John McCown authored the book *Giants of the Sea* that tells of ships and men who enhanced the world in the shipping industry. It encompasses the history and development of the modern cargo transporting business through calm and rough seas to the many ports of the globe. As a retired American history teacher, I was surprised not to have taught my high school students much about the inter-

A TURBULENT LIFE ? ? ?

national shipping and cargo container industry as it is a vital part of transporting goods to the international ports of the world. I learned more about the cargo and shipping industry in my economics classes in college.

My Grandparents on My Mother's Side

1919 and 1929

Grace Pruett lived in Hattiesburg, Forest, Mississippi. She had completed her junior year of college at Cumberland University. At age twenty-three, she married Ephraim Brevard Walker on November 18, 1915, in Barbour, Alabama, and had a small wedding with family and friends.

While living in Hattiesburg, Mississippi, my brother and I called Grace as Gaga. Papa, age twenty-six, and Gaga, age twenty-two, spent a wintry morning of December 8, 1919, in a Mississippi hospital. They were the joyous parents of their son, Brevard. Papa passed out cigars as that was the tradition then to family and friends that visited him in the hospital and the first week when he was home.

Ten years later, Gaga and Papa in 1929 in Mobile, Alabama, were having another child. On January 29, 1929, in Mobile Infirmary, Gaga gave birth to a beautiful baby girl who they named Grace Browder Walker. Brevard and his younger sister were ten years apart, which was a significant difference in those days as well as in today's times. Mother told me and my brother when she was growing up that Papa was her favorite parent! Our mother was the apple of his eye! Papa and Mother immediately bonded. From baby through adulthood, she grew remarkably close to her dad, and it was noticeable to all who witnessed their relationship; she was daddy's little girl. Papa was successful in his importing and exporting lumber business to other countries.

A TURBULENT LIFE ? ? ?

Papa had diabetes, and I recall as a child, he used PH strips to check the color of his urine because he had type-2 diabetes. That method is obsolete or not commonly used anymore as newer and better methods are used with the new technologies and the medical innovations that change to keep up with the times. I know this as I am a type-2 diabetic and use medicine, diet, and a glucose meter checking my numbers daily to keep it under control.

Sitting on their screen porch of their home almost every afternoon, Gaga would drink her vodka and orange juice with Papa smoking his pipe. When I was with her one day, sitting on the large porch, Gaga said, "Gracie Lu, I know your favorite party at my home was with your brother and his neighborhood friend playing limbo music and holding the bamboo limbo pole to see how low one could go, and there would be three winners who would each get a prize to be given away."

I responded, "That's right, and I am so glad you remembered as I had so many memorable times with you."

I recalled the times Papa would have his chauffer orderly drive him to the local drugstore to buy his one bad vice, a chocolate bar, like clockwork daily. When home, he would sit on the porch and savor every bite of the sweet confection. That was his one vice he had and the highlight of his day.

Shared Memories of James and Uncle Jack

Dad was birthed by Other on June 30, 1921, and he was older than his twin brother Jack by one minute. Born into a well-known aristocratic family in Mobile, Alabama, the children grew up for the most part in Mobile. Frank and Other maintained their beautiful home near downtown Mobile shortly after they were married. They raised their four boys and one girl during their formative years with a nanny named Martha who would prepare succulent meals, wash the clothes, and clean the home. She often cared for the children when Frank and Other were traveling and working.

James was with his family at the hunting lodge, north of Mobile. One day, while growing up, tragedy struck his twin brother Jack. He was running over hot coals from a firepit on a dare from his friend. His yelling could be heard from miles away, and James along with the family ran outside to see what was wrong. Jack was in pain and on the ground, and James immediately saw his skin become dark red. As his twin observed the burn, he knew from viewing it the burn had penetrated deeply into Jack's skin. James rode with him in the ambulance as they were inseparable growing up. It was traumatic day for James seeing his brother in agony, while the ambulance had the sirens roaring and rushing him to the hospital.

At the hospital, the doctor called the family outside of Jack's room and explained he had severe third- to fourth- to even eight-degree burns on his toes of his right and left feet. "He will be on crutches and may always have to use them throughout his life. His toes were charred, and he has no feeling in his toes as his nerve endings were destroyed. The burn damaged underlying bones. We treat with penicillin antibiotic and creams on the burn wound surface, gradually cleaning the wound and removing the infected callus skin. Keep his feet elevated with dressings of loose cloth. He was placed with a light sheet over the toes to reduce blood pressure while in the hospital. Immersion hydrotherapy would be used with warm running water continuously to wash away the dead skin and bacteria. It would help Jack not to get an infection, cleaning his wounds during the healing process."

His mother was diligent in caring her beloved son. Every day she would use warm water to take off the dead skin from his feet and toes that were knubs. With removal of all the dead skin day and night, gently massaging his feet and knubs, Jack would sigh as it felt good to him. He didn't want her to stop, but her hands were tired, and she needed to check on her other children.

Jack used crutches throughout his life and in raising his daughter and son. Growing up, I always saw my uncle Jack using his crutches and never saw him without them while raising his two children who lived with him. His story of the burns saddened me, but when I saw him, he always had a smile on his face, as if he were leaving his past and pain away but never to be forgotten.

I came to know him as an extraordinarily strong man, and my uncle endured internal and external pains he had learned to make the best of, walking and sharing his beautiful smile with others as one could look deep into his eyes and see the pain he has endured throughout his life.

James, Frank Junior, Dick, and Fran found him never to be the same mentally and are physically suffering from the ongoing agony from his burns, especially with walking. They all tried their best to give him confidence to try new things without using his crutches, and they were unsuccessful.

Dad told me the story of one day his mother had to buy them coats with the money the pittance dad would send her at that time. It was a cold day, and they wanted to go to a picture show. When they went outside, they started shivering, and his mom took them to the store to buy them all coats. They felt blessed and were cold no more, and she took her five children to the show. At that time, they were hard for her to raise pretty much by herself but with the help of Martha. She raised them reading from the Bible scriptures every evening before they went to bed. The Lord was in her heart, and she managed to raise them without a lot of drama, except for his brother Jack's accident.

Whisky Trial During Prohibition in Alabama

1923

During prohibition, Frank was one of the prominent defendants in Mobile's "whisky trials," in which 117 people were indicted in 1923. The defendants came from all works of life (sheriffs, police, chiefs, businessmen, legislators, as well as poor people). US Attorney Boyles for Southern Alabama announced Frank and others tried to bribe him. A special prosecutor was brought in named Hugo Black, a Birmingham attorney who later became a US senator and Supreme Court Justice.

Frank's trial was in 1924 when Hugo Black argued that Frank portrayed himself as a person with influence in President William Harding's administration, and the bootleggers paid him five dollars a shipment for protection. The charges were dropped after correspondence was ruled inadmissible.

Black tried him again in 1925 when a new witness came forward, testifying to Frank's misbehavior. The jury acquitted Frank of violating the prohibition and tariff laws. One day later, Black charged Frank of bribing a federal agent. Frank testified in his own defense where he stated Attorney Boyles had tried to involve him in a protection racket. After twenty-two hours of deliberation, the jury found him not guilty. He was still sentenced to two years in prison. The conviction was overturned within nine months by the Circuit Court of Appeals. They declared the indictment "fatally defective" because it did not give enough information for Frank's lawyers to form a proper defense. The family rejoiced praised God for his innocence. It was a dramatic and turbulent time in those years, especially for his wife. The ups and downs through that time made them stronger than ever!

During prohibition, for instance, my dad told me a fantastic event occurred. Frank and Other were staying at the lodge when Other entered the upstairs attic, also known as the bullpen area, to make sure everything was clean and prepared for any guests who might sleep there. When she saw a full tub of standing water in the guest bathtub that smelled a bit odd, she dipped a finger into what looked like clear, clean water to taste the liquid and realized, to her horror, it was actually *gin*. Other ran screaming in shock through the house.

"Frank, hurry, come see what I've found!" Other cried.

Frank ran up to the attic, asking, "What's wrong? How did this bathtub full of gin get here? Gin?" exclaimed Frank in surprise.

"I don't know! It looks like clean water to me. Taste it."

Cupping his hands to scoop up some of the liquid, Frank drank what he thought was water and immediately spit the alcohol out of his mouth onto the floor in total surprise before immediately pulling the plug and emptying the tub of all the bathtub gin.

Frank was never tempted to keep the illegal booze because he'd sworn off alcohol after a few years of indulging and had vowed to his children he would never drink again. He stuck to that vow and had even offered his youngsters and grandchildren one thousand silver dollars if they never drank or smoked. Robert was the only one of his five children who ever won those thousand silver dollars, and only one of his daughters' grandchildren was able to collect the prize. Because of his strict views on abstaining from drink, Frank called a staff meeting at the lodge, asking whoever had brewed the bathtub gin to confess, but nobody came forward. Throughout the prohibition era, this tub was filled with pure alcohol not just once but many times after that first incidence with no explanation as to how it was happening. The bathroom and attic were checked during every visit, and the tub had to be emptied of gin at least twenty times. Frank suggested it must be the work of Ms. Agnes, as they trusted all their employees, and there was no solid evidence of anyone mortal ever being the culprit.

A TURBULENT LIFE ? ? ?

Prohibition failed in enforcing sobriety and cost the government billions of dollars to enforce it. Congress in 1933 adopted a resolution to the Constitution that repealed the Eighteenth Amendment. The Twenty-First Amendment was ratified on December 5, 1933, that ended prohibition. President Franklin Delano Roosevelt (FDR) signed an order authorizing the sale of beer. Later he signed the full repeal of prohibition. Celebrations were held throughout the country in the north, south, east, and west.

Kounter Klan Organized to Fight Ku Klux Klan in Alabama

1924

The Ku Klux Klan (KKK) received legal status to do business in the state of Alabama as a foreign corporation on September 25, 1924, in the post-civil war times. They were throughout the United States, rioting in Eastern, Midwest, Northern, and Southern states. In 1924, they dominated the elected officials from the East, West, North, and Southern states and having control of state governments and were treacherous activists!

Frank stood at a platform, voicing his disapproval to the thousands of Southerners who refused to go along with the Klan's motives and guerilla intimidation tactics.

"We'll start a clan of our own—a Kounter Klan," Frank pledged. "It will be known as the Loyalty League. Instead of wearing white to show some assumed superiority, we will be cloaked in robes of green, Mother Nature's own color, because we are all her children, regardless of the color of our skin. The members of the Loyalty League will pledge open warfare on the Klan and all its evil purposes."

The crowd roared, and still the fires burned.

The Kounter Klan league's members consisted of Catholics, Protestants, Jews, African Americans, and other minorities. It was a multilingual membership in speaking of many languages, reflecting the fabric of a growing nation. But unlike the Ku Klux Klan, the Kounter Klan patrolled for the purpose of saving lives, righting wrongs, and protecting the weak that were deprived of the rights and privileges to be free. They were able to fight without killing anyone. They fought for the discriminated religions, minorities, and foreign races to be treated like everyone else as they were disenfranchised of having no political voice.

This second incarnation of the Klan was the first one to adopt the fiery crosses placed on the front yards of Black families. There wasn't quite as much in the way of racial killings, lynchings, or Black people being drawn and quartered like there was with the early Klan of 1865–1874. But this organization was more insidious with the KKK platforming for better public schools for poor Whites, prohibition measures, improved road construction, and other seemingly progressive steps to "benefit" society. Frank purchased over eight hundred green robes for the Loyalty League's members out of his own pocket, and it was written in his financial ledger under the heading of *suspense* on November 24, 1924, for $148.65. As Republican state governments sprouted up, so did the spread of Kounter Klan orders throughout the South, mostly rural areas. One of Frank's friends, Congressman Michael McCormack, acknowledged in the congressional records that Frank became president of the Loyalty League of Alabama, Mississippi, and Louisiana sector. He organized local Kounter Klan orders that were not centrally controlled but were instead free to act independently in the same manner of the Ku Klux Klan, yet for different purposes. It was Frank's version of "fighting fire with fire."

When a Kounter Klan representative learned of Ku Klux Klan actions against Black citizens, they would gather local members and raid the KKK meetings, mostly in Mobile, Alabama, disrupting the proceedings and defending the victim. There were many such skirmishes in Alabama, Mississippi, and Louisiana with the Kounter Klan members banding together to take down the Ku Klux Klan.

"I have information that the Klan will gather in the front yard of a home in Mobile tonight," a Loyalty League member would inform Frank.

"I'll alert our men," was Frank's response.

In massé, they'd ride their horses at breakneck speed, their green robes fluttering in the wind as they barreled down on the location like an army of uniformed soldiers. There could be nearly a hundred men, but they moved as one with a single mission.

"Stop!" Frank would shout, as he and the Loyalty League members brought their horses to a halt in front of a roaring flame.

Some of the horses reared back, frightened by the large cross ablaze on the lawn. Outnumbered and cowardly, the Klan members would disband, scattering as the League put out the last of the fire. Such confrontations were fraught with violence and danger, but there were others cloaked in robes of social respectability.

Frank told his son James the story of those who tried to reincarnate the Ku Klux Klan and lived to regret it. One such individual was Pierre Lafayette, a fearless prosecutor being considered by President Franklin Delano Roosevelt for an appointment to the Supreme Court. Lafayette was charming, seemingly principled, and mainstream. In short, a wolf in sheep's clothing. Though his agenda was based on "reform," it was in actuality a front to further causes for White folk and keep the Blacks "in their places." Under sworn examination with the president and his attending staffers, Lafayette vehemently denied the fact that he'd once been a gold-card-carrying Klan member. But the truth about Lafayette's character was finally brought to light by a journalist who was a member of Frank's Kounter Klan. The newspaperman produced a detailed, handwritten list in Lafayette's own writing of the thousand and one corrupt ways in which the politician had hoped to make money, including bribery and bootleggers and extorting money from moonshiners. Lafayette tried to bribe the newsman for the evidence, but the journalist was a sworn enemy of the Ku Klux Klan and all they stood for and would not have any part of Lafayette's generous offer of blood money. Instead, the racist prosecutor was later arrested for the attempted bribe, and he was indicted.

Thanks to the integrity of members of the Loyalty League and the journalist, a member of the Kounter Klan.

Unfortunately, the grand jury was filled with Klan members, who forced the prosecution to drop the case for lack of evidence, and in 1926, Lafayette ran for the United States Senate. With the Klan's support, he was elected, although he was taken to task in the press by outraged members of the Kounter Klan.

A TURBULENT LIFE ? ? ?

One of the few defeats Frank ever knew in his lifetime was seeing Lafayette elected, and it made him that much more determined to protect those who were wronged and to do what was right with his money, brawn, power, and contacts. Such determination was what had originally given him the vision and courage to start the Kounter Klan, no matter what it cost him financially or emotionally and no matter what threats and mental anguish he suffered as a result.

Black the Klan would gain some serious headway into US legislation. Frank was in for the fight of his life. They were known for rages of racism, against Catholics, there hatred of Jews, Blacks, foreigners, and minorities at the hands of terror the Klansmen caused more damage in the Southern states. They wore white masks and white sheet like clothing that did not represent the color of white, symbolizing cleanliness, innocence, purity, and peacefulness with which they were not known for any of those sentiments, as they were known for destruction and burning fires.

I taught American history to high school students, and in my teachings and readings of history books, I had never found references to the Kounter Klan in the 1970s to 2000s. I believe it should be taught in all schools as the Kounter Klan in the Southern states was a valuable part of history that seemed to be lost in the untold stories of history.

The unfortunate fires of the Ku Klux Klan still burn today throughout the world!

Resources

Everything Is Made for Love book by Edward Boykin, *Congressional Record*, personal letter from Frank's secretary and a letter from two newspaper cartoons of KKK, entry for robe purchase in ledger. Newspaper articles in Alabama State Archives, Congressman Michael McCormack, acknowledged in the *Congressional Records* that Frank became president of the "Loyalty League of Alabama, Mississippi, and Louisiana" sector.

The Nation's Spotlight Was Focused on the Sunshine State

Thousands of people pulled up stakes, abandoning wife, family, and home. Florida beckoned like a utopia, a place where one could invest rainy-day dollars and watch them become thousands. Bankers were not immune to the Florida fever. They crammed their vaults with notes, which if they were lucky, they could realize 10 percent return when the blow came off. Credit was limitless, and money more than plentiful. People came to Florida by way of trains, planes, buses, and rusty jalopies. The starry Florida nights of an all and fun land where leisure was the watchword, and dollars almost grew on trees like oranges. In 1924, all roads led to Florida. Men and women trotted over one another to bid on swampland and whatever they could get their hands on.

In Alabama, next-door neighbor Frank watched, wondered, and waited. Real estate was his forte, and every breeze that blew over from his tropical heaven bore the unmistakable odor of big money. Frank was ready to make a "fast buck" that is getting in and getting out the same way. Frank's friend and later to become his business partner in Florida was President Herbert Hoover's brother. He had a three-way deal with the Hoover's where they funded it, Frank would go to Florida, buy the raw land, and supply the sales "umph" with his vivacious, energetic, and determined personality to succeed in his endeavors after the necessary development. Frank paid his own expenses, but he was to have a third interest in whatever profits accrued from the enterprise. After the meeting, Frank boarded a sleeper car for Jacksonville, Florida. He had $900 in his pocket. His first task was to locate men who controlled large chunks of Florida land. His first stop was meeting with bankers who, he figured, could introduce him to people who controlled large chunks of land and found that he did better by himself without the banker.

So he walked the streets and told many he wanted to buy a million and a half acres of Florida real estate. His talk had many open their ears and listen to him. He met with the Brooks-Scanlon County, the largest sawmill people in the state, owners of vast stretches of land in the Florida. Over the phone, Frank was talking with the high-powered attorney H. S. Hoover hired, helping with the negotiations with the over a million acres of land they purchased. Frank had the maps and tax assessment receipts that gave excellent descriptions of the property.

On a sheet of hotel stationary, Frank wrote in pencil, "For five thousand dollars and other valuable considerations, I hereby bargain, sell, and convey to his full name or his assigns, for two dollars an acre, one million acres of land as described per the tax receipts and maps hereto attached. He also specified that the remainder of purchase money was to be paid within one, two, three, years after his lawyers had approved the transaction." Frank called in a bellboy to witness the paper. Frank wrote a draft for $5,000 on the Hoover's account with a bank in Chicago and gave it to Scanlon. Thus, Frank and Hoovers were a part of the land's gold rush.

The town of Homosassa, from which the big tract took its name, lies on a beautiful river that runs into the gulf above Tampa on the west coast of Florida. The purchase included the entire river down to its mouth. It was fifteen inches deep at its mouth when he purchased it. He had it dredged deeper so that yachts and other boats could sail in. It was a region of natural beauty and charm. The spring bubbling up was eighty-seven feet deep. It was considered a massive goldfish bowl. After closing the Homosassa deal, Frank hurried to see Burton-Swartz Lumber Company that specialized in cypress. He was able to talk the concern into selling him five hundred thousand acres on the same terms as the Homosassa acquisition. Now Frank owned a million and a half acres.

A TURBULENT LIFE ? ? ?

Dad said, "My father didn't come home for months at a time, as he worked day and night building roads and houses by the hundreds. His brothers were taking care of his turpentine and crosstie business."

Frank opened a big business in Tampa and kept twenty rooms at the Mayflower Hotel to accommodate customers. He later sold the hotel to Dizzy Dean, the famous St. Louis Cardinals pitcher. Frank and his lawyer from Mobile moved to Homosassa, paying him $36,000 a year to process deeds and legal papers on the sight. Frank hired a sales force. They sold mostly units, not acres. For instance, if they sold five-thousand-acre units, you would have $5,000 interest in a million-and-a-half acres and whatever development there was. It was a great deal, and people fell for it as if they were buying diamond mines.

Frank was used to the good clay soil of Alabama and began figuring out how to get out of the Florida sand and not lose the friendship with the Hoovers. One night, Frank was at Davis Island near Tampa, where a crowd was putting on a land sale under a tent. Men and women were fighting and shoving to bid on lots that were underwater at high tide. He knew at that early age he would be a success in business. He was convinced at that time the joyride could not keep going. That was one time he was wrong if he were only able to have looked into the future through a looking glass, and he would have seen land in Florida excelled in prices and has had a far better financial growth than the land in Alabama.

President Hoover with his brother and Frank chartered a special train and invited the governor and entire Florida legislature to be their guests from Miami to Chicago. Frank was convinced at that time the joyride could not keep going. The governor and over two-thirds of the legislature and other wealthy people of the area accepted. They hired a big band to meet the train when it arrived in Chicago. They paid the bandleader $500.00 to write a march that he called "Salute to Florida." The Hoovers reserved the gold room at the Congress Hotel, the biggest room in Chicago at that time, for a banquet and for a terrific high-speed selling operation. Prospective customers were packed into the expansive room by the hundreds. Frank ran the show and, like an auctioneer, started selling the units of land.

It was during that time Al Capone was running Chicago. Frank had hired eight detectives to police to watch out for gangsters and hoodlums. After everyone was stuffed with tasty food and champagne, Frank gave a sunshine-and-roses talk. The audience went wild with enthusiasm. They were on their feet to try to buy units they didn't sell in acres like today. The units were sold from the big maps he showed them. In that one night, they sold eleven and a half million dollars' worth of Homosassa land.

In that same night, Frank sold out his share for the hard cash to the Hoovers. Within sixty days of his sell out in Florida, you could not sell land in the state of Florida for the next ten years. Frank put every bit of money into Dauphin Island, Alabama, Gulf shores beaches, and timberland in his home state of Alabama.

Resources

Everything Is Made for Love book by Edward Boykin, newspaper articles in Alabama State Archives.

September 1926

At age forty-one, disaster and turbulence came riding over the southern horizon on the wings of wind. In an hour, winds were racing and screaming over Mobile like a thousand banshees. The heaven's blackened; the rains, as the expression, goes were like cats and dog's coming down. The eighty-mile hurricane left lands submerged for fifty miles northward. Soaring off with the hurricane was Frank's vision of retirement. The hurricane had wiped out the timber kingdom. His sawmills were masses of planks and sawdust. Turpentine stills collapsed. His commissary store was hard-hit. The saddest and most turbulent time in his businesses was the desolation of millions of feet of pinewoods that was ready to cut. The wind of the hurricane uprooted thousands of trees. Frank, even with the turbulence of the events, continued to bounce back and rebuild his fortune. People were impressed with Frank's unusual enterprises throughout the country.

Dad and Mom's Schoolings

1929 and 1935

Our dad James attended Murphy High School with his twin brother Jack. He also took classes at Spring Hill College and American University in Washington, DC, where he loved running track and was proud to have lettered doing it. He shared many stories of his running track with me in his younger and older years, and it kept him in great shape and always full of energy. He graduated in 1935 from the University of Alabama with a business degree shortly after he returned home from World War II.

Browder was born in 1929 into an upper-class family that was respected throughout Mobile. Our mother loved males and had many boyfriends through her school years and adult life, and her father was her favorite parent growing up. Some of her best girl friends thought she was spoiled rotten by her dad, who had perhaps abused her as she was drawn to the male persuasion throughout most her life. Mainly priest were teachers and taught classes at the visitation convent school in Mobile, Alabama. She graduated high school, and her proud parents watched her receive her diploma. They celebrated afterward at the Mobile Country Club with some of her friends and families.

She was enrolled by her father into Miss Simpletons finishing school on the Upper East Side, but down on Greenwich Village, along the highways leading to the Holland Tunnel in New York City. The school was of brick and stone marked with an American flag. Behind the orange doors was a four-story cluster of classrooms designed in 1875. English, basic mathematics, focus on music, songwriting, beauty culture, urban affairs, elementary merchandising applicable to shopping, and a little bit of business practices were taught. It was expensive to attend, and the main focus was teaching social graces and upper-class customs as a preparation of entering society. Her best friend Suga who graduated with her from the visitation convent also attended the finishing school. They would have socials with Princeton boys, and Browder's dance card was always filled as she had rhythm and could follow or lead. Suga would be doing the jitterbug as Browder and she both loved to dance!

University of Alabama and Football Stories from Uncle Riley

1930s to 1978

I grew up loving the University of Alabama football team because of Uncle Riley's stories, and he was from Carrollton, Mississippi, and was six foot two inches in height. He was proud to share his time of playing football for the university as he was known as the best all-around player! He could block, punt, kick extra points, and make field goals in 1933–1935. He won a national title in 1934 for the Southeastern Conference (SEC). His team went to the Rose Bowl against Stanford University in that year. He won the Jacobs Blocking Trophy award. He was excited when he shared that he was the first drafted player by the National Football League (NFL) for the Washington Redskins (1936–1938). In 1937, they won against the New York Giants with Riley scoring all thirteen points. He really enjoyed demonstrating how he kicked two field goals; he was running and intercepted a passback for a touchdown, and then he kicked the ball for the extra point. All the players felt he was the most valuable man on their team!

    I recall his telling those in the room he enjoyed playing more than his coaching. He was backfield coach for Washington Lee (1939–1940) and head coach in 1941. He was honored into the college football Hall of Fame. He left football to join the United States Navy as lieutenant commander during World War II. As he shared his story to all ages in the room, hearing him share it with such enthusiasm, he had a captivated audience!

He was married to my favorite aunt Fran. She was so caring to all who knew her as well as a good businessperson. Returning home from World War II, her husband became a successful real estate developer in Mobile, Alabama. In 1978, he was honored into the Alabama sports Hall of Fame.

It was a heartbreaking day for the family when he died at age eighty-eight. He was Aunt Fran's husband for many years and had two older girls, and the youngest was his son named for him. I know that their father and mother are looking down upon them from heaven and is proud of all his children. Those that had the pleasure of knowing him as well as those that played football with him.

I also liked the Alabama football team through the years because of my dad graduating from there. He loved the team as well, and through the years, when able, he would not miss watching them play on the television set, "Roll Tide."

Grandfather's First Year as US Congressman in 1935

Frank's Gulf Properties Corporation purchased in 1930 and 1935 most of Dauphin Island, which became a tourist destination on the gulf coast of Alabama. He helped organize the Alabama Deep Sea Fishing Rodeo that continues on in 2022. He and his partners sold the rights to the event to the Mobile Chamber of Commerce for just under a million dollars in 1953. He became so famous in 1935, the leaders of the Democratic party recruited him to run as a lawmaker.

When my grandfather was elected to US Congress from the Southern District of Alabama. He maintained an office and a large apartment at the Washington Hotel for twenty-eight years. On the floor of Congress, when they were in session in 1935, he became a lifetime member of the Democratic Party. He took his new career seriously. He made a point of spending his first week of service shaking hands and introducing himself to 434 individual congressperson and 25 of the senators in the nation's capital. He emphasized the point forward to personally working with each one of them, and he would appreciate their help, as Alabama needed a lot done to have the state grow!

His office had pictures hanging on the wall of family, staff, friends, and visitors. He loved photographs so much that he hung them proudly in his hunting lodge in Alabama as well. Congressman Frank's office was known for remaining open seven days a week and was never closed. All constituent's and correspondence would not go unheard or unanswered. His office staff became his extended family, and to his credit, there was never a turnover in his workforce. His chief assistant and secretary were his best friends. At a difficult time,

Frank even took money from his own pocket to pay for the extra help he had to hire in order to answer his mail, which was more than that of anyone else in Congress. Frank made sure that no letter went unanswered. Work was a way of coping with his loss of Frank Junior. He received many letters and condolences as he walked through the halls of his work from many elected officials. He would take a twenty-minute nap and feel refreshed. Although Frank functioned on little sleep, his office was a friendly place, as well as a busy place. Constituents were always welcome and treated like family members that he was pleased to see again. His office staff as well was like family, and due to their dedication and loyalty to the boss, he was well-known for putting in more office hours than any other on Capitol Hill.

Frank's joy and energy was contagious, and his loyal staff members maintained pep and vigor that equaled his own. They worked long and hard for him because of his generosity and compassion. In sickness and adversity, he stood ready to step in and help those in need. After his first years of working seven days a week, he continued working on Saturdays and, on occasions, some Sundays when all other offices were closed. His office staff could hear him down the hall, saying, "Howdy, partner! Everything is made for love," before entering his office.

The Southern delegation was the most powerful on the hill. Like all the successful Southerners, Frank knew the fine art of tooting his own horn without coming across as a braggart. He succeeded in the House and gained seniority with his unfailing drive and outgoing personality one catalyst being that he realized he was competing against more than four hundred and thirty other representatives competing for every federal dollar they could get for their respective districts.

Frank was introduced to the thirty-second Vice President Garner of Texas who served under President Franklin D. Roosevelt from 1933 to 1941. Shortly after taking his oath, Garner and Frank instantly became great friends, forming a genuine fondness for one another. Garner gave him the guideline of "dos and don'ts" for new members: "Boykin, I have made a few speeches on the floor of either House and I wish I could retract some of those I have made." Vice President John Garner retired from the political jungle in 1941.

A TURBULENT LIFE ? ? ?

Frank's great-grandson Bevo, who is my son, found this letter that Grandmother Browder had kept for many years, and she had given it to him. Then he passed it on to me to help with my authoring my new book.

June 28, 1960

> Frank wrote a three-page letter to his grandson Robby and excerpts from the letter are as follows:
> I and your grandmother have moved into the suite that Vice President Garner had occupied at the Washington Hotel. We bought the furniture, rugs, and etcetera, a long time ago. We are just sixty feet from the Treasury Building, and then the Whitehouse. I can see the Presidents study now. F. D. R. is up in the third story, where he works sometimes until one or two in the morning. He gave James phone numbers to call if he ever needed them and said call me anytime collect. I wish I had you to help and all the rest of the boys. Well, there is a lot of work to do because these communists are after us. They remind me of the devil himself turned loose on earth; or maybe Hitler has come back.
> Well, you will be hearing from us, and you will be getting some more things, and if anything should happen that you need us, you can call collect. Our telephone number in the daytime, at the Capitol of the United States is 3121, extensions 5331, 5332, and 5333; and our number at this Washington Hotel is 8-5990 Room 719. I and your grandmother have moved into the suite that Vice President Garner had occupied at the Washington Hotel. We bought the furniture, rugs, and etcetera, a long time ago. We are just sixty feet from the Treasury Building, and then

the Whitehouse. I can see the Presidents study now. F. D. R. is up in the third story, where he works sometimes until one or two in the morning. Well, there is a lot of work to do, because these communists are after us. Call if you ever need us and call us collect. I wish I had you to help and all the rest of the boys. Well, there is a lot of work to do because these communists are after us! Give our love to the family.

Frank and Other

Frank invited many of the elite in Washington, DC, to visit his beautiful and beloved state of Alabama. When some of the Washington leaders arrived in Mobile, Frank escorted his many guests on a tour of the city, which was blooming beautifully with azaleas. After that came a cruise down the fabled Mobile Bay. Then it was off to his game preserve, surrounding the beautiful antebellum plantation home that was first built in 1905 for the Agnes Miles family. The thousands of acres of pristine hunting grounds were famous for the quantity and quality of the game animals that bred and flourished there.

Many of Frank's family members came to believe Ms. Agnes haunts the home as there have been many stories told about Miss Agnes. A few were told by many relatives who stayed in Frank's and Other's room that the rocking chair would rock when no one was sitting in it and embers would burn in the fireplace with no fire burned that day. Lights would go on outside where the deer were hung, and no one was there. Squeaky noises could be heard throughout the house.

Together with his son, James, Frank made the preserve into a place where they could go to relax when work was through. The colonial mansion was the site for the entire family to get together and eat the choicest food from their land. Within that famous old hall, many trophies hung upon the wall, Mallard ducks hung from the ceiling in the entryway. While outside, all kinds of fish swam contentedly in the lakes while mallard drakes soared overhead. Because Alabama's own congressman had an ear for the dog that barks, the other legislators were able to enjoy the bounty of the Boykins' preserve as well.

The founding fathers decreed that members of the lower House must run the electorate every two years, which does not give them enough time to warm their seat in the House Chamber before abandoning the business they were sent to do in Washington to promote their states in order to campaign in their districts for reelection. This involved quite a lot of time, energy, and money, especially since a representative often had to defend his character and record against any dirt a competitor could drum up.

One of the first bills Frank sponsored freed all toll bridges in his state. It was passed, and thousands of Alabamians were grateful. With this accomplished, he persuaded the government to repay approximately three million dollars that Alabama had invested in these bridges, and the government money was used to build more state roads. My grandfather fought for federal low-cost housing for farm folk and residents of rural areas in Alabama. He championed every bill in the House, favoring veterans of the nation's wars, and opposed further loans to Great Britain while the World War I debt remained unpaid. He also voted for rural electrification of every state farm. His famous slogan was "Everything's made for love." Frank was officially sworn in as a US Congressman on July 30, 1935. At age fifty in Washington, DC, his new career started at a critical moment in US history since it was also the era of Franklin Delano Roosevelt's new deal. Frank knew at an early age he would be a success in business.

Shortly after winning the election, Frank and his wife had the unenviable task of explaining to their children that they were moving to Washington, DC. Being a devoted family man, Frank worried about how the kids would take the news, and the reactions were indeed mixed. Naturally, the children didn't want to leave their friends, but they would do anything to support their dad. Almost immediately upon arrival to their place in the nation's capital, Frank and Other's brood was left at the Mobile house with their nanny, Martha, when their mother went to see their father being sworn into office. She was anxiously sitting in the House gallery, filled with pride and with a grin from ear to ear, as her husband entered the aisle of the

House of Chambers on the arm of his Alabama colleague Lester Hill. Frank was beaming as he was sworn in as representative from the first district of his beloved state of Alabama. Speaker Joseph Byrnes even stepped down and offered his hand to welcome the newly minted member of the House.

It was a momentous occasion, yet there was much to live up to and much at stake for his beloved state of Alabama.

Frank knew this and stated, "Southern leadership was at its pinnacle when he entered Congress on August 12, 1935, and a sensation of excitement dangled over the historic chamber where much of America's destinies were shaped."

At the time of his swearing-in ceremony, the first session of the seventy-fourth Congress was coming to an end with only two weeks left before adjournment. Within this relatively short period of time, almost 25 percent of all major legislation passed and was enacted into law.

Frank moved into the Old House Office Building, and his crew instantly went to work decorating the office with historic pictures, guns, knives, a stuffed bear, and other mounted animals that reminded him of his home in Alabama. (After his twenty-eight years of service, it would become a museum of historic memorabilia, telling a story of Frank's life and service to his country.) He was assigned a desirable suite in the Old House Office Building that would normally go to a senior on the Hill and instead went to Frank. Many veterans on Capitol Hill even preferred it to the gold-plated quarters in the hundred-million-dollar range in the Sam Rayburn Building that was open to lawmakers.

Without delay, Frank's office became Grand Central Station with a steady stream of constituents and friends from all over the state and elsewhere, seeking help and guidance from a man with a reputation for great enthusiasm for serving his fellowman. His office staff, as well as his personal secretary, Alphonse Lucas, all followed him from Mobile. Alphonse was the most astute and loyal coworker and secretary Frank ever had. He stayed with Frank as his right hand and remained loyal to him for forty-seven years in and out of Congress. You might say he was Frank's best friend. Frank was already a multimillionaire by that time, so his new government salary was no inducement to serve. At only $7,500 per year, plus a travel allowance of $2,500 a year, and an additional allotment of $2,500 for office help and expenses, he could have easily made more money out of politics than within it.

Rescuer and Gifting of Many Dog Breeds from a Washington, DC, Animal Shelter

1935

Frank would stride into the big cage with the condemned unfortunates, who seemed to sense instinctively that they had found a friend for whom "everything's made for love" including dogs. This big jovial figure and cheery "dog talk" brought a clamorous response of barks, howls, yelps, and leaps. He would rub their bellies one after another, scratch their ears, and pet their backs and necks, all while talking and "cooing" to them. Of all the dogs he rescued, declared the pound assistants, not one ever bit or snarled at him. They knew he was a dog's best friend. Unfortunately, he never knew the breed of Boykin spaniels from South Carolina that he would have fallen in love with at first sight. The workers at the pound were glad to see him as he broke up some of their monotonous days with no one visiting the pound.

Congressman Frank would spend more time when he walked to his office, making a detour to the doghouse than any man in Capitol Hill. He looked over the canines waiting to be executed and selected the best to send to friends and constituents in Alabama. He came to save over two hundred dogs. As word of mouth spread of him retrieving and giving dogs away of many different breeds, he received request from nearly every state even Alaska and countries of Chile and Africa. At the pound, he found many different breeds—Russian wolfhounds, bulldogs, cocker spaniels, bird dogs, whippets, Great Danes, huskies, to name a few. He owned more than a hundred hunting dogs he kept at his hunting lodge. *Collier's* magazine did an article with a picture of him and the dogs he would rescue. He continued rescuing dogs whenever he was in Washington, DC, and his health permitted it.

US Congressman Death of the Oldest Son with Game of Russian Roulette

Friday, January 13, 1939, was perhaps the most turbulent time for James, his parents, sister, and brothers. Headlines in the newspapers was: "Congressman's Son Is Fatally Wounded." Frank and Other immediately boarded a train from Washington, DC, following the death of their son as soonest as they could get there since a snowstorm prevented them from taking a passenger plane, and they had to take a train.

Frank Junior at age twenty had much more life to live as he died so young. He was fatally wounded by playing Russian roulette and miscalculated the chamber the one bullet was in. The young son, a student at Spring Hill College, was killed instantly.

The coroner said, "The revolver he owned and was handling accidently discharged."

He was visiting a home of a friend, and they were planning to attend a movie. The investigating officer called the home and found Frank Junior lying on the hard floor with blood all around. Witnesses were saying the pistol snapped twice and then discharged. He dropped to the floor immediately and died before an ambulance could reach the residence.

In the prime of his life, he was going to transfer to Georgetown University at an early date to be with his father who was serving his second term in Congress. They were awfully close, and they thought how such a handsome man with a promising future, having grown up with hunting, could have been so irresponsible in playing a game with his life expectancy. It was a highly emotional, confusing, and most turbulent time for Other as tears flowed to the floor, unable to gain composure as they heard the news, and they were devastated!

James and Jack picked up Frank and Other at the train station. Their mother sat on a bench, unable to move as it was a dramatic grieving time for their mom and dad. They got them into the car, and James could barely drive as he was shaken by the reactions and turbulence in the car. Tears were shed by Jack and his parents. James had to stay strong and focus on the road as he drove them home. Upon their arrival, their sister Fran immediately hugged her mother and father.

Other's youngest son held Other tightly and said, "Mom, he had no pain."

James cried out, "Mom, Dad, and everyone here, you know Frank Junior is happier than ever in being with his Savior in heaven. Mom, you always quoted at bedtime to us your favorite scripture from your Father's preaching and reading the Bible. Psalm 31, 'In you, O Lord, I have taken refuge, let me never be put to shame; deliver me in your righteousness. Turn your ear to me, come quickly to my rescue; be my rock of refuge, a strong fortress to save me. Since you are my rock and fortress, for the sake of your name lead and guide me. Frank Junior is blessed as God called him to heaven early and needed his help in paradise. Your children remaining here are able to quote scripture because of you, reading to us and giving each one of us a Bible when we were in elementary school and first able to read and to say our prayers every morning and night. I am relieved in knowing my big brother is with God!"

Silence was in the room as everyone was speechless that James had the wisdom to put things in perspective. It didn't remove the pain, but it was easier to live on without the tears for at least a short period of time.

The family looked at James straight in the eyes and said, "Thank you."

Other and Fran gave him a big hug. Frank gave him a pat on the shoulder and shook his hand. Frank Junior was his father's namesake, and they grew awfully close as the children grew up. They knew he was the proud son that his father adored.

It took years for the family to cope with their grief and loss but was never able to forget Frank Junior. James told me and Robby the story of Frank Junior and had us promise him we would never play games with a gun you could shoot bullets with! "The guns are only used for shooting wild game for food and for self-defense. No game playing with deadly guns!"

"I won't," I promised, and Robby echoed the same sentiment to our dad.

My dad taught me and Robby the importance of gun safety, especially while visiting the hunting lodge at our young ages. Dad told us his older brother loved taking chances and was a real daredevil. Once while riding his motorcycle, he saw a pretty girl and wanted to show off, so he stood on the seat and waved his hands. His cycle swerved into a brick wall, and he was tossed into the road, suffering a brain concussion.

Dad said, "Neither of you be a daredevil and do stupid things!"

Frank Junior was buried at the family plot with a headstone in a cemetery in Mobile, Alabama, in 1939. When Frank returned to Washington, DC, all who knew him in the District of Columbia as well as his friends throughout the state of Alabama offered their condolences and sent many sympathy cards to him and his wife.

He fought for his district in Alabama harder and threw himself more into his work, which helped him deal with his grief. He persuaded the Geigy Chemical Company and Alabama Power Company to set up plants in his district of Alabama. He encouraged many companies to come to Alabama such as Vanity Fair Mills and International Paper Company, and funding for the Bankhead Tunnel, which he helped secure, and that was only a few industries he helped bring to Alabama.

He was a senior member of the committee on Merchant Marines and Fisheries and subcommittee on fish and Wildlife. Frank was appointed chairman to a House buildings and grounds committee. In January 1943, a new honor was conferred on Frank with his appointment as chairman of the House Patents Committee, a task he welcomed, knowing that hundreds of the nation's most valuable patents were being handed over to the wrong allies. He was well-versed in patents, as he had several of his own with his turpentine business, and so Chairman Boykin sponsored and steered through the legislative mill a bill to clarify the patent laws. The Boykin Patent Act was voted into law and was often cited as "one of the most constructive pieces of legislation affecting patents enacted by Congress in a single generation."

World War II

1939 to 1945

One day when he arrived at his office, Frank sent a telegram from Washington, DC, to his two sons, James and Jack.

> Congratulations and lots of love on this nineteenth birthday in 1940 and all other days. You have been fine boys, and I know you are going to now be wonderful men because your mother has taken such loving care of you and trained you exactly right. From now on, it is almost up to you to financially take care of yourselves and your families. We will keep helping all we can always. Love to you both, Mother, Dick, and all our loved ones.
>
> Daddy

James called his parents, "Today we received our shipping orders. We are shipping to Americus air force base in Georgia, which is supposed to be a swell place, so if you come down that way, I can see you. It is still freezing cold down here. At the present, I am a group leader in charge of quarters, and it is really cold in this building. I have my overcoat wrapped around me, but that doesn't do much good. The only way to get warm is to do like we did in Mobile when you and Dad were in DC, and that is to go outside."

The night fighters were a different breed of men, Dad explained to me. The pilots were all volunteers flying the new 1943 Northrop

A TURBULENT LIFE ? ? ?

706 P-61 Black Widow Night Fighter planes built for war and preserving freedom. My dad served as a lieutenant in what was known as the Air Corp, a division of the army and in today's times known as the United States Air Force as it became its own branch of service after World War II. Dad was a flight officer as he loved flying! He flew the P-61 twin engine night fighter with a maximum speed of 366 mph and could fly up to 610 miles and one of the first planes to have radar in World War II. They can be seen today in the Air Force Museum in Dayton, Ohio, or at the Smithsonian Museum in Washington, DC, or even in the People's Republic of China. My dad was proud to share his stories of the war.

He said, "The P 61s reached the Pacific and joined the sixth night fighter squadrons on Guadalcanal. Several P-61 squadrons were stationed in the Philippines where I was stationed."

He told me of the sustained attacks in the Philippines when the US in the weeks after they entered the war.

Dad said, "it was a heralding experience being in the Philippines when it was attacked by the Japanese on December 8, 1941, Nine hours after the attack on Pearl Harbor. Our mission during the war was to perform ground level 'Armed Intruder Sorties,' looking for railroad trains, truck convoy, barge shipping, troop concentrations, factories, and other prime targets of opportunity in order to destroy bombs. These were hazardous nighttime ventures. The most frequent objectives were done in the dark and stormy skies over enemy territory using radar. Typically, the enemy was tracked and shot down before they could attack our bases and installations.

"All flying is exhilarating and inspiring," said Dad. "You'd use by-the-book flying to fight other flyers, but flying to fight by night reaches heights of personal experience that are rarely achieved, especially as a squadron commander. One of the key factors involved in being a pilot during the invasion of Borneo, for instance, was to fly over convoys and navy ships, as the new radio IFF was the only way to communicate to the scramble room of a ship or by a visual."

Dad also told me that while flying with the Australians in Borneo, baboons would often line the runway. As they landed, the pilots frightened the apes, which scattered like flies when their planes touched down.

"It was quite a sight to see!" Dad said. "We would often do a 'flyby,' just to see the hysteria it caused among the baboons, but there was also a serious reason for our fun. We were trying to prevent fatal accidents that could be caused by sucking a baboon into the intake of an engine, and when they were clear, we could land safely. As they did their flight maneuvers, they would have to do flyovers because of the runway being full of baboons that were actively playing on the runway. We had to account for fuel used in flyovers from missions enabling us to land safely."

On Borneo, the natives' religious beliefs included killing Christians, Dad informed me. The most common way for the populace to eradicate Christians in that era was to add sugar and bamboo to clog their gas tanks.

"One night a pilot was taking off with his crew," Dad said, "and the plane started and was up in the air when the engine sputtered and crashed into the water at the end of the landing strip. The alarm sounded late at night, and I was the first in the jeep with others not far behind. I remember driving, then bumping into a ditch, hitting my head on the windshield, and waking up in a field hospital."

"Oh, Daddy!" I teared up as he shared his remembrances.

"It was okay, honey. My head was busted up some, and my clothes were wringing with blood, but my house boy, who was loyal and trustworthy because I paid him well, cleaned all the blood from my clothing and brought them back to the hospital. This sort of thing was important, as it was hard to come by clothes in that part of the world in wartime. Later, I had to undergo a complete physical examination before I could continue flying. The X-ray showed I had pneumonia. I was relieved when I finally got over the pneumonia and was granted permission to fly at last, as I hated not being a part of the action," he said modestly.

Unfortunately, another accident in the Philippines soon grounded me once more. While he was swimming in the water of Bacolod, his feet were severely cut by the razor-sharp coral in that area. He had been unaware of the danger and did not wear shoes as he swam.

Once again, he was rushed to a field hospital and grounded from flying. This time, running further tests, an X-ray found mycobacterium tuberculosis in his lungs. Deemed contagious and considered a high risk was the reason for his disability and time lost from duty for six months. He was hospitalized overseas and remained there until the war ended. Then he was shipped to Fitzsimmons General Hospital, a facility specializing in tuberculosis treatment in Denver, Colorado. There he spent another six to seven months recovering before finally being sent home for good.

"I didn't know what was wrong with me," Dad admitted. "I thought I was a leper. I didn't even know what TB was. While I was in the hospital this time, the medical staff taught me all about the disease and showed me how to take care of myself, as well as how to relax. With their expert help, I recovered."

Dad explained to me that the philosophy he'd learned from his own father during their many hunting trips were the greatest experiences he'd ever had. They helped him sustain a positive attitude during that trying time in his life.

"Your grandfather tried to expose me mentally and physically to whatever life had to throw at me. From an early age, I was mentally prepared to defend our country during war," he reflected. "The values he learned while hunting with Dad included integrity, strength, compassion, and to honor all people."

The Philippines was governed as a semi-independent commonwealth government; the United States controlled in the Filipino American army as my dad explained it to me. Filipinos in the army units uncaptured, with the communist trying to take over the country, all the troops including the US troops played a role in the resistance. The Japanese never tried to occupy many of the smaller towns. He told me he would hear stories of thousands of Filipinos that fought in the war. He told me of the houseboy he had who would take care of him in his hut and provided food to him on a daily basis.

In 1944, Allied forces liberated the islands from the Japanese control with the naval invasion. My uncle Dick, my father's younger brother, served in the navy. Also, Aunt Fran's husband, Uncle Riley, was a lieutenant commander who served in the navy. Mother's brother Brevard was also in the navy as a lieutenant and naval commander.

My dad wrote copious letters to his family during his war days. His family kept them all. My dad collected them and wanted me to have them as I read them numerous times as the originals were in a large black photo album. He also had copies made, able to read them. My stories come from the mouth of my father and what I remembered from his letters I read.

The Telegram That Changed History

1940, 1941, 1942, 1943, and 1944

Frank and Other Boykin had risen, as usual, with the firing of the cannon at Fort Myer across the Potomac. Other was reading aloud from their hometown newspaper, the *Mobile Press Register*, when her eyes lit upon a column titled "A Hundred Years Ago Today," which told the story of a group of intrepid Alabamians who, a century before, had built a dam at McGrew's Shoals on the Tombigbee River near Jackson, Alabama. While drilling and blasting for the dam's foundation, they struck a strong stream of oil that, within several days, had coated the surface of the river as far down as Fort Stoddert, sixty miles below the shoals.

A party of Native Americans set the oil afire. Flames engulfed the river, which burned like an inferno for miles and miles. Blazing oil enveloped the swamps along the riverbank, cremating hundreds of deer, bear, and small game. Turkeys, quail, and owls fleeing the holocaust were defeathered or destroyed. Thousands of trees, fine timber along the river's edge, were burned to ashes. People traveled miles to gaze in silent awe at the broad burning river that, for three days, had devoured everything within reach.

"Frank," said Other, glancing up from her reading, "this thing has given me an idea."

"I'll bet it's the same as mine," replied Frank. "And I'm going to do something about it right now."

Husband and wife had gotten the same idea at the same exact moment. They had earlier been talking about England's plight and wondering, as was the whole world, just when Hitler would invade that country.

"Why," they seemed to ask each other silently, "couldn't the British set the English Channel afire just as the Tombigbee was set afire a century ago and destroy the German invasion fleet and barges loaded with troops, tanks, and guns?"

It was just 5:00 a.m., but Frank called his close friend, Joe Danziger, who lived in Fort Worth, Texas. Joe had known oil all his life, and when he answered the phone, Frank immediately asked him if the idea was feasible. He listened alertly to what Frank said and gave an emphatic yes. Two hours later, Frank had a five-hundred-word telegram from his friend explaining exactly what to do. It would require dumping enormous quantities of oil on the Channel waters and setting it afire with bullets and flares. Early in the morning of August 1940, Frank boarded a taxi at the Capitol and sped to the White House. After hurriedly revealing his mission to the presidential secretary, Marvin McIntyre, he was immediately ushered into Franklin Delano Roosevelt's (FDR's) private office, where the president read the telegram that Frank handed to him.

"Frank," he said, "I want you to see Lord Lothian, the British Ambassador, at once and have him read this telegram. Tell him exactly what you've just told me. This information is too valuable to keep away from the British. Say nothing to anyone about this."

Leaving the White House in a rush, Frank taxied to the British Embassy, where he presented the telegram to Lord Lothian, who was impressed at its detail. He promptly communicated it to London by transatlantic telephone. What the telegram contained would change the course of history. At that dark hour in Britain's history, Winston Churchill, with eloquence that would resound through the ages, had assumed the position of prime minister and rallied his people. Months before, in May of 1940, Adolph Hitler had unleashed his long-anticipated Western offensive. His divisions blazed through the low countries and overtook France's line. Denmark and Norway had fallen prey to the Nazi party.

It was in the air over the "English Isles" that Hitler had paused at the Channel, his panzers panting for more work to do, a million of his Wehrmacht poised to resume their bombardment. Hitler's Operation Sea Lion, an invasion of England, was started dated for late September. Meanwhile, Britain got ready. Residents and visitors were urged to curtail seashore outings. Church bells were silenced and ordered to ring only to warn of parachutist invasion. The little island mobilized to meet the Nazi onslaught on her soil. By the end of June, Hitler's swastika flew over Europe from the Pyrenees to the North Cape of Norway. England was on the verge of absolute, unconditional defeat. There was talk of bargaining with Hitler, of handing over the British fleet before he crossed the Channel, and erased what the world had once known as England.

On September 7, the Luftwaffe, bombers and fighters, roared through the late afternoon toward England in London for fifty-six nights, wave on wave, Hitler's vultures discharged death and destruction on the great metropolis of the world. This was the Blitz, Hitler's next-to-last card in the Battle of Britain if his bombers could break the spirit and pride of the British people by raining sorrow, misery, and fire from the night skies, devastating London itself if need be. They would force the Churchill government to capitulate and ask for terms after thousands of the soldiers burned. Wehrmacht were transported across the Channel to complete the conquest of the British Isles. It was not to be. Many believe that Hitler's greatest mistake was the failure to invade Britain in September of 1940 when she appeared defenseless, and bombers could cause the destruction of her proudest city. Instead, on September 16, 1940, the Royal Air Force (RAF) met Hitler's invasion fleet in the English Channel and destroyed it.

In exterminating Hitler's seaborne army, the RAF used the technique suggested by oilman Joe Danziger, which had been relayed to the British through Frank via President Roosevelt and, in turn, Lord Lothian. RAF bombers covered the waters of the Channel with oil, igniting it with flares and combustible bullets. The invasion armada was enveloped in a sea of flames that incinerated or injured an estimated fifty thousand German soldiers. It also destroyed the invasion fleet, crowded with troops, artillery, tanks, and materials.

Several times toward the end of 1944, President Roosevelt brought up the subject with Frank, simply saying, "Frank, I think you ought to know your idea was used. It served its purpose amply."

Later, Frank revealed, "Lord Lothian told me in confidence that the idea had been carried out by the British, and that an attempted invasion of England by the Germans was thwarted through its use."

In 1943, the full story of Hitler's invasion was brought to light. Datelined in London, the story appeared under the byline of a *United Press* correspondent. He pieced it together from what he learned from Belgian nurses and doctors who had cared for survivors of the Holocaust and by intimate contact with higher-ups of the exiled government in London.

"I was told in Antwerp," said this correspondent, "that the Germans had concentrated hundreds of self-propelled barges, each about one hundred and sixty feet long that had been used on the Rhine and continental rivers. Belgian nurses told me that the German survivors had called Hitler's battle a hellish nightmare. Belgians with whom I talked were surprised to learn that the British and American public had never been told of the failure of the invasion attempt. It was common knowledge in Belgium.

"Renee Meurisse, a Belgium Red Cross nurse, was in charge of caring for Belgium refugees at the time. She said, 'During the day of September 17, we heard rumors that thousands of bodies of German soldiers were being washed ashore along the Belgian beaches. That night at seven, a German Red Cross train of forty coaches pulled into the Brussels station. We had been expecting a Belgian refugee train and were surprised when it was filled with Germans. A German officer, who looked tired, approached me and asked if we could give aid to his wounded.' Miss Meurisse said the German officer told her his train had been on the wrong line, and 'my men are dying from lack of treatment.' 'We sent a call for more nurses and ambulances and began taking the wounded from the train,' she said. 'The moans and screams were terrible.'

"'I helped carry one young German soldier from the train to the stretcher. He was horribly burned about the head and shoulders. The doctor and I placed this particular soldier in a corner, and we decided we could find out what happened. We began by asking him about his mother and then about his sweetheart. After each answer, I asked him, 'Where were you going when this happened?'

"'Finally, we pieced together the whole story. He said they had been told they were going to invade Britain, that nothing could stop them and that it was just a matter of getting into the boats and going across the Channel. He said it was horrible. The whole Channel was in flames. The British bombed and machine-gunned them. Hell couldn't be worse. And then he died on the stretcher. We cared for more than five hundred soldiers. Many of them died there in the Brussels station.'"

Those intrepid dam-builders at McGrew's Shoals on the Tombigbee River over a century before would have never dreamed that they would set the pattern for a future generation to save the world from the Nazis.

In a letter to the Mobile *Press-Register* in 1944, Frank's partner, Joe Danziger, wrote of the idea that thwarted the Nazi invasion of England. "It is Frank and his alertness that all credit is due in grasping the importance of ideas suggested to him and acting upon them immediately. The State of Alabama can well be proud of your great congressman, and our only regret is that he does not hail from Texas."

I am loving history, and having taught it in public and private schools, I was surprised never to read or teach about the burning of the English Channel. It was a vital part of history that was never told and should be written in school history books.

In February 1941, the Battleship *Alabama* was launched at Norfolk, Virginia. Frank was there, glorifying in the great day. (Today, visitors can tour the great ship as a historic museum on the Mobile, causeway in one of Frank's projects had also come full circle, and the Bankhead Tunnel in Mobile, Alabama, opened under the Mobile River in 1941.

Resources

Everything Is Made For Love book by Edward Boykin, interviews with Frank and Other Boykin, and article in the Mobile *Press-Register* and records in the state of Alabama Archives.

Browder Boykin (Mom) Frank W Boykin (Grandfather) Ocllo, Boykin (Grandmother)

Marriage of James and Browder

1947

James and Browder met and formed an instant attraction to one another. After dating for a period of time, James asked Browder's father for her hand in marriage as that was a tradition in those days to do. Her father granted him permission to do so. When the time was right, James asked her to marry him, and without any hesitation, she said yes. They went together to pick out the engagement ring and wedding ring set at a jewelry store.

James and Browder had a large wedding as it was hard to cut down their list of whom they wanted to have present to see their wedding vows. As custom, the bride's parents paid for the wedding. Browder's father also paid for the beautiful white gown with a white veil she wore for the large wedding held in the Presbyterian Church as she was bought up as Presbyterian. James and his parents were Methodist as his mother's father was a Methodist minister. They followed the custom of having his parents paying for the after-dinner rehearsal party held at the Mobile Country Club for close friends, the wedding party, and family that were invited. The reception was also held at the Country Club but was in the ballroom that would hold the large number of guest they invited. Dancing to the band that was hired, it was a night to be remembered with champagne flowing and dancing. A toast was made by his twin brother Jack who served as his best man! His younger brother was a groomsman in the wedding party along with Browder's brother Brevard. A sit down dinner was served, and all the guests left stuffed.

James and Browder were leaving, and the guest threw uncooked rice at them as that was the tradition, and they ran to the limousine, holding hands, and got in and waved goodbye to the guest as they were driven away by the limo driver. The groomsmen attached many cans to the limo, making enough noise to know they were just married when the limo driver dropped them off at the airport.

They checked in and boarded a flight to Cuba for their honeymoon. James spoke just enough Spanish for them to get by. They enjoyed the breezes on the beach tans and sangria with the food they would order in the restaurants, except for breakfast. My mom shared a story of my dad on their honeymoon; he had beautiful olive skin, brown hair, five foot eleven inches.

While dancing in the street, passersby would ask him in Spanish, "Where do you live in Cuba?"

He would respond, "I am from the United States, and they would give him a surprised look."

He loved his camera and took many pictures of his bride with her long wavy blond hair, fair skin, and five foot eight inches. James purchased many Cuban cigars to give to family and friends when he returned home. His sweetheart had him by some cigars for her dad as well. Returning home from their honeymoon, they shared many stories with family and friends.

Browder would go with James to his dad's hunting lodge but never participated in the hunts as she had two young children she had to attend to. She was there for holidays and participated with her children, holding me in her arms, dressed in a pretty dress my mother picked out for me to wear. The only job she ever had was a telephone agent with Eastern Airlines. She would be a pole worker for Frank's campaigns as a congressman.

Throughout their married life, it was apparent to close friends and family who would observe and socialize with them. They would be heard saying the following statement among themselves, "As the saying goes, they were opposites that were attracted to one another with no common goals in life."

The romance was strong, and in 1949 when his sweetheart told James she was pregnant, they were so excited and couldn't wait to

A TURBULENT LIFE ? ? ?

share the good news with their parents and then the other family members and friends. Great Depression began in 1929; the same year "Browder was born." She was James's first wife, and that belle was full of Southernisms, who twirled a parasol 'neath the canopy of an Azalea, Alabama, magnolia tree. She was literate with impeccable penmanship whose southern drawl was amongst her charm. Robert instantly knew she was a genuine Southern belle who became his darlin'. Robert asked her to dance, and she stole his heart.

Birth of First Child Robby

1949

The day arrived, and Browder told James to get her to the hospital immediately. He got her to the car as she could hardly walk and speeded to the Mobile Infirmary Hospital in Mobile, Alabama, emergency room.

James yelled, "My wife is having a baby!"

They immediately rolled her in wheelchair to the hospital delivery room.

Our mother would often tell people how she nearly lost her life having Robby with the lengthy, intense delivery she experienced and was one she never wanted again. She had gained a lot of weight with him as well. She had never had such cramping and excruciating pain as the contractions were extremely hard to push his head out.

Hours had gone by with the doctor assisting her in a calm voice, "I see the head."

Browder yelled, "This is taking too long, get the baby out with a few other choice words!"

Looking up at the clock, the doctor saw it had taken over ten hours of intense labor pains with Browder screaming. He finally was able to use forceps to turn his head, enabling him to come out as he was in a breach position.

Crying was heard from the baby, and the doctor said, "It's a boy!"

After several hours, Browder regained her composure and said, "Praise God! It is over!"

A TURBULENT LIFE ? ? ?

He was almost more than she could handle as she felt she was going to die. The doctor cut the umbilical cord, washed, and got his Apgar score, testing his color, heart rate, reflexes, muscle tone, and respiration. Robby scored 10 as he was such a large baby. He told her he weighed fourteen pounds and three ounces, which was the largest baby I had ever delivered. She didn't want any other children after having such agony she experienced in the delivery room with him.

The doctor was concerned about Browder and took her blood pressure and pulse, which were high. Her temperature was in the normal range, and her face coloring was almost white. They bought her some chicken soup to eat, and she threw it up. They took her to a private room that James had requested for her. The floor nurses checked on her every thirty minutes as Browder was exhausted and needed some sleep. Her vitals still had to be checked on a time schedule to follow.

James was ecstatic that his sweetheart survived the birth and had Robby with his thick dark hair as a baby that eventually turned blond as his mother had blond hair. They were both proud parents and had advice from both sets of grandparents on how to care for the infant. He was born in the original Mobile Infirmary Hospital, and the nurses in the nursery raved about how cute and how big a baby he was! Many of the nurses had not seen a baby that big before. James and Browder were jubilant, and the proud father passed out cigars to family and male friends who visited his wife in the hospital, as it was a time-honored tradition in those years. So many came by to see their son. James ran out of cigars and drove to the closest store for more as he didn't want to be known as one not to honor the tradition of passing them out.

It was an exciting time for the delighted parents, but Browder was unable to nurse him, so she bottle-fed him. The obstetrician and her regular doctor kept her in the hospital past the customary time of a delivery of a baby. They would not release the baby to his father until his mother was stable enough to be released. James packed some of Browder's clothes and toiletries that included her makeup she didn't like being without. She always wanted to look her best to family and friends.

Gaga and Papa were the first to visit their grandson who was the largest baby they had ever seen, looking through the glass window of the nursery as he was easy to spot in the crowded area. PaPa couldn't believe his baby girl could deliver such a big baby.

He said, "We are giving you a years' worth of cloth diaper service to be delivered to your door when you need them."

"Thank you so much, Dad and Mom."

When the nurse bought him in, they were both able to hold him. Then they gave him to his mother who was still weak from the delivery. They didn't stay long and left her in the good hands of the nursing staff.

Other and Frank came shortly after her parents left when James was in the room. They both loved Browder and could see how tiring it was for her. The nurse brought Robby into the room and handed her to his mother. Then she handed him to her husband, and he let his mother hold him as he cooed in her hands. Papa B was chomping at the bit to hold his new grandson, and Other put him in his arms, and Robby appeared to him to give a giggle. Papa B said he was a heavy baby and sat in the room in a chair with him for a couple of minutes. James's mother and father gave Browder the present they bought for Robby, and it was a sterling silver fork, spoon, and baby knife and rattle and teether with his initials engraved on them. Browder thanked them profusely for the wonderful gift. They noticed how tired she was and made their goodbyes.

The day finally arrived at the end of the week, and Mother and Robby were allowed to go home. James had cleaned the car and made it comfortable for his wife and Robby to ride home in. In the ride home, Mother and son finally bonded as she held him in her lap. Neighbors and family members who were unable to see him in the hospital rushed over with food and baby supplies they didn't have. It was an exciting time in the proud parents' lives. They had cloth diapers in an unlimited supply as they had a service deliver them to their residence that Papa and Gaga had given them as a present.

James had a crib placed in their bedroom and the antique mahogany rocking chair her parents had given them. So they could

A TURBULENT LIFE ? ? ?

watch over Robby as his father was very protective of both mother and his firstborn son. He was a handful for his mom to carry.

He would cry every time he wanted his bottle and to be fed. He also sucked his thumb, and after two months of trying to get him to stop at age three, they were successful and praised him. As his reward for doing, they took him out for ice cream. He consumed it and was a happy little boy.

Browder was pregnant with another baby, and James was ecstatic about it. Browder was skeptical as she did not want to experience the pain she did with Robby. She had a portrait done of herself as portraits were common to have done in her family from the 1800s. She was twenty-one, getting ready to turn twenty-two when she had it done. She had always told me I was in the portrait as she was carrying me then. At age three, Robby was glad he would have someone to play with. Mom didn't gain as much weight as she did with Robby, and the family prayed for an easier pregnancy for her this time.

Robby would ask his mom, "How much longer before the baby comes?"

Numerous times, she would say, "Not much longer, but when I am ready, you will know."

He would say, "Hurry up, Mom, I want to know if my new playmate will be a boy or girl."

Mom would reply, "I can't either, and I hope it is a girl because I already have a wonderful son."

Baby Gracie Lu Is Born

1952

The day finally came when the contractions were close, and James was at home, and on the way to the hospital, they dropped Robby off at his grandmother and grandfather's house. He called them Gaga and Papa. It was close to the Mobile Infirmary. Then he speeded to the hospital as Browder's contractions seemed to be getting stronger, and she was yelling, "Get me there now!"

Arriving at the emergency room, some of the hospital staff recalled Browder's almost dying with her baby boy of fourteen pounds and three ounces that she and James named Robby on his birth certificate.

Commotion at the Mobile Infirmary began, and the doctor was immediately called as they entered the hospital. The doctor got to the hospital and had time to wash up before delivering a little girl seven pounds and four ounces.

He immediately said, "It's a little girl. She was a lot easier to deliver than your big boy."

He cut her umbilical cord, and her baby tolerated the birthing process well as she immediately began crying.

The doctor said to James and Browder, "Her color is good, heart rate is normal, her reflexes on hand and feet are good, she has a small muscle tone, and respiration is good. She has an Apgar score of seven, which is in the lower end of the normal range. In other words, you have a healthy baby girl. What is her name to be?"

The proud father answered Gracie Lu.

James said, "She is a beautiful baby girl with little blond ringlets and her five fingers and toes."

A TURBULENT LIFE ? ? ?

Her mother asked to see her. She was beautiful as she was able to hold her before the nurse took her to the nursery. I was born in the new updated section of the Mobile Infirmary.

On January 31, 1952, on a foggy, icy cold day, President Harry S. Truman was president, and Allen Barkley was vice president and elected by Democrats. Truman left office in 1953 as an unpopular president serving four years as a one-term president. Through history of the years passing by which seemed to move rapidly through many peoples' lives,' the world was increasingly growing in populations in many countries! After President Truman's death, he was in later years ranked as a particularly good president by historians. James called all in their families, giving them the good news.

He then left and told his sweetheart, "I will be back in a bit with Robby."

His son had recently learned how to talk nonstop at age three and eight months older than his baby sister. Robby could not wait to hear from his dad if he had a sister or brother. Gaga and Papa were as anxious as he was. They played jacks with him and taught him how to play pick-up sticks while waiting.

James arrived at their house and said, "Your mom had a healthy, beautiful little girl."

They were all excited to hear the wonderful news.

His dad picked up Robby from his grandparents and took him to see his baby sister for the first time at the hospital. He was anxious to get to the hospital to see his sister.

When they entered his mother's room, he hugged her and asked, "Where is my baby sister?"

James replied, "The nurse is getting her from the newborn babies' nursery and bringing her to the room."

She was born healthy with a loud set of lungs when she cried. The nurse entered the room and placed Gracie Lu in her mother's arms. Robby climbed on the bed to get a better look at his sister.

He uttered the words, "She is so little. Was I that small?"

Mom replied, "You were larger and heavier. Gracie Lu weighed seven pounds and four ounces."

Robby asked, "Can I hold her?"

Mom reached over as he was on the bed with her and lay Gracie Lu on his lap. Gracie Lu cooed as he was holding her, and she made a sound like giggling with the strange faces he gave her. Mom told him to hand her back, and he didn't want to give her back. He loved her and was so glad to have a baby sister.

James walked over to Robby and said, "Hand her to me," and he did.

Robby climbed off the bed and was getting restless and wanted to go home. The nurse entered the room and took Gracie Lu to bottle-feed her as Mom could not breastfeed.

James and Robby kissed Browder and Gracie Lu and said, "We will see you tomorrow."

Browder was tired and fell asleep until the nurse would enter and take her vitals temperature and blood pressure.

On the next day, both sets of grandparents visited Gracie Lu and Browder at the hospital at different times of the day. Gaga and Papa thought the baby girl was cute as a button with her little blond curls and her hazel eyes. She started crying, and they hit the call button for the nurse, and she came in with Gracie Lu's bottle as it was her feeding time. The nurse gave Browder a refresher course as the bottle she was given was different than the one they gave her with Robby.

Gaga and Papa said goodbye, so their daughter could have alone time with her precious little girl.

Other and Frank were in town from Washington, DC, and were delighted to see the newest member of the family and gave her a sterling silver rattle to play with. James and Robby entered the room when Robby's grandparents were visiting. Dad gave his mom and dad a hug, then Robby hugged them and was glad to see them. When they left Browder gave James and Robby the great news that she and Gracie Lu were being released tomorrow morning.

The next morning, James and Robby were dressed in their warm winter clothes and in unison said, "It is bitterly cold outside. We bought some winter clothes and a warm coat for you, honey, and two baby blankets you received from the baby shower that was given to you to wrap Gracie Lu in."

A TURBULENT LIFE ? ? ?

The nurse entered the room with Gracie Lu wrapped in a blanket given to them from the hospital staff along with instructions for caring for their new baby girl and her birth certificate and a picture of her babies' two feet they had blue printed.

Browder and James both said, "Thank you for the memories."

The nurse handed Browder release papers to sign for the happy family to go home.

The outside air was freezing that morning, and Gracie Lu was bundled up with blankets and Browder with a warm coat to return home. When they arrived home, the nursery was painted pink, and she had the same crib as Robby. James began rocking her to sleep in the antique mahogany rocking chair Gaga gave them. As he held her close to him, calming her down from her crying, she fell asleep in his arms. He gently placed her in the crib without waking her.

Browder was put to bed as she was worn out from all the excitement. She began working on Gracie Lu's baby book she received from a friend at the baby shower she was thrown by Gaga in her home. She immediately placed the many cards she received at the hospital and the items from the nurse in it. She was diligent in keeping up with it throughout Gracie Lu's early life as she was with Robby's as well.

My brother was so glad to have his mother and sister home. He learned to feed me with the bottle. When I was old enough, my brother would spoon my baby food in my mouth, and we got things messy for our mom to pick up.

Old Papers and Pictures in File Cabinet Found in a Barn of the Congressman

1950s and Beyond

Tarasee had me at age forty-six, driving in my SUV to the lodge where she met me. Taking me into the red home that was once Isaac's, Frank's head caretaker on the plantations home, he maintained the acreage and lodge. As Tarasee explained to me in Isaac's old house, they moved the old, musty, cobwebbed, wooden-looking cardboard file cabinets from the barn where they had found them and cleaned the cobwebs off before taking them inside. With the current caretaker in present times, Hobby carried the files to my car. As I siphoned through them, they were stuffed full of business papers, personal letters, memorabilia, and song sheets titled "Everything Is Made for Love" written by local friends, in hopes it would be a theme song for his movie. Frank and Other would decide which song would be selected for the full-length picture show to be seen in theaters around the country.

It was a bonanza to me as I felt like I had hit the jackpot into learning of my beloved father's family's history and their untold stories. I felt like I was in heaven; I had the history buzz, especially of my family roots! Having taught geography in Dunedin, Florida, public schools several years after graduating college as well as teaching my favorite subject and love of American history, I learned more of my heritage about my grandparents and their untold stories with some as untold history. I felt as though I had died and gone to heaven!

A TURBULENT LIFE ? ? ?

Ciphering through thousands of telegrams, letters, song sheets, and movie script of Frank's life titled "Everything's Made for Love," he had earned all this through his own labor and of his own hand and brain. Using all the injection of enthusiasm of his philosophy "Everything's Made for Love," Frank was no stranger to the small screen. For several years, he did the Ted Mack telethon fundraiser, for which he received the following letter:

February 6, 1951

Dear Mr. Boykin,

>Words fail me when I try to express my very deep appreciation for the enthusiastic support you gave me, both last year and this, toward the success of the VIP shows. You are one of the kindest, most effective, and most beloved persons it has ever been pleasure to know. Anyone who has you as an ally is fortunate indeed.
>Indebted to you immeasurably are the Ted Mack staff, the Women's National Press Club, and the USO. Some time, I hope all of us will find a way to repay you. At least, in part.

>Ever so sincerely and gratefully,
>Hope Ridings Miller
>Associate Producer of the VIP Amateur Shows

He had an article in *Collier's* magazine with picture along with him saving dogs at the pet shelter. Numerous articles in newspapers in Alabama and throughout other states about him.

I was surprised and fascinated sifting through his files to find Frank made a contract as a US Representative with Breedlove Production Company in Los Angeles, California. I had never heard of his efforts of making a contract with Breedlove, granting him authority to act as his exclusive agent in bringing his story to the screen, radio, television, and other literary media. Also, when necessary, he would perform duties of technical director for the studio to assure accuracy and good faith in production. Breedlove would obtain the highest price and best terms possible for the story, but every offer would be submitted to Frank for approval. Frank received letters from wannabe actors and songwriters, many of whom sent bios and lyrics to a theme song titled "Everything's Made for Love," a full-length movie in the late fifties and early sixties. While I was growing up, none of my relatives had mentioned it. The following letter was written by Frank's secretary to Mr. Breedlove:

> All of us here, including many congressmen from all of the states, are very pleased about your proposition to have Mr. Boykin help make a human-interest picture. We, of course, know that he can do it with ease. As a matter of fact, during World War I, he had a very flattering offer from Hollywood to make a picture, but he was working day and night in the manufacturing of ships, running his turpentine stills, sawmills, etc.
>
> Since the article in *Collier's* by our friend, Mr. Davenport, we have received many, many letters which might be of interest to you. Also, some of his old friends have composed several songs on his slogan, "Everything's Made for Love."
>
> Just make any suggestions that you think might be helpful, and I will try to have everything in shape by the time he returns.
>
> Sincerely yours,
(Miss) Avis Mallette

*****

A TURBULENT LIFE ? ? ?

February 11, 1952
Marshall R. Breedlove
615-3/a Kelton Avenue
Los Angeles, California

My dear Mr. Breedlove,

    A photographer from the *Saturday Evening Post* joined me on a hunt at the Boykin Hunting Lodge at McIntosh, Alabama, where Aaron Burr was captured, and he came all the way from Philadelphia to take a picture of our living room at the Hunting Lodge where we have many trophies. He told me that they wanted to write a story about the place with pictures of the deer, wild turkeys, quail, doves, foxes, coons, bobcats, and bears, but I believe this picture of the living room will be in next month's issue of *Saturday Evening Post*. Anyway, the judgment, everybody in Washington and Alabama, or almost anywhere else, will cooperate with us. I was in a show to raise money for the Heart Fund, along with about forty other congressmen. We had a show in Constitution Hall here and had an overflow group, including the president and our leaders. Then we went to New York, and some young lady that was in the theatre, whom I never met, composed a song about me. They call it "Everything Is Made for Love," and I am enclosing a copy of it and return it to me as soon as you finish it. Some man with a good voice in New York made a record of it, and we played it Christmas Day in Mobile, and we thought it was pretty good.
    We have at Mobile facing on Mobile Bay the great Brookley Air Depot, the largest installation of its kind in this country. They have every

kind of airplane that is made, hundreds of hundreds of them from the smallest to the largest. They work about fifteen thousand people there. We can use any planes or any part of this great Air Depot for the movie.

I also forgot to mention that Fort Morgan where we have the hotel is the place where our great-great-grandmothers landed, and if you know that part of the history of the country, they were called the casket girls (where French orphans came to Alabama as wives for colonists). I believe it would be a great thing to reproduce that particular part of Fort Morgan. I would be glad to send you the data on this.

With every good wish, I am
sincerely your friend,
Frank W. Boykin

Awed by Frank's international connections, loyalty to his friends, and humility in the face of success, Mr. Breedlove wrote directly to Frank, stating: At age sixty, Frank had emerged as a national figure, and his life was exciting and enjoyable. His exuberance jetted him into the spotlight in a manner unlike anything seen in Washington in a generation. He walked with kings, queens, presidents, prime ministers, popes, and head of governments, yet never lost touch with the less exalted of his friends and constituents.

Worldly honors had fallen lightly on his shoulders. He had earned all this through his individual labor and of his own hand and brain. On the way up, he had fought many a grueling battle. He had enemies, but this applied to most men struggling from the very bottom to the top and remaining there. Considering the kind of presence my grandfather had, a deal for a movie based on his life was being worked out in 1951 with Marshall Breedlove Productions, Inc. in Los Angeles, California, I desperately want to see if it was ever made.

A TURBULENT LIFE ? ? ?

Those to be involved were quite impressive names with lots of credits in their bios in the 1900s. Marshall R. Breedlove was producer, along with George J. O'Brien, a producer and contract actor with 20th Century Fox, who, in 1947, was in *My Wild Irish Rose*; in 1948, in the John Ford-Harion Cooper production *Fort Apache*; in 1949, in the Ford-Cooper production *She Wore a Yellow Ribbon*; and in 1950 to 1951, in his own production, *Gold Raiders*. Many of the movies can be seen on Turner Classic Movies on television or specials offered in theaters in 2022.

On May 21, 1953, Mr. Breedlove wrote to Frank:

> Negotiations are underway with a major studio for a deal whereby we can lease space and facilities and also arrange for distribution of the film under their organizational setup. The studio executive has demonstrated considerable interest in the project. He saw the publicity regarding it last week and is now investigating the possibility of working out a mutually acceptable plan of production with my company. Under this plan, his studio would lease space and equipment to us, would generally supervise the production, and would follow through with the release of the picture to theatres in this country and abroad.
> They are also interested in participating financially with a percentage of stock coming to them in proportion to the amount of money advanced. I've told them that we were planning on $900,000.00, which, as I explained to you, contained a contingency amount which would assure an outstanding finished product. Should we work out a satisfactory plan this total amount probably could be scaled down to about $750,000.00 to $800,000.00. Upon receipt of finished script, 5 percent of the actual outlay is due. That would mean that you, Frank,

and your associates would have to come in at about seven or eight dollars to one dollars subscribed by the studio.

We are in an excellent bargaining position now. The transition to wide-screen and 3D-plus inroads of television has left a shortage of product and a picture of this nature would be received with open arms. Produce pictures that will help build relations between Western countries, besides being good entertainment for consumption at home and abroad. We are in an enviable spot now if we can only follow through "fastest with the moistest," or better still, the best damn picture that has come out of Hollywood in many years.

Frank would make an appearance in the picture, but that a professional actor would be chosen to play the regular role. It would show him shooting wild turkeys from a moving automobile on his game reservation at McIntosh, Alabama. Another would show Frank jumping from a horse to a moving train. He did just that in proposing to his wife Other.

The screen story was written by Marshall R. Breedlove from 1950 to 1953 and titled *Everything's Made for Love!* based on the life of the Honorable Frank W. Boykin, a member of Congress. It was dedicated "to the members of the Congress of the United States of America and to all men who have dedicated their lives to the service of their fellowman, their country, and their God—appreciation is gratefully acknowledged for their unselfish devotion to duty and for their wholehearted cooperation, which made this picture possible."

As the news spread to newspapers around the country, the *Atlanta Journal* had the following headline: "Everything's Made for Love."

A TURBULENT LIFE ? ? ?

Representative Boykin of Bama to Star in Own Film

Washington (AP) Rep. Frank Boykin of Alabama said today he has yielded to Hollywood pressure to film the story of his life. Now sixty-eight and silver-haired, the onetime water boy on a railroad said, "The script is written, and the contract awaits signature." He declined the name of company.

He said, "Filming will begin when this session of Congress ends and will include a scene reenacting his proposal to his wife after jumping from a horse to the train she was riding through Malcolm, Alabama."

"'Everything is made for love' has been his motto for forty years," he said. It has been booming in capital corridors since he came to the House from Mobile, Alabama, eighteen years ago.

BOYKIN SAID the filming would be done in his Alabama Congressional District (First and in Washington).

The movie would depict Boykin from the time he got his first job as a water boy on a railroad through his business career in real estate, farming, and timber and his eighteen years in the House of Representatives. "Everything's Made for Love" is Boykin's trademark.

*****

The surveying of all possible sources of financing for the script was being done and should break the bottleneck. In March and April, the result of local and national publicity would coincide with the campaign, which should be in May. At that time, they could actually be shooting the picture, which would not hurt the reelection. With an early fall release, I plan to take advantage of the extreme interest being created in the national elections to insure a good box office turn out for our picture.

My organization stands ready to move on the following schedule contingent on the success you have this week: February–April: Preproduction phase. Do additional research, write shooting script. May: Shooting phase. Actually, shoot film in Mobile and Washington, DC; June–August: Finish film. Edit, music, sound recording, make prints, preview for audience reaction, make final changes and corrections. Prepare for early fall release. June–August: Finish film. Edit, adapt music, sound recording, make prints, preview for audience reaction, make final changes and corrections. Prepare for early fall release. Jack Moffitt has been alerted and is keeping the period open for writing the script.

*****

February 1954

The Mitchell Gertz Agency, which is handling Harold Schuster, has offered their services in packaging the deal and negotiating for best possible release. I have been assured that once the shooting script phase has been accomplished, that with my qualified organization, studio and/or bank financing can readily be arranged for the balance. When I get your call this week, I will immediately forward the necessary information and papers for executing the transaction. My best regards go with you and Mrs. Boykin and your family on your return to Alabama. May your efforts be rewarded by the most successful campaign ever. That you will return to Washington, I have no doubt, but even more important is the wonderful message we can bring to the world through your example in living the golden rule or more aptly stated by yourself "Everything's Made for Love." Good luck and may God bless you. I'll be awaiting your call.

Yours sincerely,
Marshall R. Breedlove

*****

  With an early fall release, I plan to take advantage of the extreme interest being created in the national elections to insure a good box office turn out for our picture. Too, I'm planning a tie-in with our schools whereby all school children can, by seeing the picture "Everything's Made for Love," get an authentic portrayal of how a citizen gets to Congress and the work he does while there as a representative of his district. This should serve to focus attention on the duly elected representatives as the servants of the people under our constitutional government. Dramatizing the story will give the theater-going public an entertaining film of Americans and a story which proves that by living your motto one can have a happy family, business, and political life.
  I have been assured that once the shooting script phase has been accomplished, that with my qualified organization, studio, and or bank financing can readily be arranged for the balance.

The last letters of any consequence, on record, regarding the movie were the above one dated February 2, 1954, from Marshall R. Breedlove and the one below, dated February 3, 1954, from Frank:

February 3, 1954
Mr. Ben McPherson
c/o Mrs. Hazel Gentry

Dear Mr. McPherson,

I have your letter of January 24. Sorry to learn that you have been confined to the hospital but glad you have now been discharged and are slowly getting your strength back. We have been completely swamped with congressional work to give any time to the movie; however, Colonel Breedlove called me from Los Angeles several days ago, and he's still interested in making the movie. I have received scores of songs, which I am holding in a file until such time as there may develop the possibility of using them.

With every good wish, I am sincerely yours,
Frank

In 1967, below is a simple song with his favorite motto set to music, with lyrics by Frank, set to the tune of the famous song, "Oh, Susannah!" John P. Philpott and Jimmy Dixon, who wrote the following:

EVERYTHING IS MADE FOR LOVE
OF ALL THE PLACES IN THIS WORLD,
THE PLACE I LONG TO BE IS MOBILE, ALABAMA WITH
A HARP LEANING ON MY KNEE.
EV'RYTHING IS MADE FOR LOVE IN
ALABAMA

A TURBULENT LIFE ? ? ?

> EV'RYTHING IS MADE FOR LOVE, SO THEY SAY.
> THE BIRDIES AND THE BEES,
> THE FISHIES OF THE SEAS
> YES, EV'RYTHING IS MADE FOR LOVE
> IN GOD'S OWN WAY, EV'RYTHING IS MADE FOR LOVE IN
> ALABAMA
> WHERE THE SWEET AZALEA BLOSSOMS SCENT THE AIR.
> EV'RYTHING IN ALABAMA
> A IS A MAJOR MELODRAMA
> MADE FOR LOVE WHEN YOU ARE THERE.
> EV'RYWHERE.

Above was just one of the song sheets as I found more when sifting through the papers I had from the old file cabinet.

Marshall R. Breedlove also wrote in a letter dated February 24, 1954, that they were investigating the possibility of casting Will Rogers Jr. or Charlton Heston to play Frank and of having Frank appear in the picture.

I was disappointed when I could not find any more documentation or correspondence of the movie. I don't know if it was previously filmed other than the screen script written by Marshal Breedlove. I have contacts in California in the film industry I am reaching out to, seeking their help if they can help me find out if it is in a can in a studio somewhere.

Resources

Books and movie deal about Frank W. Boykin, *Everything Is Made for Love* by Edward Boykin, *The Southern Hunt* by Grace Boykin, movie story to be titled: *Everything Is Made for Love* movie contract (1950–1953) bio on all involved. Studio (20th Century Fox). Original sheet music scores newspaper announcement (*Atlanta Journal*), congratulatory letters.

A Marriage Crumbles

1955

As children growing up, it didn't take long for my dad and mom to realize they did not relish the same things in life. I was age two, and my brother was five and a half when we lived with both my dad and my mother. We were comforted, secure, and felt safe with Dad in our home.

In my adult years, I came to find out that one day my dad came home from a hard day's work at a local paper mill that he managed. Walking past a parked car in front of the home, he saw his wife in the car, making out with another man. When she entered the house, James was fuming and began yelling at our mom when she walked inside.

"How could you be making out with another man? Don't you know what our vows meant when we said them to one another? I have to be alone to think what my next move will be." Giving her no chance to answer, he stormed out and slammed the door so hard it felt as though it shook the house.

My brother and I heard the argument, and at our youthful ages, we didn't understand why our dad left without saying goodbye as he always did. Our mother was sobbing and hid in her bathroom. Robby was trying to comfort and protect me as his little sister who was crying. It was confusing to both of us. He was unable to comfort me as he had always done. It became one of the most traumatic, turbulent, and confusing moments in our lives. We could not understand why he left us and didn't return home.

James was a proud, strong man and could not get over his wife's infidelity that she displayed. He divorced our mother in 1955. Robby was five and a half years old, and I was two when my father left. Robby and I came to miss our dad, especially the many times he would lift me onto a stool and have my brother and I take turns, looking through his large prized-possession telescope from the second-story window of our home. Dad was instructing my brother and I the names of the constellations and stars that he knew oh so well and loved to reference them throughout his life. James returned home to gather his belongings when we were not home.

Many times, he would come to each of our first-floor bedroom windows and scare the living daylights out of us by tapping on the window in a scary mask. My dad was playful, and I and my brother loved that the most about him! When we returned home one day, we were playing around the house, and we entered the room where the telescope used to be, and we yelled to Mom, "Dad's telescope is gone." Mom entered the room and tried to explain that our dad took it, and he would not be returning to the house.

Robby asked, "Why not?"

She said, "Your dad is divorcing me."

Robby asked, "What is divorce?"

"It is when two people can no longer live together, and it's not because of you or your sister."

"Will we see our dad ever again?"

"Yes, a visitation schedule will be set up by the court."

My brother and I were silent and felt bewildered.

A Marriage Crumbles with a Divorce Finalized

1956

Because our mom's and dad's differences could not be settled, they went to court to have a judge grant divorce papers.

Our parents' divorce was finalized by the courts in 1956. It devastated and angered us being left alone with only our mother. No one knew how many times I sat in my room by myself, withdrawing into oneself as I was unable to describe my feelings even to my brother. I felt letdown by my dad for what felt like rejection to me as I found the word to describe my feeling to express as a teenager. Tears would flow down my face when I thought of my dad.

In my room by myself, I had bad thoughts of hate that would enter into my mind. "How could he leave my brother and I behind?" I ultimately would gather strength and learned to love beyond one's faults. I cried in my room with the door closed into my pillow to fall asleep. I fought battles within myself that no one knew about as I began talk with a whisper when I answered questions asked to me. Mother and Robby would find it difficult to get me to speak my mind. I was only two years old when I withdrew within myself and had just learned how to say a few words.

Great-Grandmother Mama Dies

1957

I was my mother's namesake, my grandmothers name was Grace, and they would call my mom by her middle name Browder throughout her life as it would be confusing to call her Grace. Gaga's father's dad my mom never knew personally as he had died before she was born. His name was Browder, and she was named for him. She knew only what her parents told her about him, and as an adult, she had his portrait hung prominently throughout her life in the dining room.

Gaga's mother was Ella Hill Parish who was my and Robby's great-grandmother, and we called her Mama. We were blessed and fortunate to know her as she lived with Papa and her daughter in her older years when her husband died. She had an old white French provincial furniture in her bedroom that later I and guests would sleep in as it became a guest bedroom at Gaga and Papa's house after she died. I inherited it when Mother gave it to me when I had a home, and it was my guest bedroom furniture.

It was my fourth birthday, and I recall Mama giving me the first toy rifle, and it was a toy but looked real to kids and had no play bullets. As I was a tomboy from an early age that was my favorite toy to play with. My mother had a birthday party and dressed me in a dress with an organdy slip underneath and I hated it as it was an itchy scratchy material to me! The party was held at Lion's park in Mobile. My mother invited some of her friends' children, and family were in attendance. It was a fun party, and my favorite part was going down the ladder on a swing set but not in a dress. Then we had cake and ice cream as I developed a sweet tooth. Gaga came, but Papa and Mama were unable to. Mama was frail, dainty, petite, and quite a lady. I loved my great-grandmother and was told, as an adult, I looked like her, and I found that to be a complement. A picture was taken with her, my grandmother, Mother, and I being of four generations and was in the Mobile, Alabama, *Press-Register* newspaper.

Mama died in 1957 shortly after the picture was taken, and I was age five, and that was a traumatic day for me as I cried at the loss of my great grandmother. I felt blessed to have known her for the short period of time. I was unable to attend her funeral as my mother felt I was too young to go. Many condolences of sympathy were given over the telephone, and cards were received from some of Gaga's friends as most of Mama's friends had died. We rejoiced that she was with her friends and family in heaven.

Mom Marries Second Husband Hudy

1957

Mom would call us for breakfast downstairs and serve us lunch and dinner at the table.

My brother would say, "That is delicious, Mom."

I liked some of the stuff she prepared, and my favorite meal was breakfast. I was a very picky eater and was never made to eat everything on the plate. As an adult, I still don't eat vegetables. I will eat grilled onions, celery, carrots, avocados, and artichokes—that is the extent of my eating vegetables even in adulthood. I regret not developing a taste for healthier foods such as vegetables.

I recall the time my dad and I were at a restaurant for lunch, and he made me eat green beans, and after the first bite, I threw them up onto the table. That was the last time he forced me to eat anything as it was an embarrassing moment for both of us. Dad would return me home to my mother's house in Spring Hill.

I was age five, and my brother was nine after my mother married her second husband Hudy. I remember little about her marriage to him. He was overweight and would prance around the house like our mom, and he displayed his gestures like a girl to my brother and was not sure if he ever abused him. As an adult, I had a feeling that my strong-willed mother and Hudy contributed to his being gay.

We would visit him at the car dealership he owned in Downtown Mobile as it was on the parade route. As my brother and I would go with our mother to park in his lot and watch Mardi Gras parades, we each were given sacks to put the goodies in that we would catch. When home, we would count the Cracker Jack boxes and could not

A TURBULENT LIFE ? ? ?

wait to open them to see the prize within. We would each count the pieces of taffy and other candies, eating one or two while doing it. We felt lucky if we were able to catch a stuffed animal and the beads that were thrown.

Robby served as an equerry in the Mobile Mardi Gras Court and was in costume at the old Battle House Hotel for Thanksgiving as the ladies in waiting and Queen were introduced to Mobile Society and their eligibility to be able to marry. He was going to be in a parade, and his mom ordered boxes of snacks for him to throw. The parade was cancelled that day because of rainstorms. My brother was disappointed!

Mom said, "You can have a parade here with your red wagon and put your boxes of throws in it and toss your goodies to children in the neighborhood in Spring Hill."

Some children gathered around as he threw his treats and cars with children would stop and gather some of the goodies as they parked on the side of the road. It was no cancellation to him as he wanted to ride on a float. We chose the throws we wanted before he threw them to the neighborhood kids.

Mom explained to us in 1866 that Indian Joe Cain, a clerk of the market and was sometimes thought to be the town wit, began a celebration all his own. He commandeered a charcoal wagon on Fat Tuesday and dressed as an imaginary Chickasaw Indian chief. With his hand up his nose as he paraded, he thumbed the "damn" Yankees. Cain's actions showed the city of Mobile's spirit was not broken by defeat as large crowds formed to watch him. Every year that followed until his death 1879, he repeated his parade. Large crowds formed, and in time the celebration became known as Mardi Gras.

Mardi Gras evolved as a celebration of European heritage. "Mom was in Mardi Gras Court in 1948, and your dad did it in 1947 when mules were used in the evening parades with torches as lights. Those were some of most memorable times, and I had the time of my life!"

I recalled how honored I was at the age of ten when Aunt Fran's daughter Sandy asked me to be her serving girl when she was introduced to society as an available woman at marital age at Thanksgiving.

Mom Divorces Second Husband Hudy

1958

I opened the door to my brother's room one day and immediately closed it. I saw my mother in bed with another man while married to Hudy. I went downstairs and told the maid what I saw. My mother dressed and told me to lie to the maid that I didn't see anything and that I made it up. I did what she asked, and later I came to find out his name was Carlin.

Shortly after that day, my mother had an argument with Hudy and told him she wanted a divorce and to pack his things and leave right now! Hudy moved out of the Spring Hill house they were living in which Dad had given to Robby and me in the divorce decree. Once again, my brother and I were confused as to why our mother would divorce again. Our mother divorced Hudy, and he moved out of the home. As an adult, I figured out it was because of the other man I saw her with that she had me lie about.

I remember so little about him or their marriage. Was it something I witnessed and blacked it out of my memory, or was it because I was too young to recall those years? It didn't take long for that marriage to come to an end.

I had heard a rumor of my brother from time to time that he was physically abused from a boy at the military school he attended and who later had hung himself. It traumatized Robby, and he began creating turbulence through the home. It was like my brother became a different person.

Father Marries Second Wife Cora

1959

Two years after our dad divorced our mother, James met Cora and fell in love, and they wedded. Cora was raised in an air force military family. Her dad was a general at Brookley Field Air Force Base in Mobile. As a child, Dad and Cora would take us to play bingo on the base. I, shouting bingo, was able to select a prize from many displayed, and I chose my first camera, a brownie, and began taking pictures immediately. The base was later closed in the 1960s.

Cora had one older brother who followed in his father's footsteps by joining the air force. He retired as a colonel in the service in Destin, Florida. His children did not follow his military career path as they pursued their own interest.

Her younger brother lived on the west coast in California with his wife, where they lived a quiet and peaceful life. Like his sister Cora, he had a wonderful sense of humor and a smile that would have all around him light up and smile with him. I was fortunate to meet him several times.

Once was in Lake Tahoe where we stayed at the Harrah Casino Hotel, and Dad treated the entire family to a vacation there. Dad and Cora enjoyed the gambling, while some of the children went snow skiing, and fun was had by all.

Cora grew up as a tomboy and pursued high board diving throughout her youth and high school years. She traveled extensively through the years to military bases where her father would be stationed. She loved hunting and fishing and the outdoors as James did. They had a lot in common and liked the same things. She became James second wife and his last. They had two girls who were the oldest of their children they had together. Gracie Lu and Tarasee were the oldest girls and seven years eight months apart with Tarasee being the oldest from his second marriage. She looked like her mother's twin and became her mother and father's favorite child as it was obvious to all that saw their interactions together from near and afar. The two sons were younger, and in the year 2022, the children's ages ranged from the midfifties to sixties.

My brother and I, in our youth, only spent two weeks during the summer and for Christmas, Thanksgiving, and Easter vacations visiting our wonderful, loyal, giving, responsible father and stepmother Cora who made my brother and me laugh. Cora, with her facial expressions and tone and affliction in her voice, could tell a joke like no other. I felt she could have been a world-class comedian if she pursued it as a career. I often did not get jokes but was able to understand and laugh at many of Cora's. In adulthood, I still don't get many jokes. Dad didn't always catch on to them either, and Cora would explain them to us. Robby caught onto all her jokes and would often interrupt her to explain them to us. Robby was Dad's and Cora's favorite and would often comment on how smart he was. I learned how to be second at a young age, or you may say last as I was the only other child my mom had. I observed and always knew my mother Browder favored males and my brother. As an adult, I thought it was because her father spoiled her as she grew up.

A Tragic Memory in the Attic at Grandmother's House

1959

My tear-jerking memory at Gaga's house occurred in her attic, where my cousins, my brother, and I would play often, opening the old steamer trunks that were filled with old clothes we would try on and other treasures. It was a great area to play hide-and-seek. They also had a basement in the home that was very cold and could act as a bomb, hurricane, or tornado shelter if they ever needed it.

One day at age six, my brother and I rode on top of the elevator from the second floor to the attic. Robby had made a bed among all the old steamer trunks and a curtain hiding the bed. He started fondling me at age six, and he was age ten going on age eleven. He played with me on the bed and caused me to run down the attic stairwell into Gaga's open arms.

"Gaga, I am bleeding. Look!"

Gaga gasped and calmed me down, taking my under pants off and said, "Your cherry was broken."

I asked her, "What's that?"

Gaga tried to explain the anatomy of a girl and a boy the best way she could to a six-year-old. My relationship with my brother was damaged after the incident. Robby acted like he was in a lot of trouble, but he never was. It was a secret for many years to only he, Gaga, and me. With my mother never ever knowing about it, she went to heaven never knowing what happened.

Robby didn't realize what he had done was wrong. Gaga didn't have the right words to explain to him the act he performed should never had happened. When I became an adult, I believe Loraine, the housekeeper, might have known what had happened but never mentioned it to me. She knew most of the things that happened in the house. In adulthood, I mentioned it to a friend and psychologist. My life was beginning to unfold with my feelings not fully understood to myself.

Sunday Brunch at Gaga's House

1958

I was living in Mobile with my mother and brother in our house in Spring Hill. Every Sunday, except when one of us was ill, after church, we would have brunch at Gaga and Papa's house. Loraine would be busy in the kitchen, preparing scrambled eggs, ham, bacon, sausage, grits, and handmade biscuits with apple butter. I was often in the kitchen with her, watching her prepare my favorite desert cup custard with brown sugar in the bottom of the ramekins she served it in. The best part of the meal was the handmade cup custard, and many times I would ask for another, if any were left. Loraine was like family to us all. Loraine would ring a handbell when it was ready and served it buffet style.

Uncle Brevard, Aunt Betty, and their two sons were there, playing with us. We were double first cousins because our aunt was a Boykin and married my mom's brother, and my dad was as well, and my mom married his first cousin.

Eph, Mathew, Robby, and I would have fun with the Persian cat Gaga had, and she called her Purr. They enjoyed petting her long gray hair. I would pet her but never wanted to stroke the cat for a long period of time as my brother did. It was the start of my brother loving cats. I had dogs.

Papa and Gaga had a storyteller in the neighborhood, and we would often go to her house, or she would come to a birthday party in our home and tell adventurous kids' stories, and as children, we all paid attention as her face would show drama, humor, and excitement. Her voice carried even when she whispered. It was a wonderful way for her to make a living in the public library, birthday parties, and any event calling for a storyteller.

Living at Home in Spring Hill, Alabama, with Mother

1958

One night while at our home in Spring Hill, sirens were roaring. I was such a sound sleeper; the alarms didn't waken me. Robby and my mother started shaking me and told me to wake up. We went outside and watched the blazing house fire two doors down burn down to the embers. It was the Volkert's second home as the husband was an engineer and had his own firm. Praise God they were not in the home as the fire blazed it to the foundation. The next day, the Volkert's had flown from Virginia to Mobile, Alabama, to access the damages, and they met with the insurance agent as well.

They were close friends of Mom, and she offered them to stay in our home, but they had a hotel room. The Volkert's sold the ash-ridden lot and moved to Virginia full-time on a horse ranch. They had two children later in life that enjoyed riding horses and purchased a ranch in Virginia. Mom stayed in touch with them through letters and cards over the years, but she was never to see them again as they lost touch as their lives became so busy and hectic over the years.

My brother and I were playing outside with Craw who lived across the street getting tadpoles that would turn into frogs and put them in a jar. The pond also had goldfish. Craw got upset and lost his temper. He ran across the street to his house and came back with a butcher knife and was running after Robby and me. We both started yelling in unison at the top of our lungs, and our mother was in the kitchen and heard us screaming, and she witnessed what was happening.

She immediately called Craw's mother who was at home and said, "Come get your son! He is chasing my children with a butcher knife, or I will call the police!"

His mother instantly hung up and came out with her older son, and praise God he was home. They both tell Craw to stop, and my brother and I ran to safety with Mom opening the door to the kitchen that was locked. Once we were inside, she locked it behind us. Craw's big brother was able to get the butcher knife safely out of his hand, and they went home. We were not to see nor play with him again as that must have been his punishment, and we didn't want to play with him ever again.

Robby would walk the two German shepherds named Ham and Sam that lived outside in a chain-linked fence area. One day he came home from school and noticed Ham and Sam were dead. He ran crying to his mother, and she went out and had no idea how they died. Taking their dead bodies to the vet, they discovered they were poisoned. We immediately felt it was a member of the country club or a neighborhood child that might have done it, but we never gathered any proof of who did it.

Mother let us pick out another dog, and we chose a red Irish setter who, of course, we named Red. I had a recurring dream as I told my brother and Mom when I woke up and over breakfast.

"I was in the TV room, watching a show, and Red came to the door and was pulling on a man's pants and removed the pants from him. I thought it was a burglar, and I froze unable to speak as he was trying to get in."

Mother and Robby both said, "That never happened."

I went outside with my brother the next day, and we found a knife in a window that had a large antique mirror completely covering the window from the inside.

Robby said, "That could have been there from a long time ago."

To this day, I don't know what the truth was and if it wasn't just a dream. Did they feel it would scare me if I knew the truth? That is a question that wouldn't be answered.

A TURBULENT LIFE ? ? ?

We could walk to the Mobile Country Club, where we were members, and my cousins were members also. One day there was a swim meet, and my cousin Mathew pulled me aside and told me no one was swimming in my age-group of being seven years old for breaststroke. He took me to the other pool at the club and showed me quickly how to swim breaststroke. He took me back to the meet, and he entered me into the breaststroke for my age-group. I swam twenty-five meters and received a first-place trophy. I thanked Mathew for teaching me breaststroke.

First Commercial Airplane Ride with Dad and Cora to Washington, DC

1959

At age seven and my brother age ten, we flew on our first airplane trip with Dad and Cora to Washington, DC, to see our grandparents. We enjoyed the flight and was ready to go anytime as we both learned to love traveling.

I was on top of the world visiting the Washington monuments and the Lincoln Memorial as it captivated me when my father read the inscriptions to us and visiting our grandparents at the Washington Hotel, where they lived for so many years was a thrill.

Our father would tell us stories of when he was a teenager and lived there. How he, his sister, and his brother would play hide-and-seek.

Dad said, "I would hide in the dumbwaiter that went to the kitchen. My last time doing it, I got stuck and could not get out, and the kitchen staff tried pulling me out of the dumbwaiter, and they couldn't. So they tried ice and corn oil that after thirty minutes, I was able to squirm out and was shivering from the ice. I felt like a was a frozen popsicle! I was so embarrassed and humiliated as the kitchen staff were laughing so hard at my dilemma. I was glad to be out and ran out of the kitchen and straight to the elevator and rode up to the apartment.

My mother asked, "Where have you been?"

He was so cold. "I have to take a hot bath, and then I will tell you, Mom."

A TURBULENT LIFE ? ? ?

When he got out of bathtub and dressed, he told the family the story, and they all had a good belly laugh. Cora had not heard that story and found it very amusing.

He said, "I will never ever do that again!"

Frank gave Gracie Lu along with the family a tour of his office and introduced her to his faithful staff. Frank was nearly six feet tall, weighed more than two hundred pounds, and dressed elegantly in statesman attire, always making him look like a congressman as he would enter a room, and it was as if a thousand butterflies were turned loose. His white hair flowing back from a full face distinguished him from many others. The pictures on the wall were like telling his life story and with the many dignitaries and influential people he worked with. The families' pictures were all hung together prominently on the wall as a focal point. When at the hunting lodge, he wore his hunting clothes. I never knew Other to hunt but saw her to tend to the kitchen staff and needs at the lodge.

His office many visitors would describe as a Noah's Ark, for the rooms contained photo of the rich and famous, all dedicated to the congressman. He had two huge rattlesnake skins, five mounted deer heads, a nine-foot wolf hide, and old campaign posters and snapshots of hound dogs at work. The tables and cabinet of his so-called private office were loaded with curios, trophies, antiques, and mementos. He had a large cuckoo clock from Germany's Black Forest, two six-shooters that once belonged to Jesse James, a machete assorted rifles, and a chastity belt is a locking item of clothing.

Frank was famous for his party-giving, and one that is especially notable was for Speaker of the House Sam Rayburn, with nearly a thousand friends in attendance. They served salmon, elk, bear steaks, venison, turkey, and opossum, with lots to drink. My grandparents, we would hear from others, would say, "The host and hostess with the mostest."

It was exciting to me to have breakfast in the House of Representatives dining room with many of the legislators gathered, and Frank introduced the family to many of them. After breakfast, we walked to the House Chamber, or it is often called the Hall of the House of Representatives.

In my later years, I believe the visit in Washington, DC, was where I became interested in history and in the government.

I didn't want to leave my grandparents or Washington, DC, but Dad and Cora would say, "You have to get back for school."

Neither Robby or I liked school!

Papa and Other said, "You have to get educated as the country has changed, and you need to be schooled and go to college to have a good career."

They hugged and kissed our family goodbye as they ordered a limousine for us to ride to the airport. That was a thrill for my brother and I as it had soda, waters, and snacks for us to enjoy and the luxury in riding in such a roomy car.

I was thankful for my dad giving us such a wonderful, memorable, vacation, and one I would never forget! I feel blessed in my adult years to be able to write about my grandfather and grandmother as well as reading and researching them in newspapers, magazines, and books.

The articles in whatever media outlet in which it was found. The journalist would stop just short of being able to be sued for slander. I spent countless hours in the Mobile Public Library downtown, researching about him, and a lot of information I found in the Alabama Archives and some older magazines and newspaper articles. I had written a lot of their political years and stories in a three-hundred-page book I had copyrighted but never published called *South of the Hill*. I received many rejection letters as they were not interested in the politics that was over fifty years ago. Perhaps I will get it published one day.

My Shared Memories of Killing My First Buck with My Dad in 1959

My dad and I were walking alongside the railroad tracks with our guns to kill a deer, and he would tell me stories along the way. I carried a .22-rifle small and light enough for me to carry. My dad carried a .243 rifle to kill the deer with. He told me in a whisper Aunt Fran had driven to the lodge one afternoon and got there just after the "playboy" had killed our pet deer Fawny who would come into the lodge.

Our mother told us she could kick you with her hind legs and injure one of you for life. She remained outside on the lawn and not allowed in the lodge ever again. Aunt Fran cried for a full ten minutes before she could wipe the tears from her eyes and compose herself. Then she began screaming at the young man, who hadn't realized Fawny was a pet deer. He felt terrible about the whole thing and was not to be seen for many years after the event. I was glad 'cause I might have taken a poke at him. We all loved that deer.

"No! Not poor Fawny!" I knew how the family loved the deer, and that was a sad story for me to hear.

We stopped and set up to kill a deer, and there was no more chatter as the early morning fog began to lift. All was quiet, and suddenly we heard the brush and trees whistling on the cold blustery morning. A white-tailed deer buck (male deer) appeared along the railroad tracks. My dad raised his gun and shot it, still moving. As the deer ran away, we tracked the blood to where he nested, and Dad told me to finish it off as it was struggling to get up and away from us.

He said, "Put the deer out of his misery."

I raised my rifle and shot my first deer that I killed off with the second bullet. It was a six-point buck, and my father and Grandfather Frank were immensely proud of me!

Following tradition, we returned to the front of the lodge with deer from the hunt that icy wintry morning, the workers hung deer as the fifty-pound drums were cut in half to collect the blood and guts of animals killed. Gracie Lu's joined the crowd on the outside iron rack, where Frank's slogan prominently displayed, "Everything is made for love." Isaac, one of Frank's trusted workers, cleaned and hung my deer. Later, putting the skinned deer in the icehouse, and the meat would be cut and handed to hunters that wanted the venison to take home, and often the nape and head would be taken to a taxidermist forever lasting memories to hang on a wall in one's home.

Frank had the honor of the tradition of smearing blood all over my face, with cousins, aunts, uncles, and friends gathered around his beloved granddaughter. I experienced the ceremony of my killing off my first buck. It was a cherished moment in my life. As my grandfather spread the deer blood all over my face, my dad was busy snapping pictures of that proud day with his daughter, which has been shared throughout the years with others.

Entering the lodge with my grandfather who took me to my grandmother in their first-floor bedroom with the fireplace roaring and sitting in her rocking chair near it to stay warm, Grandmother stood up and immediately took me to their bathroom and proudly washed the dried blood from my face as I, with enthusiasm, told her the story of my killing the deer. The servants were busy preparing breakfast for the hungry, tired, hunters, and all in attendance but especially for the hunters who were on the hunt and up at dawn. While waiting for breakfast, my grandfather and I bonded after grandmother cleaned me up. He walked with me in camouflage clothing and he in his brown overalls, shirt, and boots as his attire. Walking through the lodge with him was like seeing it for the first time. Stuffed ducks hung prominently from the ceiling, as well as other trophy game on the walls. Walking the stairs to the second floor, he explained the pictures of previous hunters of which many of whom were famous, distinguished businessmen, politicians, athletes, and businesspeople of the era. Pictures of whom he explained was his friends he had gone into business and worked with over the years. He explained to me that with challenging work, due diligence, sweat, and tears, lots of energy, which rang true throughout his life, there is nothing one can't do! "I was able to maintain my marriage to your grandmother for many years." It was a bonding time, and the most special day for me and my grandfather as we talked and came to know one another. I listened attentively. He had told me not to read or listen to all the negative and exaggerated articles written by journalist as they exaggerate or tell lies to sell their newspapers or magazines. I felt like I came to know my grandfather and grandmother that day as we talked had chuckled and learned about one another.

I also read many exaggerations and falsehoods about my grandfather, which made me feel determined to prove them wrong, and the reader can decide from the glimpses I write about him, the man and character of who he truly was. I listened attentively as their stories were captivating, which kept me yearning to hear more. The outside bell was rung by a maid to come get breakfast. I was disappointed as I didn't want our conversation to end. We walked to the long wooden dining table, where I wanted to sit by my grandfather but was unable to as he sat at the head of the table and started every meal with a blessing to God. He would sit down, and all would start eating.

The traditional breakfast was served buffet style with scrambled eggs, ham, bacon, grits, biscuits and jelly, jam, or honey. It was devoured by all. Complements were given to the staff. That was my favorite meal of the day at the hunting lodge but also the last meal served before returning home that day.

In the car with Dad and Cora, I could not stop talking of my time with my grandfather and grandmother and how I felt for the first time in my life that I knew their compassion, love, and a miniscule part of their lives. Dad and Cora dropped my brother and I off at our mother's house. I was a chatterbox, telling Mom all about my finishing off the deer. My mother was delighted to hear me talking as I was so closed mouth around her in the past.

GRACE BOYKIN

Grace Boykin with traditional blood on face after killing first deer with Papa Boykin as I called him (Grandfather).

Holidays with Father James and Cora

1959

Dad had shared the story of his twin brother Jack with me, and he had been married two times and later divorced from both. He had a son and daughter he helped raise, playing one day with them at hunting lodge and the other hunting preserve was not far from the lodge known as Gulf Pines. We had good times together in our early childhood years.

I would be playing outside with Jack's son and daughter one day and was running when a peacock's spurs also known as *kicking thorns*, as it began to fly, hitting me near my right eye. I was crying so loud my dad and Cora ran to help me. I was bleeding, and Cora washed the blood from my face, and a scar formed on my right side of the face for the rest of my life. The good thing was many people thought it was a beauty mark from birth.

Cora said, "You are so lucky that it didn't get you in the eye."

James and Cora's favorite events when they were first married was taking me to wrestling matches. Chairs were thrown from the ring, wrestlers being thrown out of the ring and into the spectator's area. I would get scared as anything would be thrown around and jump into my dad's lap. Once I recalled a wrestler's pants coming off. The wrestler had a huge body and bulging muscles.

The spectators were laughing as his odor permeated through the room. It stunk!

I said, "Pee you!" The wrestler was left with only his tight underwear and looked as though he had pooped in them. Spectators began laughing as the words *pee you* caught on to all the onlookers. Laughter resounded throughout the arena. The wrestler was so embarrassed he ran out of the ring into the locker room. His loud cries of anger were heard in the arena. The ringmaster announced the next wrestlers match, trying to gain the audience's attention. The odor was so horrific people in the small arena began standing up from their chairs and exiting the event.

It was heart-wrenching for the ringmaster who could not get control of the spectators who continued leaving and the announcer calling them to come back into the arena. No spectators remained to see the next match, and the ringmaster called it off and closed the small arena early that night. The wrestler had sunken to rock bottom as he would not allow himself to be ridiculed again from fellow wrestlers who did not want to wrestle or see him again or the audience. Fellow wrestlers turned against the pantless wrestler and didn't want to wrestle with him again. The writing was on the wall for the stinky wrestler to find another field of work. It was also the last wrestling match for him as he was embarrassed to put himself into a situation like that to happen again.

When taken home, I shared my experience at the wrestling matches. My mother was appalled at my story. She argued with my dad, taking me to such events at such a young and impressionable age. He conceded he would not take me to anymore wrestling matches. I later heard from my dad the wrestler opened a judo school that he owned and operated and was an instructor to students who attended. His shop was doing well. I grinned and was happy to hear he moved on and owned a judo shop, where he was the instructor and was happy in being his own boss.

Later they would take me and my brother to watch them bowl in the league they were in. They would also take us bowling with, which I could win every time with my gutter balls, and spectators were often heard laughing in the background as some would cross over to the other lane.

James favorite expression was, "Let's go, let's go now! We are leaving you behind." The kids knew not to play around as they knew he meant what he said! The door would close behind him, and his children would hop to it and run to the car. Once he went to pick up a prescription in a drugstore, he left Robby and I in the car, and my brother just turned ten, and he got in the front seat of the car from the backseat and put the car in gear and hit the sidewalk, causing no damage to the car, but the jolt caused some bruises on my body.

It was a short visit with our dad that day because Dad came running out and immediately put on the parking brake. He gave my brother a scolding as he could have run into the drugstores window and totaled the car or even killed someone. He gave my brother on the spot fifteen switches.

"I am telling your mother what you did."

Robby started crying, saying, "I am sorry and please don't tell Mom."

Our dad replied, "I must tell her the truth!" He took us back to Mother's house in Spring Hill and told her what had happened.

She turned the table on James and said, "How could you leave two young children in the car by themselves?" She added, "You are the irresponsible one!"

Dad shook his head and left, closing the door behind him. We were puzzled that he didn't give us the usual hug and kiss goodbye.

On other visits with our dad and Cora, all would laugh as Robby would throw strikes and spares. The bowling alley was lots of fun, having pool tables, and video games. I was allowed to bowl and watch Dad and Cora bowl in their league. It was fun to watch but even more fun to play.

Our mother would call James whenever my brother and I needed discipline. Dad would drive to our home in Spring Hill with his new wife Cora. They carried a switch in the car with which we would get five switches each. In today's times, it would be considered corporal punishment and enforceable by law. The switch hurt and stung, leaving red marks on both of us as we cried.

On a Halloween night, my brother and I were with some neighborhood kids, and we were caught throwing eggs at cars. Dad and Cora were called to come and handle the situation. Dad was hot under the collar and tired of coming to discipline us; he gave us a tongue-lashing and fifteen switches with a thin stick to where we were bleeding. At times, he and Cora's two girls would be sitting in the car, watching us getting switched by our dad. He would drive back to their house. We would go back into our house, crying.

I was age seven in 1959, and we were visiting our dad and Cora in the apartment they shared as a married couple. I loved playing with their old telephone that hung on their wall, which they would often tell me no, and I would obey them. We were the oldest of his children. If we didn't obey our dad, he would switch us, and we didn't like it. Dad would come home from the paper mill he managed in Mobile, Alabama. He would often smell like rotten eggs to us. He would immediately enter his home and go straight to soak in the bathtub with bubble bath as he entered his house after work. Robert, who managed the large paper company, also served as the secretary treasurer of the family-owned business in 1947 while still working at the local paper mill. He later left the paper mill to work full-time as president of the family company, and someone else took over his duties at the paper mill.

Our times spent at one of his and Cora's favorite places was at the family compound in Fort Morgan, Alabama. Summers with Dad were often spent in my father's home, his two brothers' homes, and sisters home, as well as his parents beachfront home. At dawn, all would get in their beach buggies and drive down to the beach to fish for their lunch or dinner. After catching fish, Dad and my brother skinned them underneath the house on stilts in the sink. Later they would walk them to Other and Frank's home handing them to Martha to cook. The families would gather around the large rustic wooden table with a big lazy Susan turntable in the middle, which made it easy for us children to grab condiments and what we wanted to eat. It was special moments made as the families gathered around to eat the succulent red snapper or flounder fish they would frequently serve.

One of my favorite childhood memories with my dad was when he had his private airplane stored in a hanger in Southern Alabama. Early in the morning at Fort Morgan, Dad would get his Cessna airplane out of a hanger, and he would fly Cora, me, and my brother from Fort Morgan to Dauphin Island and do flybys and touch and goes over the small runway. Laughter was heard throughout the cockpit as it was such fun to see the gulf and then turn scary when we saw sharks swimming so close to shore out the windows of my dad's plane. I often recalled my time in his airplane as a bonding time with Dad, Cora, and my brother. I was unable to recall a lot of memories of my childhood with my dad and Cora, but those that I do were some of the highlights in my life.

The most unforgettable memories at the Fort Morgan family compound occurred in Dad's home, Jack his twin brother, youngest brother (Dick), sister (Fran), and parents' (Other and Frank) homes that were located as a family compound in Fort Morgan. On the beach, while fishing and playing and calling each other by nicknames were heard by many who found them to be appropriate to each child. They are embedded in this author's mind and memories. I would hear the nicknames from cousins, friends, and family members what we called each other. Tarasee was often called the Guppy, the oldest boy was called Carp, youngest boy child was Jellyfish, and the youngest girl child was Sea Slug. Those were nicknames given to my dad and Cora's children while playing outside at the Fort Morgan compound with family. I was called Cuddle Fish, and my brother was called Flounder. She could never forget their nicknames as they were said often by their cousins when they were playing. We would call our cousins guppies. All were named for fish of the sea because all knew fishing was their favorite past time while growing up and playing at Fort Morgan Beach.

Often as dusk would fall, Dad drove us in his beech buggy down to the shoreline, collecting their lights, spears, and nets to catch flounder, walking along the shoreline at the Gulf of Mexico as the moon would shine bright on the water. My head just barely popped out of the water and when Dad speared one.

I asked, "Can I try spearing one?"

My dad handed me the spear, and we saw one, and I missed it.

Dad said, "When you are a little taller, I will let you try again."

The next morning as the sun was rising at the gulf house on the water's edge, I was running and playing with my cousins as my father and Cora were fishing. While my dad was casting, a fishhook got caught in my eye while I was running. My dad and Cora told me to stay still as they were afraid I could lose my eye. I was in agony, and it was over two hours or so to get to medical help. My dad and Cora took turns as they tried getting the hook from my eyelid, and neither of them had any success. Dad drove to his parents' beach house and, in a panicky voice, asked his family for help. They drove Martha to where I was standing and unable to move far. Martha was the only one able to remove the fishhook gently with her steady hands. Many family members tried but were unsuccessful. If Martha were unable to get it out or move it a fraction toward the pupil of the eye, I would be blind today in my right eye. Praise God, Martha removed it! When Martha was driven back to the house, I was dropped off with her at my grandparents' house.

The family profusely thanked Martha, and she was given a raise as well as my grandfather giving her a bag of one hundred silver dollars as he always kept on hand. They felt that was the least they could do for her saving the day in her aid to their beloved granddaughter. That day, Frank and Other and James, Robby, and I could not stop thanking Martha for saving my eye. Martha was thankful she was there and able to help. Martha became my hero, and I did not want to leave the kitchen as I wanted to stay with her as I felt safe. I had a crying fit when my dad and Cora would not let me eat in the kitchen with her.

Martha hugged me and said, "I have to work and go with your dad and Cora to the table to eat."

I continued sniffling and crying through the meal and didn't eat. I couldn't understand why I was unable to eat with Martha in the kitchen. I was never given a proper explanation.

When James and Cora took Robby and me home, Mother had heard the news and was furious at James when he bought us home from summer vacation. "How could you let that happen?"

James replied, "She was running and playing with her cousins as I was casting, and she ran into the line. She had to stay still as that was quite a challenging task for one barely five-years-old and watching her cousins and brother playing in the surf of the waves. I was proud of her for listening and staying still."

A TURBULENT LIFE ? ? ?

Fort Morgan was Robby and my favorite place to play hide-and-seek outside. We often went to the arsenal with a small opening in the sand, where we would hide from our cousins who couldn't find us. It was close to a quarter of a mile away from the family compound of houses. Our cousins would often never find us. We saw lots of graffiti on the walls in the arsenal, and it was a suitable place to hide as long as the weather was good.

One day, my brother and I were late for dinner, and Dad was looking for us. Around 10:00 p.m., we walked into the dark house.

James asked, "Where were you?"

Robby replied, "At the fort in the arsenal."

Dad said, "You missed the delicious dinner that Cora made. I was calling you and hollering for you to eat dinner." Dad grounded us from playing at the fort for the rest of the summer.

They both cried over the punishment Dad gave us and thought it was obsessive as we went without dinner that night. We had lost all track of time while reading all the graffiti on the walls.

Summer Vacation with Mother, Robby, Gaga, Papa in Cherokee, North Carolina

1959

Summer was ending, and we were driven back to Mom's house after being with Dad and Cora for two weeks. I ran to my mom and immediately began, bragging to her how Martha (the maid) saved the day in saving my eye with her gentle touch. She maneuvered the hook exactly right to get it out of my eye.

James said, "Praise God there was no damage to her eye."

Her mother was relieved to see my eye was normal and gave me and my brother great big hugs as we returned from the two weeks with our dad and Cora.

I said, "I missed you terribly."

She asked us, "How was your time with your dad?"

Both of us replied in unison, "It was great!"

Our mother was jealous and envious as she didn't want to hear we had a fun time. She would change the subject to what fun we would have, going on a vacation to North Carolina and seeing the Native American Cherokee Reservation with Gaga and Papa and what other conversations would keep us distracted from sharing the good times we had with our dad.

Living in a two-story brick home in Spring Hill with my brother having his own room filled with Lincoln Logs and metal toy soldiers. Next to his room was my room with dolls and a Barbie doll playhouse with which Barbie and the Ken were my favorite dolls to

A TURBULENT LIFE ? ? ?

play with, and Barbie was the craze in dolls at that period. I also had Chatty Cathy as a favorite doll as I loved her talking to me.

There were two weeks left before school started, and Gaga, Papa, and Mom drove us to Cherokee, North Carolina. We visited Native Americans on the land they owned with their tepees, and it was quite a tourist destination. They were able to enter one of the teepees to see how they lived. We were having a blast watching them dance and seeing them in their headdresses.

Mom took us into a shop, and my brother and I both bought headdresses with the feathers we wore for a couple of days and took home with the moccasins Mom purchased for us to wear as slippers. Night was starting to fall, and we went back to the hotel.

At the hotel, we had dinner and went to sleep. The next morning, Mom had us brush our teeth. She bought a stand in the bathroom for me to stand on, and while I was brushing, I fell from the stool to a small white tiled floor and immediately started crying. Mom ran into the bathroom and saw me in a puddle of blood.

She ran in the hall, yelling at the top of her lungs, "Help! Is there a doctor nearby?"

Meantime, Gaga and Papa came from their room next door and called the front desk, asking for a doctor.

Mom was still screaming in the hall, and a man ran to her and said, "I am a doctor. What's the emergency?"

She took him in and showed him her young daughter lying in a pool of blood. He gently removed blood from her scalp with a clean washcloth, and he noticed the large gap in her skull. "We must get her to a hospital immediately!"

The hotel operator called for an ambulance as she was losing a lot of blood. The ENTs put me on a stretcher and took me down in the elevator with my mother. Robby was left with Gaga and Papa. My mother was a nervous wreck! We arrived at the hospital where the ER doctor had nurses immediately taken my vitals as they did in the ambulance as well. "We need to sew her skull with stitches and keep her overnight to see if she has a concussion."

Mother said, "I will stay in the room with her."

They had to shave my scalp to see the skull and gash better. He observed the other raised scars that were keloids on her skull from older injuries to her head. They gave me some anesthetic to dull the pain from sewing me up. I had to have nineteen stitches in my skull.

When they finished and took me to a room, the ER doctor came in and asked my mother, "How did she get the other keloid scars on her skull?" He was suspecting child abuse.

My mother explained to him, "They are from kindergarten when she played on six-foot wooden boxes. She is a tomboy and was following the boys as they did. Ambulances were called several times from the school, and she had passed out. The last day of school, she was climbing on the six-foot rope ladder, and she fell on a tree stump and was taken to the hospital from the school, and I met her in the ER as they rolled her in on the stretcher and had to have her head shaved and eleven stiches. But the worst of all was as a baby, she had rolled out of her crib onto the hard floor with uneven textures in it as well as being uncarpeted in her nursery. She cracked her skull open from her forehead." She showed him her scar to the back of her skull.

"She was in surgery for four hours while they put the cracked bones back in place as she was a baby. It was explained to me that they repaired her along the suture lines, which were spaces between the skull bones, and that was why she had some blood from the opened wound. She was in the hospital for two weeks as they observed her reflexes, vital signs, and checked for any brain injury, and Praise God she made a full recovery with no damage to her brain. Her dad helped aid in her recovery as he would do anything for his baby girl! He made sure the crib was safe, and she couldn't roll or climb out of it again. It was a very trying time for both of us."

Doctor asked, "Where is he now?"

She said, "We are divorced, and he is in Mobile, and we are here on vacation with my parents."

They cut the vacation short and drove back to Mobile for me to see my doctor.

A TURBULENT LIFE ? ? ?

Upon examining me, he said, "The stitches are not ready to be removed yet. Make an appointment next week, and we will take them out."

Later, Mom returned me to the doctor and had them taken out, and things returned to normal as my hair was starting to grow back.

Burglary of Frank and Other's Home

1962

A burglary of Frank's home in Mobile, Alabama, occurred on the memorable night of March 5, 1962. Police were called, and the report stated it was a professional craftsman. Entry was achieved through the large French doors that opened onto the front porch, yet no piece of the knickknacks on a table, just inside was out of place.

Frank and Other were in Washington that month as congress was in session. The crooks picked a Mardi Gras carnival night. The time of year, Mobile came alive, and most citizens were enjoying the merriment of music, revelry, and parades; it was the perfect time to break into the Boykin home. They could not have picked a better night.

The day before the robbery, an anonymous man phoned the Boykin home. The maid, Martha, told the police investigating it that she was the nanny for forty-six years of service to Frank and Other. She answered the phone, and the person asked, "Are the congressman and his wife in town?"

"No, they're in Washington, but I expect them home in a few days," replied Martha.

"Do you stay in the house at night?"

"No, I'm just leaving now, but I come in several times a week to dust a little and see that things are all right."

The next morning, at about seven, Martha entered the house and knew immediately it had been robbed. In hysterics, she ran next door to the neighbors, and they opened the door with Martha anxiously, saying, "Frank's house has been broken into during the night."

A TURBULENT LIFE ? ? ?

The neighbor volunteered that when she went to bed around midnight, and she thought she heard noises in Frank's house. Her suspicions were so aroused that she turned on her yard light.

The detectives found no clues or fingerprints with a diligent search and examination of the premises. Silverware and valuable jewelry worth thousands of dollars were untouched. The master bedroom was ransacked, and the lock to a huge wardrobe was sawed out so neatly and replaced that the circular scar was barely noticeable. Inside the wardrobe were several large drawers with locks that were jimmied open. The contents were scattered everywhere on the floor, with mementos, baby curls, old love letters, and many keepsakes, none of which the vandals wanted.

Upon examination, the mantle in the room had been torn apart with a fine-toothed electric saw, pried out and replaced. From deductive reasoning, the police and family believed they were after incriminating papers, of which there were none. The burglars continued ruining much of the furniture, looking for hidden crypts. Dozens of pictures on the wall were destroyed, with the backs torn off and tossed away for nothing. Hundreds of papers were found scattered and tattered throughout the rooms and halls. Many, many books were taken from the bookcases and shaken out for what might have contained concealed papers.

"They must have been in the house for hours," commented Frank later. "They were reckless. For instance, we have some fine trunks we brought back from Hong Kong. They have all sorts of things in them, and they have complicated brass locks. They broke into all these, investigating everything in them. For instance, forty years ago at Palm Beach, we had a party for President Harding, who was an old friend of mine, and we saved some of the absinthe from that party. We used it at the weddings of our granddaughter's. We also had in there some old papers from the old Ku Klux Klan trial that framed about fifty Mobile citizens, including myself. The case was thrown out of court. They also took one of my pistols, and a good one at that."

Frank told the detectives, "Not only did they break into our home in Mobile, but they also rifled our rooms at the Emerson Hotel in Baltimore during my Baltimore trial, and they were looking for papers which I would gladly have handed them if I had them."

Frank and his office staff had sent the federal attorney all the letters and books showing where he bought the land in question, the price of the land, and what county seat it was recorded in, as well as the income taxes he paid on it. "The burglars preferred to pillage our rooms, invading our privacy, even with us absent. They must have been desperate, as they broke into my automobile that I used during the trial. They twice ransacked my office in the House Office Building."

My father told me, "We thought we knew who sent the robbers, but couldn't prove it. The phones were tapped for months before my father's trial and while it was going on." When Attorney General Robert Kennedy moved to New York, he left behind accusations that he had employed unlawful undercover methods to get evidence that convicted a teamster boss Jimmy Hoffa. In December 1965, a committee of the United States Senate was probing into wiretapping and bugging operations of the Justice Department. The committee just skimmed the surface, with Robert Kennedy being a senator from the Empire State. Of course, the politicians' "club" is very protective of its own.

Whoever pirated Frank's home, offices, and car had been given an "unrestricted hunting license" to bring Frank down. They used electronic and other technical aids, as well as such investigative techniques, surveillance, undercover work, etcetera, including burglary. The politically motivated raids on Frank was never broadcast or noted by the national media in 1962. James felt it could have helped lead to the backdrop of the scandals that developed into Watergate.

On October 29, 1965, Drew Pearson of the *Washington Post* stated, "The man who really started the eavesdropping was none other than Robert Kennedy when he was attorney general." None of these points were bought up during the trial against Frank to the jury that tried him!

Browder's Third Husband Carlin

1962

Mom married Carlin, who worked selling insurance. While Mom was married to Carlin, she would tell me at age nine after dinner to go upstairs and watch TV in bed with him. Night after night I did so, and Carlin would pull me on top of him and fondled me. When he heard Mother coming up the stairs, he would throw me off him. I was so confused and felt rejected! I didn't understand what was happening. My brother was away and attended a camp at Lookout Mountain in Tennessee.

One day, Mom told me we were moving to Macon, Georgia. We moved into a two-story apartment in Macon, and I was enrolled in a public school there in fifth grade at age ten. My brother stayed with Gaga to complete his school years as he didn't want to move.

Carlin, my mother, and I moved without my brother. He had two sons from his previous marriage, and they came over on a few occasions. When school started, I met Louis who became my best friend. He would come over, and we would play with our sleds whenever it snowed, and we would sled down the hill at the complex. When there was no snow, we played games and always managed to have fun.

One night, I was sleeping, and my mother woke me up from a sound sleep.

She said, "I am killing myself." She left my room, she went to her bathroom, and she had a razor blade in her hand, ready to cut her wrist. I was awake and looked at the time on the bedside table in my room, and it was 2:15 a.m. I ran to her bathroom and told her to stop!

"You can't kill yourself! What would I do without my mother?"

Mom continued on, and I grabbed the razor blade from her trembling hands.

Then we heard the door open downstairs, and Carlin was back, and as he was walking up the stairs, we heard him bumping into the wall.

He entered the room stumbling and asked me, "Why are you up?"

I replied, "Just helping my mom."

I was afraid of him, and I ran to my bedroom and could hear the fighting between them. He had been drinking at a bar and was drunk as he was slurring his words. I assumed he passed out on the bed as there was a sudden silence in the room. The door was open to their bedroom, and I looked inside, and he was still in his clothes on top of the bed, and they were both asleep. I went back to my room and saw the clock had 3:45 a.m. on it. I was so confused and cried myself to sleep as it was such a turbulent night for me. I had no one to talk about it with as the next morning, my mother acted as if nothing had happened.

When fifth grade was over and it was summer, we moved back to Mobile. I was sad to say goodbye to Louis who was my only friend in Macon that I played with. We wrote for a while to each other, and then our lives got so busy we lost touch with one another.

Once again, I was bewildered, and would I ever be able to understand what separation meant? Shortly after the move back, my mom divorced Carlin. Later, Mother began dating again. Robby, me, Uncle Brevard, Aunt Betty and my cousins were at Gaga's on a Sunday for the usual brunch served by Loraine.

While all were in the dining room, Browder asked, "Should I go back to my third husband or marry Howard?"

Robby stood up. "I will not go with you if you go back to Carlin."

I stood by him and said, "I won't either."

That made Browder's mind up to marry Howard and was the best decision she had ever made since things didn't work out with James, our dad.

A TURBULENT LIFE ? ? ?

Still to this day, I praise God for his giving my brother the strength to stand up to his mother that day. All in the room, I clapped and praised him. I give him the credit for my being somewhat normal, which is all in one's perspective and outlook on life. My brother and I rejoiced when Mother told us her divorce was final from Carlin. Alleluia!

I had been so sheltered, confused, abused, and timid to say anything until he did. I don't remember if I had told him what had happened and how baffled I was. I did not grasp or understand what I was feeling at that time. Then again, I think I must have said something to him to stand and say no to his mom that day. He was always the stronger of us physically, mentally, and displayed confidence in whatever he did. There is no wonder why girls and boys alike were friends with my brother who was a little chubby then. As he grew, he became slender and close to six feet tall and had beautiful blond hair.

Mother was busy helping her mother and Loraine as her father was dying. She took us to see him before he died. He looked the same to us as he always looked old because of his diabetes. It was a somber day when Papa passed away on August 7, 1966, at the age of seventy-two in Mobile, from his ongoing battle with diabetes. Our mother took it hard as she loved him so much as he was always there to help her when she needed it.

He was buried in a cemetery plot in Mobile, Alabama. Gaga never remarried after her husband died as he was the love of her life.

Shared Memories of the Courtroom Verdict

July of 1963 was the most turbulent year for Grandfather Frank as his heart started racing and blood pressure rising like a thermometer, facing a conflict-of-interest charge as well as charges of conspiracy relating to land deals in Maryland and Virginia. Accusations were swarming about Washington, DC, of his using congressional influence to gain dismissal of mail fraud charges, which was an extremely broad in scope charge. Frank's mail charge incorporated elements of a scheme to defraud and receive kickbacks from real estate transactions. His judgment was not good when working with the wheelers and dealers that were known to others as cons. Frank paid his team of attorney's exorbitant sums of money to defend him of the charges and to fight to the end of the judicial process for his innocence. Among several other people he trusted, he were named in the suit. He was facing criminal charges because of trusting the wrong people who were also known for sucker punching people to obtain money in their unethical ways of conducting business.

With his four living children as adults and their wives in the courtroom, they were anxiously waiting for the verdict. The jury entered the room after several hours of deliberation, came back with the verdict, was read by the foreman of the jury, and we found the guilty as charged on all counts. Gasps were heard from the family throughout the courtroom in astonishment of hearing the verdict. Others were named in the suit, and all were convicted as they were the ringleaders that conned and persuaded Frank who always looked to the good in people to do the deal. The cons named in the suit received more time as they were the instigators and promoters of the land sales.

All were convicted, and Frank served six months under house arrest and paid a $40,000.00 fine.

Frank was trusting of others and had never met a stranger in his life as he was jovial and loved people, which would later be found as a flaw in his personality in letting others deceive him as the cons approached him with their unscrupulous business plans that possibly led to his unfortunate death.

As an adult, after hearing of my grandfather's trial, I continued to sift through thousands of papers and millions to possibly billions of words about him and from his own mouth that documented his life well lived. The family all believed the conviction was a travesty of justice and a quest for an honorable man's execution. The heart condition Frank had before the indictment flared up during the trial, and on the advice of his doctors, consistent with that of his trial counsel, he was not allowed to appeal the verdict; all who played a part felt it would endanger his life.

Shared Memories of Frank and Other

1960s

My father quoted his father as saying, "Even Jesus, in picking only twelve disciples, had one traitor." Frank made it through his anguish with his characteristic cheerfulness, hard work, and friendship toward all who crossed his path. The year 1963 took a toll on all his family, especially my grandmother. With his children and their families, all were trying to gather evidence to prove it was a fraudulent lawsuit. It was perhaps the hardest years of his life as well as the entire family! It took a toll on Frank's heart. He knew President Johnson well, and he pardoned Frank in 1965 at the request of Departing Attorney General Robert F. Kennedy. Frank was in his eighties, and lawmakers didn't feel he deserved any jail time.

The chambers of the Capitol with both Republicans and Democrats celebrated his departure, honoring him with many of his friends and family in attendance. Many of the legislators said, "We will miss you terribly!" During his departure, an audit of his non-reimbursed expenses revealed that during his twenty-eight years of service, he had spent a million dollars or more of his own money and was far more than he received from the government. He owned more land (where his wealth was concentrated) the day he entered congress than when he left. It was a joy in his life with his jubilant personality and endless energy to work for the people of his beloved state of Alabama.

Frank and Other were married for almost fifty-six years. Their fiftieth anniversary was serving the most delectable food. It was a night of celebration that lives on in many people's memories that

A TURBULENT LIFE ? ? ?

heard about it from word of mouth. His faithful, trustworthy servants who were still alive and faithful to him throughout the years were his servers at the large event. Many friends, his large family, celebrated with them and danced to music, as champagne flowed throughout the night, including other beverages.

The next morning, Frank being an early riser walked to the kitchen in his Mobile home, and he thanked his staff profusely for the wonderful job they did at the anniversary party. Showing his appreciation and faithfulness to him throughout the years, he handed Martha (the nanny and maid), as well as George (his faithful butler), a red velvet bag filled with one hundred silver dollars. They were so pleased Martha gave him a hug, and George shook his hand and said, "Thank you, sir."

They both uttered the sentiments and said, "It is a pleasure to work for you and your lovely wife where 'everything is made for love!' We witnessed you exemplifying your love and graciousness through most of our lives working with you."

The former congressman remained active. His lumber business doubled since he left Congress.

"We work day and night," he said. Frank was chairman of the board of the family-owned company he started. His sons and daughter were doing most of the work in running the business. The firm has been in business since 1900. His daughter Fran was the only female president of the company and grew the company to larger proportions. James had done the same thing as president, following in his father's footsteps with his philosophy of the land holdings.

Frank, who said his future consisted of building his business even bigger, expressed hope that he would get back the $40,000.00 he paid in connection with the fraud case. He said he understood that since he had received a full and unconditional pardon, his fine would be returned.

It was a turbulent year that took a toll on all his family, especially his wife Other. With his children and their families, all were trying to gather evidence to prove it was a fraudulent lawsuit. Along with others of the family's third and fourth generations, as though the conviction was a travesty of justice and a quest for an honorable man's execution.

James quoted his father, saying, "Even Jesus, in picking only twelve disciples, had one traitor." But Frank made it through his anguish with characteristic cheerfulness, hard work, and friendship toward all who crossed his path. James also said that Frank's personal motto that he learned for himself, perhaps from watching his mother and father, was: "Integrity in taking care of family, showing respect to all people, and being good to those that work around you."

After hearing of my grandfather's trial, I continued to sift through papers about Frank from his own mouth, newspapers, magazines, Alabama, Virginia, and Missouri archives that documented his life well lived. Because of fires and lost records and the case being so old, I was unable to find any courthouse records of the trial other than what had already been written in print.

Throughout Frank's life, he was hated, envied, admired, hardworking with turbulences of ups and downs, but always loved by family, friends, and colleagues who knew him well! Reporters had embellished stories of him that cast him in a bad light just to sell newspapers. They stop and go just far enough not to get sued for liable and deformation of character.

He was robust in statue, jolly, and often reminded me of Santa Claus with his goodness and kindness to all. I added, "My grandfather had more friends than most in those days. He will always be remembered for his twenty-minute naps, and he always replied, 'I'll be good to go.' For Christmas, birthdays, and special occasions, he would give his servants and grandchildren shiny bright one hundred, 99.9 percent silver dollars. In my later years, I wish I had kept the $100 pure-silver dollars under my mattress as they were worth far more than a dollar in today's times, being made of sterling silver with no copper as seen in today's coins! Hindsight is twenty-twenty!"

On Christmas day, my brother and I would celebrate with our dad at Other's and Frank's home in Mobile. Before getting into our family cars and heading to the lodge to hunt with our cousins, we celebrated Christmas coming together with their grandchildren at their downtown home in Mobile. Grandmother would have Martha prepare a buffet and a butler to serve the food for everyone to eat, as it was a growing, increasingly large family. Pictures would be taken as Dad's two brothers' and sister's spouse and children gathered around the organ, playing music and overlooking the living room on the small second-floor rotunda with the beautiful lighted freshly cut pine tree that Frank and his sons cut down from their country property. Then all the young cousins would gather around to have their pictures taken sitting on the deer statue outside. Those were everlasting memories of the past that I was still able to recall from my tender age of two and through adulthood. I grew up in what is known today as the baby boomer generation that I was never to forget the few times I was with my father's family.

I communicate these words to my blessed children. I trust you to face the challenges life presents before you as your great grandfather Frank did. Lift your head up high as you help those for the greater good. If you get depressed, remember these words: "Keep on climbing the ladder of life and what those words mean to you personally." Continue smiling and be your congenial self. We are caretakers of vast acres of God's magnificent lands. We as a family unit take great pride in the wild creatures as Frank helped teach his family to do. It is a continued family tradition taught to the future generations to care for.

His son James would say, "To me, there is nothing more beautiful than the sheen on a turkey's wing in sunlight and the leaves with multicolored variations in the season of the fall. The natural things to me are the beautiful things as words are a vehicle of expression."

The speeches he made to the House floor included his annual orations on the widening of the Tombigbee River in his native Alabama to accommodate ocean-going vessels. Even though the house operated on the five-minute rule for speeches, they would let Frank talk on and on.

Frank died of his heart giving out on him in 1969 at the age eighty-four at George Washington Hospital in Washington, DC. During his twenty-eight years in the House, Frank was a conservative and a loved congressman. He was eulogized as having traveled his life in "unique splendor." No congressman has ever had a greater love for the First District of Alabama than Frank did.

If we could throw back the white robe around the throne of God, we would see him leaning on Jesus, saying, "Come home, loved ones, weep not for me." Friends, he is not dead; he is bigger than life as his memories live on and on into the third and fourth generations and beyond with his world-famous saying and his motto, "Everything's is made for love." Our grandfather today continues on being remembered as an idol to the family and also to those of all colors, including White and Black alike, whose hope was centered in him.

I remember at age seventeen, sitting on my grandmother's lap in my blue pantsuit, trying to comfort my grandmother as her tears flowed like a sprinkler in a garden. He was escorted to his grave site by many police and cars that followed the black hertz carrying his coffin.

Over fifty years later, on March 7, 2009, I held a book signing at the hunting lodge for my book *Southern Hunt*, based on my research about the life of my father and his family and my grandfather and grandmother. I can say in sincerity, "My grandfather and father had more friends than you could count in one lifetime, and that is how I remember him." Frank bought and sold land well over three million acres during his lifetime.

A monument was erected at the cemetery in the family plot. Frank and his wife were married for almost fifty-six years. His name lives on as a school was named after him in McIntosh, Alabama. Road was named after him, a scholarship at Cumberland College, and buildings as well. An African American community is named for him after he secured federal funding for it to supplement his own personal money to support it. Driving through the state of Alabama, there are many remembrances of him. He had a total of eighteen different businesses in his lifetime known to Gracie Lu and could have been more, and as you read, I include the ones from his early childhood that my father never included as he would mention the eighteen businesses.

A TURBULENT LIFE ? ? ?

Frank's Businesses:

1) Milk delivery, whitewashing fences, cleaning outhouses, and other side jobs
2) Church bell ringer for services and occasionally for funerals
3) Queen bee business
4) Selling raccoons
5) General store in 1920s, selling anything from coffins, guns, Coca-Cola (you name it, he had it)
6) Mobile Real Estate Company
7) Baldwin Timber Land Company and Naval Stores **1936**
8) Lumber, Crossties, Naval Stores **1940**
9) Land and Timber Company from **1957 to 2022 and beyond**
10) Washington Lumber and Turpentine Company **1957**
11) McIntosh Logging Company
12) McIntosh Wood Company
13) Bilbo Livestock Selling Cattle and Land Company
14) McIntosh Logging Company
15) Alabama Salt Corporation
16) Developer of Homosassa Springs Florida with President Hoover and his brother
17) Gulf Beach Land and Development Company
18) Built and owned Fort Morgan Hotel (A hurricane tore it down)
19) Gifting and shipping dogs to other countries and those that wanted them in the states
20) Breaking in mustang, stallion horses and selling them
21) Livery Stable
22) Taxi service of the day
23) Negotiating a movie of his life **1950s**

He was instrumental in bringing industrial companies to Southern Alabama. Many letters, cards, and tributes were sent to the family at the passing of their father. There are many reminders of Frank throughout the state of Alabama as one drives the state and sees the industry he helped bring to the state. Brookley Air Force Base was now closed and used for other purposes. He was influential in having the Bankhead tunnel built in Mobile, Alabama, as well as buildings and other things you can see throughout the state.

After Frank died, family members would look after their mother. She lived in the house near Downtown Mobile. Family members went to Washington, DC, and gathered all their belongings at the Hotel Washington in their suite that they lived in for so many years. Other dispersed the items to family members that wanted them as her Mobile House was full of their massive furniture.

Many letters, cards, and tributes were sent to the family at the passing of their mother. A remarkable woman with a strong heart, discipline of mind, and smart as a whip. She was the backbone of my grandfather and often kept him on the straight and narrow with her integrity and teaching him the many lessons he learned from her.

Visiting Dad and Cora as we drove to the lodge for a weekend of hunting for white-tailed deer. Sitting in a shooting house, I had taken a nap. I asked myself, "Where did the day go?" A fast and furious wind suddenly blew into the hunting house, rousing me just as the sun was setting in the west. Wide-eyed and hungry, I peered into the field where two does, a buttonhead, a ten pointer, and the granddaddy of all bucks stood on the edge of the field, which appeared to the naked eye to be at least twelve points, if not more. At dusk, three bucks entered the field, with me counting the antlers of each deer through my binoculars. Determined to shoot the largest bodied with the best rack, gasping, I immediately raised my gun and, looking through my scope, focused on the dark-skinned, deep, heavy muscled buck, appearing to have a swayback and a potbelly with a Roman nose coming from the swamp. The first deer I killed by myself while sitting in a field attentively. I kept counting a rack of twenty points. In awe, and with my adrenalin pumping, I recounted, again getting the same number. Taking my safety off, I took aim and fired at my target, approximately sixty-five yards away, and immediately he dropped to his feet. It was a large dark-skinned swamp deer as the others ran away. He dropped right in place on the ground with the perfect shot to the heart. Running to the deer, it was a ten-point nontypical rack and beautiful! I was so proud, alerting all nearby of my large deer. It was the biggest killed that day.

Elated, I walked out of the hunting house in shock to behold the most beautiful rack I had ever seen. The body was so large I'd have to wait for the other hunters leaving their fields to come after night had fallen. My dad was the first to pick me up and could not believe what he saw; his eyes grew round as he gazed at perhaps the largest deer ever killed in the area. He immediately radioed Bevo, Wes, and Hubby to come help. When they arrived, the truck headlights shone brightly on the deer as the three men dragged the trophy buck from the field and lifted it onto the truck. They were anxious to get to the lodge to see how much it weighed. To their amazement, it weighed two hundred and fifty-one pounds, which they thought might be a state record. People in the lodge ran out with cameras, snapping many pictures of me and the largest deer ever killed in four generations on the hunting preserve. Just as I hoped, I was able to return to school and show my class the many photos of my award-winning trophy buck.

To my surprise, when they returned to the lodge, my son Bevo had shot his first deer and was being inducted into "the first buck's deer slayer club." It was fun looking at my son with blood smeared all over his face by his granddad he was living with at the time. I hated taking away from his thunder by killing the largest deer that day.

On Bevo's twenty-first birthday, a year or so after killing his first buck, Granddad gave his grandson a female Boykin Spaniel, a pedigreed hunting dog he bought from a breeder in South Carolina, where the breed originated some sixty years ago. Granddad had raised several Boykin Spaniels over the years and had a male that lived to be almost ninety-one in dog years.

Mother Weds Fourth Husband Who Gracie Lu Called Papa

1970

They had a small wedding as they had both been married before. We stayed at the Fountain Bleu Hotel on Miami Beach for a few days until the ship sailed. My brother and I joined them on their honeymoon with separate staterooms on Carnival Cruise Line from the Port of Miami. We had a blast, seeing the shows on ship and playing bingo. My brother enjoyed Nassau and the beach. He negotiated at the market and purchased a five-foot tiki, and he struggled carrying it back on the ship. My brother and I appreciated Papa inviting us on their honeymoon. They were able to find time to enjoy each other without my brother and me.

Papa had a son and a daughter from his other marriage. His son became a lawyer, and his daughter worked for the state of Kentucky, and they were both married. We moved to Clearwater Beach, Florida, and stayed in a hotel on the beach for two months while the home they purchased was being renovated. I soaked up the Florida sun and enjoyed every minute of the carefree life along with my mother as we had adjoining rooms. My brother came later when we moved to our home in Dunedin, Florida.

Papa was a dad like I never had continuously in life. He was a man of honor, and as I reflect on my past, he perhaps saved my life with his love and kindness, sheltering me from taking drugs or following unscrupulous people and keeping me on the straight and narrow in learning the scriptures that one should follow on a daily basis.

A TURBULENT LIFE ? ? ?

He surprised me with a twelve-foot scorpion sailboat and built a pontoon to put it on and anchored in the bay in front of our house as we crossed the street to get to it. There were many fun times on the boat. The most dramatic ones were when Dede, my summer best friend, and I were in the boat with a boy, and the wind was strong, and Dede was holding on to the line in the water. Suddenly, we saw a five-foot hammerhead shark in the bay and was motioning to her to get in the boat as we sailed toward the pontoon. She finally realized we wanted her in the boat, and as she got in, the shark was circling the boat. We were all scared for our lives and made it to the pontoon in shallower water and pulled the boat on top. As we looked around, the shark had left. It was safe to swim to shore and climb the rocks to go home. Her bother Jeep would sail at times with us.

Their mom, Dede, Jeep, and two sisters and younger brother would visit their grandparents' home in Dunedin in the summer as they lived in Shaker Heights, Ohio. I met them at the Dunedin Presbyterian Church, and Dede was in the same Sunday school class as I was, and we became friends. They would often take me along with them for a day of fun in the sun and sand at Clearwater Beach Pavilion.

Another time was when Papa took the boat out around 5:00 p.m. when he had arrived home from work. He was gone for hours, and my mother panicked and called the police. They arrived and lined the streets of Edgewater Drive to find him, and the coast guard was looking as well. Suddenly he appeared with the low tide, and when out of the channel, he was walking the boat to shore. His face was red from embarrassment of seeing all the police lined ashore. That was his last time to take the boat out, and he was upset with Mother that she called them.

I was sailing alone in the sailboat, and my mother, looking through binoculars, saw me on the other side of the bay near houses, and by a seawall, I capsized the boat. It appeared to her I was struggling to turn it back over. As I was getting it over, a police car arrived and asked if I was okay. I answered yes, and I sailed back home. I was angry for my mom calling the police.

When my brother came to live with us, we would have a blast in the windy days with the boat. Those were wonderful times and memories with my brother. After sailing, he would go to his apartment over the garage, and I would go to my room.

Browder loved to entertain and hosted a large Kentucky Derby Party in our home and in the large backyard. She hired a bartender serving the traditional mint juleps and other beverages as well. A photo booth that she made as she did painting was quite creative. I manned the photo booth throughout the day with others as we took turns. My mother was always considered around time as the hostess with the mostest. They hired car parkers from the school I attended to park cars on the busy street of Edgewater Drive in Dunedin, Florida. Tents were set up in the backyard with televisions sets up to watch the derby. A betting booth was set up, and everyone had a great time, and luckily the weather held out with no rain. There were around fifty to seventy-five people in attendance. Papa was a gentleman and loved my mother so much he would often give her free reign until he retired from being a lawyer and becoming a circuit court judge.

I was introduced to Ed, and he was dressed in a yellow suit, looking dapper at the Kentucky Derby Party hosted in our home on Edgewater Drive in Dunedin, Florida. He was older than me and had graduated from Fordham University in New York with a BS degree in business. He worked for Four Roses Distilleries in Tampa, Florida, as we were talking with one another, and we began dating. He would show me his workplace, walking me into the promotional room with items to give away to customers of Seagram's Distilleries and Four Roses Bourbon, which were subsidiaries of the company. We entered the room, and I was in awe of the great giveaways. Ed told me to pick two pieces I would like to have. I chose a lounge raft for a swimming pool or any body of water, and it was in the shape of a bottle, and I also chose a bottle-shaped radio. Ed and I were inseparable for a number of years. I was going away to college, and he gave me space as he knew how important it was for me to get a degree, and he was eight years older than me. I attended night school for six weeks and graduated with a diploma from Clearwater High School in Pinellas County Florida, and the football mascot was known for their school

A TURBULENT LIFE ? ? ?

colors, which were gray and crimson as tornadoes as well as it being the name of our fight song.

While I was at college, Ed surprised me as he went to University of Florida and obtained his law degree. He was roommates with Papa's son and our neighbor's son on Edgewater Drive in Dunedin, Florida.

My Favorite Memories of Gaga

1970

I recalled my favorite memory of Gaga. I was in my freshman year of college on the east coast of Florida, driving Gaga in the passenger seat of my yellow and black-topped Camaro from my mother's home in Dunedin to visit Flagler College on the east coast in Saint Augustine, Florida. While driving from the west coast to the east coast of Florida with me behind the wheel, suddenly and unexpectedly in traffic, a white cattle bird hit the passenger side of the vehicle, where Gaga was sitting. Cracking the windshield and luckily not hitting the driver's side, it hit the passenger side front window. I couldn't stop in heavy traffic. I kept asking Gaga, "Are you okay?"

She responded, "I am fine, but your poor windshield cracked."

I replied, "That's all right, as long as you are not harmed as your well-being is the most important as a beloved passenger in my car!" I explained to Gaga, "I have always considered you my second mother, especially in the younger years of my life! We shared secrets and many fun times together at your home. The attic with all your old steamer trunks made great hiding places while playing hide-and-seek with my cousins and my brother. You and your home were the host to many of my birthday parties, and as a debutant, I would stay with you in your home, and escorts would pick me up, and you were so gracious in entertaining them."

I took Gaga when we arrived and checked her into the St. Augustine hotel across the street from the Bridge of Lions. She rested, and then we walked to a restaurant nearby the hotel and had dinner. The following day, she saw my room and was amazed at how large it

A TURBULENT LIFE ? ? ?

was, and she enjoyed seeing the old Flagler hotel, and we ate in the main dining room. We rode the elevator upstairs, and I showed her the library and took her outside to see the beautiful view of the city. After three days, we had seen most all of the sights and the Fountain of Youth. I drove her to the Jacksonville Airport to fly home where her son would pick her up at the Mobile Airport.

I attended a weeklong Christian school teacher's conference in Pensacola, Florida, in 1978. She left from visiting my grandmother for the last time as she laid on her soon-to-be deathbed. I tried my best to hold my tears back as I loved Gaga so much. I excused myself to go to the bathroom and cried for a long period of time. I was thankful I was able to see Gaga for the last time. Loraine was by her side and took excellent care of her as Gaga and Papa had done for her. I said goodbye to Gaga and Loraine and drove back to Florida. Shortly after I returned home, I received a telephone call that Gaga had died.

It was as if they were saying my second mother died. It was a turbulent time for me as I felt I had lost a part of myself. She died on November 7, 1978, in Mobile, Alabama, at the age of eighty-one and was buried in a cemetery in Mobile with a grave marker next to her husband. Gaga outlived her husband by twelve years. When Gaga died, she had left index cards with numbers of things that would go to Browder and her son Brevard. Then the four grandchildren starting with the oldest who would choose one item and then the next, and I was the youngest and picked last.

Gaga loved bridge and taught me as a fill-in if one of her bridge group was unable to play. I found bridge as a challenging card game and lots of fun playing with partners, but who would I play with now? It was a question that lingered in my mind. Gaga had many friends and would go across the bay to play bridge. When it came to her turn to host the meeting in her home, Loraine would serve a delicious lunch and pass refreshments as well. My mother never played. I never found anyone to play with after she died.

A sentiment: Standing at the unknown year and facing the days ahead, I trust you may meet all they hold in store. With composure, one lifts their heads. I hope this will be your most gratifying year in trying to do the greatest good. Tiresomely, we are doing the greatest good for the largest number of people. Today the wall that can't be scaled may reveal a door to let you through. The soil produced from stones may grow. The life you sought for, sick at heart. He rises to greet you, like the dawn, around the corner face-to-face. So keep on keeping on! As custodians with vast acres of God's beautiful land, we take great pride in his wild creatures. Finding dogs or cats as our best friend. To me, there is nothing more beautiful than the sheen of portraits hanging in sunlight and the leaves with multicolored variations in the season of the fall. The natural things to me are the beautiful things as words are a vehicle of expression. They are wonderful tools of a trade to work with. The perfect ordering of words is a special gift of God.

Gaga often taught me to deal with the secrets that we had shared in the best way I could, even when I didn't fully understand why. Now your helping God with you having no worries, pain, or sorrows, living in the grace of God in heaven! Oh, what a wonderful place it must be, something drawn of its loveliest aspects of color as Gaga often taught me to do with the secrets that we had shared. I recall vivid memories through the years of her and often brings a smile to my face.

My cousin Mathew hired Loraine to be his nanny and maid with his wife and children. She was wonderful, and I was relieved she was still a part of the family until she died, which was a sad day for us all.

Dramatic Years Attending College
1970, 1971, 1972, 1973, and 1974

I attended Flagler College in St. Augustine, Florida. It was in the old Flagler Hotel, and my mother and Papa moved me into the room. The room was filled with her belongings as they rented a U-Haul trailer towed on the back of the car. My mother helped set it up and cried as she left her at the college a freshman year in 1970. My bicycle to ride around town was placed under the carport in an old storage area where others were placed as well. We saw steamer trunks and luggage stored in that space when it was operated as a hotel.

As a freshmen in 1970, I was age seventeen. My mother would call almost every day and ask me what I was wearing. She would often tell me to change my outfit and described the outfit she wanted me to put on that day as well as how to wear my hair. As my mother picked out all my clothes for me and packed my steamer trunk, she knew everything I had.

The telephone was in the hall, and students passing by could hear my response, and I was often ridiculed from girls hearing how I responded to my mother. I would be bullied again like in grade school, but this time I was older and in college away from home. The freedom from my mother was short-lived, and I found myself withdrawing into oneself and away from people once again. I had no roommate in my freshman year. I made a few friends from Indiana who attended and a Georgia girl who was across the hall. She was an artist, and she gave me one of her paintings of a wide-eyed girl with brown hair and blue eyes from her room. My friends were at Flagler for one year, and I was saddened that they transferred elsewhere and did not return to Flagler. Two of my friends went home that year and stayed in Mother and Papa's home in Dunedin with me for the weekend. Years later, when I was married and went to California for a Rotary National Convention my husband, I visited Anita in Irvine California. She married an architect whose sister was a TV and movie star. We lost touch with each other over the years.

The freedom was going to my head, and the only thing to do at that time for a college freshman was to go walk to Dairy Queen and see the attractions the town had to offer. The Lightner Museum, Fountain of Youth, Bridge of Lions, and going to the beach where you could ride your cars on, I would ride the old town trolley. Castillo de San Marcos National Monument Fort and often when visitors would visit me at the college, we would see the attractions. Ripley's Believe It or Not was a favorite, also St George Street with shops and stores with an excavation site for archeologist. The old school and old jail were also sites to see. By the end of my freshman year, I knew all the attractions to see in St. Augustine and could be blindfolded and lead visitors to the sites. I was put on probation that year, and I had to do better the following year to be able to graduate from Flagler College. Summer of 1970, Papa and my mother signed me up for an intercollegiate tour of Europe with Betty Tours from Spring Hill College in Mobile, Alabama, to receive college credits.

Spring Hill College Intercollegiate Tour to Europe

1971

Papa agreed with Browder as they arranged and paid for me to go on intercollegiate tour in Europe. When I came home from college in May, Mother had packed my bags for the trip. Papa had my steamship tickets that Betty sent to those participating in the intercollegiate tour for college credits with Betty Tour Company that operated with her husband who was a professor at Spring Hill College.

Mom took me to get passport pictures and my passport, which I had to have to enter each country we would visit as well as taking me to the doctor for a vaccination certificate. The Betty's had been given tours of Europe for years, and Browder knew them and felt it would be an opportunity of a lifetime for her daughter as well as receiving college credit by joining the intercollegiate tour with Professor Betty and his wife of Spring Hill College in Mobile, Alabama.

My boyfriend at the time, Ed, was from Statin Island, New York, and we flew to New York together. It was a good time for him to see his mother who still lived on Statin Island and would take ferry to visit and stay with his mother while there. He took me to dinner at Rodney Dangerfield's restaurant, and we listened to comedians telling jokes in which I did not catch on too many of them told that night.

Ed was laughing so hard and asked, "Why are you not laughing?"

I replied, "I often don't get jokes as many of them I don't comprehend as I am more left-brain dominant than right."

He replied, "That explains it." He took me back to the Hotel Edison on Forty-Seventh Street West Broadway on June 16, where the tour group was staying.

Embarkation was at 9:40 a.m. when we boarded the SS *France*, which was owned and operated by the French. It set sail from Pier 88 at the foot of West Forty-Eighth Street. We were shown to our cabins, which were near the bottom of the ship, and considered the student section. We had bunk beds and a small bathroom. The cabin was just above some of the crews' cabins as we were in second class. There was a first class, and they were not to enter that section. After seeing our cabins, we went on deck to wave goodbye to those on the dock, yelling. After seeing their cabins, they went on deck to wave goodbye to those on the dock, yelling "bon voyage." The ship's crew spoke both English and French.

Set Sail on the SS *France* to South Hampton, England, on Intercollegiate Tour with Betty Tours from Spring Hill College in Mobile, Alabama

Onboard passengers at 1:00 p.m. on June 17 heard the ships engines, and shortly after they were on their way to the South Hampton Port in England. I waved to Ed as we set sail, and I noticed he had tears streaming down his face as he was crying. As the ship departed the port, I was the only one in the group who had someone giving us a send-off from the dock as other pedestrians and families were waving farewell to other guest.

We set sail on the SS *France* to South Hampton, England, from Spring Hill College in Mobile, Alabama. We were out to sea, and a shipboard party was given by the Betty's as the tour directors us students in the group in the main lounge that began at 10:30 a.m. The Betty's provided the appropriate refreshments since some of us were under the drinking age for alcohol at the bon voyage party.

Shortly after setting sail, we had a drill where everyone put on their life preservers and went to their assigned stations and given instructions by the ship personnel. As crew members walked by, they made sure we all had our life preservers on properly and adjusted them if not. Then the alarm would ring, and they were able to go to their cabins and take the preservers off, putting them back where they found them.

As I considered myself an explorer as well as adventurous, it didn't stop me from sneaking up to first class during the five-day voyage. It had a beautiful library for guest with games such as chess, scrabble, and cards. Also, lots of books. Walking casually and trying to blend in with the first-class passengers, I peaked in some of the staterooms that had their doors open, and they were roomy and luxurious compared to the student room I was in. During the cruise, I ventured into first class several times.

No one went hungry as the French meals we were able to choose from on the menu were written in French and English. Breakfast was served in buffet style. Hors d'oeuvres were offered on the luncheon menu. Breakfast was buffet style, and the food for all three meals throughout the voyage was delicious. Red and white wine were served in carafes, and for finer wines, they had a wine steward with a wine list of the better wines.

I found the voyage to be wonderful and departed the ship on June 22, 1971, in Southampton, England. I observed the many tugboats and other liners that were in the harbor. I looked out at the green lands across the harbor, and they were beautiful, lush, and seemed so foreign to me living in Dunedin, Florida, and Pinellas county, where it was known at that time for having the least amount of rainfall in the state. Brown lawns were seen throughout the county as water restrictions were set for two days a week, using sprinkler systems to water their yards and only certain times of the day, and they had officers from the water department issue tickets and place on your door if you were found watering at different times or days.

We boarded a bus, and in transit, we made stop in Stratford-upon-Avon. The stone streets and buildings were impressive. Stopped at William Shakespeare's birthplace, which was built of half-timber and stone. It was quant with low ceilings, wooden furniture, and short beds. The garden was beautiful with all different herbs, trees, flowers, and the grounds were a gorgeous thriving green.

Passing Shakespeare's school reminded her of his house but was on a larger scale and had a tower adjoining it. The architecture was of the same style. Ann Hathaway's cottage (William Shakespeare's wife) was originally a farmhouse. It reminded me of something out of a fairytale. The building dated back to the fifteenth century, and the structure comprising of timber, framing, wattle, stone, brick, and the roof being thatched, I found fascinating as I had never seen one before as I had only read about such English architecture. The house was beautiful and on a smaller scale than Shakespeare's.

London, England

Later that day, we went to the Royal Shakespeare Theatre, which overlooked the Avon river and park. We saw like *The Merchant of Venice*, which was fantastic! The staging and scenery were spectacular. It seemed as though the stage had a hydraulic system that would bring the gold, silver, and bronze coffins up for her majesty to choose from. The bronze coffin was the right one to win her love. I found the acting to be superb. We stayed in the Mount Royal Hotel Leamington Spa in Warwick, England.

We visited Warwick Castle, with which I found no words to describe the landscape and gardens. They were planned perfectly with greenery and no lovelier flowers anywhere. Peacocks were roaming about the gardens with which I stayed far away from as I recalled almost losing my right eye as I was running as a little girl, and one started flying and touched my with a toe that caused a scar near my right eye. To say the least, I was afraid of the beautiful birds as they spread their wings with beautiful colors and patterns. Inside the castle, the tapestries, frescos, and furniture were interesting as the curator talked about them.

We boarded the chartered bus to London. June 23 to 27 for four nights. Many of the students were marveled at the beauty of gardeners maintaining the lawns, trees, and landscape with rolling hills and curves. The style of architecture was regally English. We visited the Houses of Parliament and Big Ben situated on the North Bank of the River Thames and was so picturesque as well as being thrilling seeing it for the first time. They learned the lantern above "Big Ben" reaches to the skies with all of its spires, and with its age, it still gave the correct time all the time as it was well maintained. Westminster Abbey was huge, magnificent, with Gothic architecture, and the great

A TURBULENT LIFE ? ? ?

height pointed architecture and tall splendid columns that rose from the floor to the stone framework of the ribbed ceiling. The Abbey's stained-glass windows told some of the religious stories. The floor plan was unique and in the shape of a latent cross. The English poet Geoffrey Chaucer was best known for his *Canterbury Tales*. William Shakespeare and Prime Minister Winston Churchill are among the numerous head figures buried there.

All except two English queens were crowned there since William the Conqueror built it in 1066. The twin towers were in the west and looked so high up. I was surprised when our guide told us they were 325 feet high, and the central tower was square. Visiting the National Gallery of Art in London had a wide range of paintings by countless artists.

Giovani Bellini, an Italian Renaissance painter of portrait, painted *Doge Leonardo Loredan*, which was my favorite portrait in the gallery. The portrait was encased like a mummy in state robes. The "Doge" ruled Venice when Europe was leagued against her. Velazquez's The Rokeby Venus, a nude of a woman, I purchased in the gift shop and had sent to my brother Robby.

On June 25, we had a tour of the Tower of London, which consisted of a group of stone buildings in the eastern part of London. The ancient fortress and dark prison are where Sir Thomas Moore was imprisoned, and Ann Boleyn was beheaded on orders from her husband King Henry VIII. A shallow moat surrounded the tower. The Royal Crown Jewels housed in the tower were exquisite. The crowns, scepters, and other glittering royal treasures of English rulers are closely guarded by Yeomen Warders and Beefeaters.

Being among the crowd, with my camera, I caught a perfect photo of Queen Elizabeth II. Took numerous photos of the changing of the guards with the horses marching down the street with infantry in perfect formation. There hats looked heavy for them to wear. There were many guards in uniforms with weapons dating back to the Tudor period in the late 1400s to 1600s. Buckingham Palace had been the home of England's king and queens since 1837.

It was onward to St. Paul's Cathedral with its beautiful Renaissance architecture, which is used in manor houses and churches throughout

England. Some of the distinctions I observed had enormous, wide interiors and formality shown in intricate detail. The dome in the church were vast and breathtaking.

On June 26, the group visited the Houses of Parliament, which I was most interested as I loved history and also political science. The Victoria Tower entrance was opened for tourist, and the guide led us as a group and also individuals through the building. The guide explained there were 1,100 rooms and two miles of passageways. Thirteen rooms are open to the public. It the year 1941, a bomb destroyed the House of Commons, and the new House of Commons reopened in 1950, which was two years before I was born. The guide showed the group the sword line (red line) in which no speaker could cross in the early years of the house.

The woodwork was of English oak cut from two- and three-hundred-year-old trees. Various nations of the British Commonwealth contributed to the furnishings of the House of Commons. The king or queen was not allowed to enter the Chamber of Commons, as only the House of Lords could. The guide explained a special room for other members of the royal family, where they could hear the proceedings. The government sits at the left and the opposition at the right, and the speaker was placed in the middle. At this time, there are about eight hundred and fifty members in the Upper House of Parliament. House of Lords don't receive any pay for their services as it was more for prestige to be a member. The guide proceeded telling us that women were not seated until the year 1958. "Pecos Corridor" held three poses of Charles the First with the finest details painted by Sir Anthony Van Dyck, a Baroque artist, and became the court painter in England, Southern Netherlands, and Italy at that time. He captured it on canvas to have the eyes follow you wherever you stood.

St. Stephen's crypt was the exit, and the crypt and baptistery had served many purposes, and at one time, it was a stable for the horses. The speaker's state dining room today serves as a chapel, another the Speaker's state dining room, and today serves as a chapel for the members of the two houses. It is used for the celebration of Holy Communion and on occasions for marriage of members and baptizing their children.

A TURBULENT LIFE ? ? ?

West Minister Hall dates from 1097. It was principally used for Courts of Justice. St. Thomas Moore and King Charles I were sentenced to death in this room. It had beautiful stained-glass windows from the year 1840 and six medieval statues of kings under sturdy hammer beam roofs. Today it is used as a conference room and the scene of the nation's tribute to its monarchs and leaders. I was quite disappointed as I would have loved to have seen the House in session. Our guide led us to the barracks for the royal guards, which looked like large modern apartment buildings in the United States. The guards were paid very well. They returned to hotel in the bus to get dressed for dinner at Beefeaters restaurant.

I was getting over the most Turbulent night I had in London when the Betty's had the bus take the group to Beefeaters restaurant, which was mainly for tourist. I was wearing the long blond fall my mother packed for me. I had one glass of mead, which is considered a wine and an alcoholic drink of fermented honey, water, and sometimes with added fruits, spices, grains, or hops. The alcoholic content were served by female wenches (servers) depicting those of the eighteenth century in costumes of that era. They handed out small glasses of mead as it was 18 percent alcohol. Strong! After having one glass, I was feeling it. Some of the male students with the group were lit, and some were considered drunk as they had two glasses.

The Betty's had everyone board the small bus to return to the hotel. They went to their rooms with which some were on the balcony and had open windows. One of the boys came to my window with which I shared with other Mobile girls. He started stroking her fall and accidentally pulled it off which scared him. He was angry at me, and I felt belittled and didn't want to see him or the Mobile girls in the room with me. I was humiliated and felt like I was two feet tall, and he ran back to his room, telling the others what happened. Of course, the next day everyone knew including Professor and Mrs. Betty. They tried to put an end to the gossip, but I became the laughingstock of the group. I threw it in the garbage as to never see it again. To myself, I blamed my mother for doing that to me. All because my mother wore them all the time at age nineteen with a full head of hair.

London, England, a day at People's Corner, Madame Tussauds, Planetarium, I certainly didn't need to walk around. It almost ruined the rest of my trip in London experiencing my most turbulent time on the trip. I sank further into myself.

On June 27, I ventured out on my own as it was the last day in London and needed to be away from the group. While walking, I entered a shop that sold Royal Doulton China figurines. I purchased some and had shipped to her parents' home. The others in the group remained in the hotel playing cards as it was raining or drizzling.

As I was walking with my parasol in hand, a young Scottish man began talking to me. "Where are you going?"

I replied, "Madame Tussauds wax museum."

"I am going there too. Do you mind if I walk with you?"

I responded yeah as we introduced ourselves to each other. Along the way, we stopped at Speaker's Corner in Hyde Park, where anyone was able to talk about any subject we wished it had no time limit. A lady with an open parasol was feeding peanuts to the numerous pigeons gathered around her while singing and dancing about the park. An elderly man exhibited tattoos on his head and all over his body and was shouting about religion. It was quite interesting to me and Sam as we discussed how a citizen could talk to the public on Sundays without being apprehended by Bobbies (English policemen). We continued our walk to Madame Tussauds and were enjoying getting to know each other. We finally made it, and Sam wanted to pay for me, but I would not let him as I paid my own way. They entered and found it well done but overrated as it was the original wax museum.

The guide told us that every distinguished victim in the guillotine was molded by Madame Tussauds or her uncle. The grand hall of the museum featured top prominent men of the current day. The Battle of Trafalgar was shown as it really happened on a small scale. Guns, cannons, smoke bellowing out from machines, and you could hear them yelling or speaking softly as they were dying. I was terrified walking through the Chamber of Terror and held Sam's hand. Executions by the last executioner of the time before abolition of capital punishment were displayed and disgusted me as well as Sam. I found it unnecessary to display and inappropriate for children to see. Adjoining the building was the Planetarium, it had a penny arcade with slot machines in which me and Sam tried our luck with no success. Sam and I decided to go together and enter the London Planetarium built in 1958 that adjoined the museum. It was the most modern planetarium in the world. Sam and I were in awe of the F 100,000 Zeiss projector with two thousand, nine hundred parts and showed the shy as they had never seen before. They would be seen from any point on earth at any moment in time, before the birth of Christ to two thousand years into the future. Each of the forty-two brightest stars had its own projector, which forms images accurate in brightness and colors, against the constellations as the narrator showed the outlines.

Upon exiting the planetarium, I told Sam I wish my dad could see this. I explained to him at two years old I recalled the earliest memory of my dad taking turns with my brother and I to look out of his prized telescope he had set up looking out the second bedroom window. He would take turns placing my brother and I on a stool to look out at the stars and constellations and explain what each one was that we saw.

Sam replied, "Your dad sounds like a cool guy."

I answered immediately, "Yes, he is."

We got lost in Regent's Park and walked past the Regent's zoo, which had everything from elephants to monkey and animals in between. We had lunch together in an English Pub and had the traditional English dish of fish and chips, and neither could resist eating without having a beer as the most economical drink for students than sodas as they were too expensive then to have. We could not stop talking with each other as we found we had a lot in common and enjoyed the same things.

After lunch, we walked past the Regent's Open Air Theater, which appeared to be a block wide and surrounded by a fence. Sam walked me back to the hotel room, where the others in the group were still playing cards.

Sam asked, "When are you leaving London?"

I replied, "Unfortunately tomorrow." We were both sad as we were just getting to know each other and found we had a lot in common. Neither thought to get each other's address. He hugged me goodbye and said, "Safe travels to you." I echoed the same sentiment back to him and closed the door as he left. We were never saw or heard from each other again. Neither of us thought to get each other's address.

Girls asked, "Who was that?" They uttered the words *he is handsome!* I walked away as if I didn't hear them as I had nothing to say.

Sam had cheered me up after having the most embarrassing, turbulent night before. Of course, I did not share that with him. Sam still lives as one of my fondest memories of my days in London. Often thinking what would have happened if we had exchanged our contact information and stayed in touch. I regretted that we didn't have the foresight to do so.

Train to Thun, Switzerland

The bus dropped the group off with luggage handed to porters at the train station. Luggage was passed through the large windows by the porters at the train station to where we were sitting. Exiting the train, we passed our luggage to the porters at the Thun, Switzerland, station. A bus took the group to the Schloss hotel Friedhoff, and Professor and Mrs. Betty checked the group into the hotel for three nights.

In Thun, Switzerland, from June 29 to July 1, it was free time and shopping days for souvenirs and gifts to take back home. On the way to walking from the train station to the bus taking our luggage to load on the bus to the hotel, I noticed they rented bikes at the station. After the Betty's checked us in and assigned the rooms and were settled, I was walking alone and entered a jewelry store and purchased a 14-carat gold Swiss watch that fit her wrist perfectly. Upon reaching the train station, I rented a bicycle to ride around town.

Suzie from Chicago, Illinois, and Kitty from Fort Lauderdale, Florida, asked where they could rent a bike. I told them the train station. They responded in unison where it was as they were not sure how to get there. I got off the bike and walked with them showing the way to the station as they were not far from it. They each rented a bicycle, and from that day on, the out-of-towners not living in Mobile, Alabama, teamed up together. We were the adventurous threesome as we concluded those from Mobile were limited as on the last day of London, playing cards all day. Suzie and Kitty felt they had to join in.

"Gracie Lu, you are courageous and a brave soul and awesome to hang around!" They had me smiling and laughing as we rode together about town on our rented bikes for the day.

Some students on the tour asked, "Where did you rent the bikes?"

I replied, "The train station."

"Where is that?"

I pointed the direction they should walk in. The three of us continued riding our bikes through town.

I found it hard to make friends with many of those that had their nose up in the air. I had been bullied enough in my life, and I wasn't going to let anyone daunt me from enjoying and getting the most out of the trip. I chose not to speak to those who talked behind my back as they ridiculed me in London. I felt like I was in the private grade school I attended where I was bullied a lot.

Suzie and Kitty told me, "They are jealous of you and the initiatives and adventures you have made by yourself on this trip. Now we want to be a part of your escapades."

I had a big grin on my face, and those were the kindest words they could have said, as they were my peers and best friends on the trip.

I said, "Thank you for making my day with your kind words coming from two individuals I find to be honest and sincere."

Hotel de Calais Paris, France, and Louvre Museum

Suzie and Kitty agreed that we should get a room together. Suzie called the Bettys who were resting and asked, "May we come to your room and speak with you?"

Professor Betty said, "I will meet you down in the lobby in five minutes."

We replied, "Okay."

When we saw Professor Betty, Suzie explained to him we would like to start rooming together as we really didn't fit in with the snooty girls.

He said, "I understand. When we get to Paris, France, on July 1 to the seventh for six nights, you will be placed in the same room for the rest of the trip."

We became the trio and found we enjoyed each other's company.

Professor Betty says, "I liked your initiative, Gracie Lu, and admire you for going out in the rain and seeing vast parts of London as the others had not seen all the sight and sounds of the beautiful city. Instead, they stayed in the hotel all day, playing cards. Boring. Just be careful when you are alone."

I replied, "I will."

On July 1, I walked to the Arc de Triomphe that stands at the Avenue Champs-Élysées. I met some Frenchmen, who proudly told me the Arc symbolizes nation, honor, and patriotism. It also stands where the twelve avenues meet and resemble a giant star. I was looking in all directions, and they pointed it out to me. Oh, I can see it now, and I am in awe of the engineers that designed it. They continued telling me the eternal flame burns there for the unknown soldiers of France. I thanked them for telling me about it, and as I walked by them, each one of them pinched my behind.

I turned around and asked, "What was that for?"

In unison, they said, "That is the custom for Frenchman to do and be aware you will receive many more as you walk along."

On July 2, the tour leaders had the students board the chartered bus to Montmartre on the hill, and Montparnasse on the left bank in Paris. It was known as the artists' center as living was inexpensive and picturesque compared to other areas of Paris. It was a center of nightlife with private clubs and native bars. While at Montmartre, we visited Sacré 'Coeur (Church of the Sacred Heart) where the statue of the Sacred Heart in the entry. The bronze doors were decorative, and the white dome was 262 feet high. Mosaics were seen throughout and statues inside; however, the famed stained-glass windows were destroyed in air raids during World War II. The upper windows had been replaced, and the lower ones were being restored at that time.

Kitty and Suzie met up with me, and I told them what happened.

Suzie said, "We can't leave you alone as you always have an interesting experience to tell us about."

We walked together to the Church of St. Mary Magdalene with its impressive Corinthian columns facing the Place de la Concorde at the end of Rue Royale. Walking up the steps, there was a moving sculpture of the Last Supper, and as I walked in, the pipe organ was playing holy music. I felt the Holy Spirit with me as I walked through the beautiful church. Leaving there, we visited the Notre Dame Cathedral, which stands on the Île de la cité, an island on the Seine river. It was Gothic in style, and the facades were lovely with the central portal rose window. There is a picture of David on the inside. I began to understand why it took from 1220 to the early 1500s to construct with such details of beauty. It was restored in the 1800s. The statues of twenty-two kings of Judah could be seen across the facade. People could not read it as it was a Bible cast in stone. The gargoyles were a carved form in stone and divided how the water would flow from the roof. Unlike the majority of Gothic architecture, the towers had no spires.

A TURBULENT LIFE ? ? ?

On July 3, we walked through Tuileries Garden, which is one of Paris's magnificent public parks, aside from the pony rides and a puppet theatre for children and would often feature the famous Punch and Judy puppets. The Louvre Museum is of Renaissance architecture at the east end of the garden. The Louvre is of Renaissance architecture which was applied to the great palace and chateau of France. The group were one day at the Louvre; it was just a small study of its hundreds of galleries. I watched a fruitless effort of an artist struggling to recapture the one and only *Mona Lisa* by Leonardo da Vinci. Her exquisite eyes and hands seemed to want to comfort him. Winged Victory of Samothrace was my favorite sculpture as it was placed on its perfectly preserved ship of stone. The impressionist prints, tapestries, and contemporary works were in a different part of the museum. The impressionist forms of art were my favorite forms and paintings as they conveyed reality in the full aspect of color of nature and people without details and would let one use their own interpretation or imagination. Many in the tour group were disappointed not to have more time in the museum. Kitty felt it would take at least a week to see the museum in its entirety and properly.

On July 4, we walked to the Eiffel Tower on the Champ de Mars in Paris, and it was a huge wrought iron skeleton tower. My friends and I rode the elevator to the top, where we saw breathtaking views of Paris from the east to the west banks of the Seine river, trying to capture picture of the beauty with her camera. They walked part way down the different platforms where they had lunch on one of the platforms and another had a weather station, television transmitters, and experimental spaces. A guide told us it was designed for the exposition of 1889 and was the tallest structure in the world until the Empire State Building in New York City. Walking back to the hotel, we stopped and purchased postcards, a black and red tam hat, a miniature bronze statue of the Eiffel Tower, and took it to back to hotel to pack in luggage. As we walked by café's with people sitting outside, rather in the morning or evening, the French would be drinking green concoctions.

I was curious and went inside to the bar tender and asked, "What is the green drink?"

Speaking a little English, he told me it was crème de menthe and sweet and sour mix.

He asked, "Would you like one?"

I replied, "Yes, and what is it called?"

He handed me the drink and called it a stinger. I found it to be tasty, sweet, and refreshingly good, especially as a summertime drink.

On July 5, our leaders took the group to Versailles Gardens, which we were told covered around two hundred and fifty acres. The grass was maintained by gardeners and kept in the shape of fleur-de-lis that frescos and statues throughout. The sixteen rooms we saw were void of furnishings. The royal chapel had gold and white columns and adorned with statues. The crystal prism chandeliers were throughout the enchanting palace, and many on the tour felt it was sad that it wasn't being used in today's times! It was onward and upward to Gothic Chartres Cathedral with the New Tower (the oldest) was the taller spire and dated back to the year 1134. The Old Tower was built in the sixteenth century and is part of the Romanesque form of art. The stained-glass windows in the church were of all different shapes, designs, and colors that blended in nicely together, despite the lack of sunlight shining in.

"The Worshipped Virgin" portrayal was awesome! July 6 was a free day to shop and explore Paris on your own or as a group. Kitty, Suzie, and I rode a cab to the Louvre and stayed a half a day exploring rooms they were interested in and unable to see the first day. Walking the streets of Paris, we stopped at an outside café and had chicken crepes and chocolate crepes for desert, and they were delicious! There was nothing more delectable to their palates than what they ordered and had crème de menthe to drink.

I said, "That was yummy, yummy in the tummy like a coat of sugar honey."

Kitty and Suzie were laughing at that expression as they had never heard it before. Walking back to the hotel, we entered a few more shops, and I purchased an unusual cane and a music box. Kitty and Suzie bought some small items as we were running out of spending money that each had come with. I had called my mother to sell the Singer sewing machine I had that Mom made me buy for home economics class in high school. The one pattern I made and cut out and sewed together was two sizes too big for me, and as only my mother could sew on buttons, that was all I could do as well. So my mother sold it and sent me the ninety dollars. I received for it and included a little bit more money for me to have.

Relaxation and Fun in Cannes, France, a Riviera Paradise

From July 7 to 10, the tour operators checked us into a scheduled rest stop in Cannes, France, and checked us into the Hotel Mediterranean on the French Riviera. The group rode on a large catamaran sailboat for half a day as they put up the sails they were flying as it was a windy day. Other guest not with our group was on the boat as well. All in bathing suits, soaking up the sun, and snorkeling in the cold southeastern side of the Mediterranean Sea. Fun was had by all!

July 8 was a day of rest, but not for me, Kitty, and Suzie as we walked and soaked up the sun on the beach and watched all the action in the water and those walking the public beach. They put their cover-ups on over their bathing suits and began walking the Boulevard de la Croisette and stopped at an outside café for lunch. As they walked, they found it to be a ritzy, stylish place for the rich and famous to visit.

On July 9, we had breakfast and went back to sleep as we were exhausted and realized traveling from one place to another and having to pack each time we visited another country was grueling. Even me with my vim and vigor, I was ready to go back to sleep after having breakfast. We had to pack to leave on July 10 to the Grand Hotel Baglioni hotel in Florence, Italy.

From July 10 to 14, the Bettys checked us out of the hotel. It was unpleasant to say goodbye to Cannes as we felt the water was beautiful and wished we had been there for the Cannes Film Festival.

Florence, Italy

Our tour group boarded a bus to travel to the Grand Hotel Baglioni Palace in Florence, Italy. We had a packed lunch from the hotel on the bus as it was over a seven-and-a-half-hour drive. When we arrived in Florence, everyone was antsy to get up and move around. We got our luggage, and a bellman took it for us to our assigned rooms as the Bettys checked us in and handed each of us a key to the room. We had dinner that night in the hotel. Our tour group boarded a bus to travel to the Grand Hotel Baglioni Palace in Florence, Italy. We had a packed lunch from the hotel on the bus as it was over a seven-and-a-half-hour drive.

On July 11, they toured the Gallery of the Academy, where I was fascinated with Michelangelo's *Statue of David*, which had maintained its absolute perfection, and somehow it reassured us it always would. His twelve feet of "agony and ecstasy" are a heritage for all art lovers. The lovely tapestries in the gallery were interesting and were from Brussels, but all were overshadowed by the wondrous David. As we exited through the gift shop, I purchased an eighteen-inch-high statue of David on a pedestal and had it sent to her mother's home as it was a gift for her.

Visited the Maria Novella or called the Dominican Basilica with upper façade and a central doorway done in Renaissance persona. Contained therein were Gothic tombs of families to right of the façade, and the interior was designed in a T-shape cross. The main alter had a crucifix in bronze.

July 12 was a shopping day for Kitty, Suzie, and me. We bought some beer glasses in the shape of the country Italy and had them shipped home as well as some postcards. We had lunch in an Italian pizza pie restaurant. We each ordered our own pizza pie and was surprised to see it in a deep-dish soaking in olive oil and had to be eaten with a knife and fork unlike those found in our home cities. Taking a bite, it was succulent and delicious! We could not eat it all as it was very filling. We walked back to the hotel and got dressed to attend with the group the opera house and to see *Madame Butterfly* written by John Long, with music by Giacomo Puccini. We found the acoustics disappointing in the opera house even though they had choice seats. I had studied the opera in my humanities class at college. I found the picturesque Japanese life and the tragic story of Madame Butterfly were magnificently portrayed. Her superb soprano voice brought tears to my eyes when she sang "Someday He'll Come." Lieutenant Pinkerton had a rich, colorful, tenor voice. Sharpless, the American consul, had a well-controlled baritone voice. Seeing the opera performed on stage, it became my favorite.

On July 13, we traveled by motor coach to Uffizi Place and Gallery, which Suzie, Kitty, and I were unimpressed. The paintings were repetitious, and the colors faded. We knew nothing about the collection as it had not "boned up" on the collection and perhaps that was why we found them to be uninspiring.

Returning to the hotel, the group decided to enjoy the nightlife and went drinking, and some were dancing. Walking back to the hotel and as we entered the lobby, I noticed my watch was not on my wrist. It became a turbulent moment in my life as the watch was expensive!

In hysteria, I yelled, "I lost my watch!"

The students with me started consoling me and said, "We will find it."

The front desk manager gave us directions to the bar they had been in. So some of the male students and Suzie, Kitty, and I walked back to the pub, and one of the guys in the group asked if anyone had seen it, and no one replied as he didn't speak Italian. They walked back a different way to the hotel at 3:00 a.m., and the street cleaning truck was working. I began thinking it was a hopeless effort. All of a sudden, looking at the gutters in the street, I saw something glistening, and lo and behold, it was my 14-carat gold Swiss watch. Those with me were amazed I found it and rejoiced with me. Being so happy, we danced and ran back to the hotel. The night manager was elated to hear my good fortune in finding it. We made it to our rooms and slept.

From July 14 to 18, many of the students were groggy, having hangovers from the night before. They were woken up by the Bettys on the hotel phones in their rooms to come eat breakfast. The Bettys checked us out of hotel. We boarded a short ride on the bullet train that took around three hours to arrive in Rome, Italy. The train was like the previous one as they had taken and followed the same procedures for retrieving luggage, endured it for even one day. Our guide told us the scratches in the walls designated the length of time they survived, and the longest endurance was eighty years. We stayed close to the group, visited the Catacombs (Domitilla), which was twenty degrees colder than the outside.

Vatican City, Italy

On July 15, the walls felt as though they were closing in on you as the walkway was extremely narrow. I could not envision how a prisoner could the guide as one could get lost easily in the underground maze. Rome was captivating to all the students with its history.

On July 16, the tour group boarded the bus for Vatican City, and upon arrival, we walked through the Roman Museum. It was thrilling to see Raphael's designed tapestries that had been sewn in Brussels with full detail. The geographical maps, which Dante and his pupil's created, and his pupil's created took over twenty-five years to design. Walking into the famed Sistine Chapel was a vision of beauty. The chapel's frescoes were being cleaned, and we missed an audience with the Pope as he was in his summer residence.

St. Peter's Basilica was known as the largest Christian church in the world. It rises on the site of the Prince of the Apostles and has many statues and monuments of past popes. The confessionals with their green and red carpets and gold columns were most elegantly decorative. The *Glory* by Bernini is in gold and resembles a sunburst clock covered with angels. The lettering above the columns were six feet high, and the statues were eight times the size of a human body and was masterfully created.

While visiting the basilica, an old man entered with a gun, yelling to everyone, "Sit down!" He proceeded to each student in the group, whispering in their ear, "Have mercy upon you." The Betty tour group began shaking and didn't know what he meant. He was shaking his gun wildly about with many of the students shivering. As he approached, I stood up, grabbed, and began stroking his free hand. As I had grown up hunting, I knew how to calm him down and took the pistol from his hands. The male and female students were astonished as how I obtained the gun and calmed the old man down. He actually was a priest in the church.

He proceeded to the altar and said, "You have one in your group having the gun that is calm, cool, and collected as I watched others of you unable to grasp the situation."

He called me to the altar and had me demonstrate to all how I obtained the pistol from him as some were unable to see how I did it. He then had me return to my seat as he preached the word of God to us. He reached for his Bible in his pocket and read Proverbs 4:6–7, "Do not forsake wisdom, and she will protect you; love her; and she will watch over you. Wisdom is supreme; therefore, get wisdom. Though it cost all you have, get understanding." Wisdom's seven pillars, according to Scripture, are fear of the Lord, instruction, knowledge, understanding, discretion, counsel, and reproof.

He continued to say, "Wisdom is the ability or gift from God to judge correctly. Without God's help, man does not have true wisdom. Gracie Lu was a perfect example of knowing how to control the situation with her sensitivity, alertness, and what she had learned from God while walking in nature and hunting game to eat as that may have been the only way for many to eat and survive in this world, especially if they don't know the Lord as we hear about the miracles he creates around the world. Be kind to all as you never know who might be one who saves you by having God in their heart. One does not have to be afraid as you were when I threatened you with a gun." He held the revolver up, showing it had no bullets in it. "Gracie Lu had learned from her hunting experiences and love of the Lord how to handle the situation. One with an open heart and mind to God's words will be able to handle most all conditions in one's life. Bow your heads, and we shall pray."

Many of the students as well as the Bettys were Catholics but knew the scripture he quoted and understood his method of illustration with the gun. I, that day, turned the minds of the Mobile students, and they stopped bullying or talking about me behind my back as it was unchristian like behavior, and one day, I could be the one to save our lives in a threatening situation.

We left the Basilica with a better understanding of how God works in one's life who is a true believer in him. I chalked it up as another turbulent moment in my life, but this time I came out on top! The group returned to the hotel with a better knowledge of how God can work in one's life.

From July 17 to 18, the group visited the Colosseum and Amphitheater that was built in AD 72. It was sad to see the decay, and only one section remained with the original benches. One pair of steps remained, allowing entrance to the fourth floor. Three remains were composed of arches supported by piers with four entrances into the arena. I found myself reliving history vividly while there. It was onward to the National Museum in the Barberini Palace, which was being remodeled. We were able to enter with caution the remodeled area. Raffaele's gorgeous *Foramina* was displayed with her hands, eyes, and face, which seemed as though it was coming alive. It was a small wonder why it was the most treasured in the museum.

I stayed behind to find my aunt Contessa Casati of Italian nobility who lived in an apartment there. She was an elderly, and I introduced myself as I handed her a box of chocolates I purchased for her. Her servant (as known as an English word) prepared some tea and sweets for us to partake as we talked. It was a short visit as it was hard to communicate with knowing little English, and I knew no Italian. The Contessa enjoyed reminiscing of old times in Italy, and I told her about the family as other members had visited her in the past. I didn't stay long and gently hugged her good by as she looked very frail. I rode in a cab back to the hotel and began packing my suitcase to check out of the hotel the next morning.

Galaxy Cruise of the Greek Isles

On July 18, in Athens, Greece, the group checked out of hotel and took bus to board MT's Galaxy ship in Piraeus, Greece, for a four-day cruise of the Greek isles. Luggage was taken to the cabins by the stewards. The students explored the boat and observed the boat drill.

On July 19, our first stop was Delos in the center of the Aegean Sea, where remains were sparce, and the most impressive were the four lions carved of marble. Professor Betty explained the archeologists had a hard time predicting the ages of ruins.

The resort in Mykonos had many windmills, and the homes were sparkling white like fresh fallen snow. Yachts and fishing boats packed the harbor and a place for tourists! It was fun enjoying the isle and taken over by a boat tender for a short period of time. It was back to the boat.

On July 20, we stopped at Rhodes off the shore of Asia Minor. The pre-Hellenic temples, monuments, fortresses, and ruins were well preserved. The ancient stadium and theatre had been restored. We were unable to see the Valley of the Butterflies as it was too great a distance to travel and make it back to the boat in time to leave for next destination. Rhodes beaches were breathtakingly beautiful and a relief for the vacationer to relax.

On July 21, we docked in Crete, the largest of the Greek isles, where remains were found by the Cretan and Minoan cultures. The archeological museum has well preserved remains of the civilization. They had a traditional Greek lunch of a salad with olive oil, which was the known as liquid gold to the Cretans. Cretan cheeses with which Feta cheese with olive was my favorite, and I would gain a one hundred pounds if I lived there. I tried fried snails, and to my surprise, they were delicious. To drink, we sampled the national drink of ouzo, an aromatic mixture of alcohol and aromatic herbs. Many Cretans were seen to be on the heavy side as the food was so rich and delicious. Seeing the Greek islands was a highlight of my trip, and it was beautiful.

Athens, Greece Tour

On July 22, after debarking the boat with our luggage in hand, the group boarded a bus to Athens to tour the Parthenon, which was a temple dedicated to the goddess Athena Parthenos (Athena the Virgin) and Acropolis. We saw Doric, Ionic, and Corinthian columns with the Corinthian being the most ornate. The Parthenon was completely surrounded by columns. The Doric columns were slender, more decorative columns, which were used in the Acropolis.

Dubrovnik, Yugoslavia

With passports in hands, luggage was transported after going through customs. The group flew into the airport that serviced Dubrovnik, Yugoslavia, and took bus to Hotel Astarea that overlooked the Adriatic Sea with a view that could not be beat. The Bettys checked us in for two nights and found it to be quant. The houses were constructed on the right and left of the city steps, and laundry lines hung from one house to the other. The gloom of the people and drab surroundings made one deeply thankful to live in America. Dubrovnik and Malini had little to offer but a craze for the people to obtain the USA dollar. Other than the views of the water, I found it to be a depressing area. They ate a thick chunky stew made with butter beans, onions, and red peppers for lunch. For dinner at the hotel, they had ground beef with potatoes.

On July 23, walking around the grounds of the hotel, Kitty, Suzie, and I saw a little girl riding a horse in the distance and were happy to see the grin on her face as I was having fun. We had noticed a country that we considered to be poverty-stricken.

On July 24, we enjoyed swimming in the water and soaking up the sunshine at a nearby beach and had a buffet breakfast at hotel before leaving for next destination. We had breakfast and dinner meals at the hotel and had a snack for lunch.

Venice, Italy

On July 25, we checked out of hotel and boarded a plane to romantic Venice, Italy. The water taxies and buses could be seen as we landed. We had a chartered bus from the airport, driving us to the Hotel Luna on Piazza San Marco, and checked into hotel for three nights. Gondolas were seen gliding rapidly and accurately about picking up passengers. The quaintness, friendliness, happiness, music, and history percolated through the buildings, and it was far more than expected by the group. It was a welcomed site coming from Dubrovnik. There could be no place in the world like Venice! As it was known to be sinking, the Bettys had us pray, interested people, ecologists, engineers, as well as creative people with imaginations could save the city without causing more damage to the city.

On July 26, we attended San Marco Church on San Marco Square in Venice. The interior and altar were all of gold, and it was very dark inside. We walked to the Peggy Guggenheim modern art museum, which displayed modern paintings, wood carvings, metals in plastic squares to new statues. We exited through a small gift shop, and a few in the group purchased postcards. Walking the Piazza San Marco, pigeons were everywhere and would follow you all over the place in hopes to be thrown peanuts or food. They were a nuisance when you picnicked in the piazza.

That evening, Kitty, Suzie, and I had a pizza pie for dinner, and it was delicious and filling. They rode in a Gondola with the gondolier rowing them about the canals while singing to us. It was a night to remember!

On July 27, Suzie was not feeling well and stayed and rested in the room while Kitty and I went to explore more of Venus. As we were walking, two men whistled to us and started conversing.

They asked, "Would we like to go to Lido Beach Lagoon sheltered from the Adriatic Sea and famous for its music festival with us?"

We said, "Okay."

The guys rowed us in a canoe with a little motor to get there. The sandy beach was nice with the calm seas in the lagoon. We enjoyed each other's company, and it was getting late, and we girls told them they had to get us back to the tour group.

After a day of fun in the sun, we said, "Goodbye and thanked them for the day."

Arriving back to the hotel, we checked on Suzie, and she was feeling better after a day of rest. We told her about our day.

Innsbruck, Austria

From July 28 to July 30, the group boarded the train from Venice, Italy, to Innsbruck, Austria, the capital of Austria's western state Tyrol located in the alps. It was a beautiful and peaceful ride, looking out the windows at the rolling countryside all the way up to Innsbruck. As a group, we had Bratwurst served for lunch, and it was delicious. We arrived and boarded a bus to the Hotel Grauer Bär in Innsbruck. After checking into hotel and settled in their rooms, the group met in lobby to walk over to board trolley to the top of Hungerburg Mountain and took the trolley back down. We all enjoyed the invigorating altitude.

The homes had beautiful green vines growing on their roof as extra protection barrier from the extreme weather temperatures. Innsbruck was known as a ski resort and for hosting winter sport competitions. The mountain ranges were striking, and the slopes were narrow and looked treacherous to me. Innsbruck is considered to be one of the most beautiful places to see in Austria. They spoke Austrian German, and some of the younger people spoke English as well.

On July 29, as a group, we walked to the center of town and had lunch in a restaurant in the middle of town and visited some of the shops. We found many shop owners and employees in restaurants who spoke English. Walking the medieval streets was a challenge as they were busy with motorist, bicyclist, cars, and pedestrians. Summer skiing was nearby as well. There were no takers among our tour group. Seeing the beauty of the Alpine peaks and placid crystal-clear lakes was something I had never seen before. We were in Innsbruck in its hottest month of the year with no humidity, and everyone in the group found it refreshing. The Bettys told us to always say our name when asking a question as they would consider it rude if you didn't.

Salzburg, Austria

From July 30 to August 2, the Bettys checked us out, and they chartered bus to Salzburg, Austria, to the Egmont Hotel, where we were checked in and assigned our rooms. We had dinner on our own, and Suzie, Kitty, and I had a sweet tooth, and all they wanted was the apple strudel, and they were told they must have. It was like apple strudel they had never eaten before and knew why it was considered a national food of Austria as it was succulent to the taste buds and finger-licking good.

On July 31, the group rode a bus from Salzburg to Germany to tour the salt mines near the border of the two countries. They put on the furnished miners outfit, and Professor Betty took a photo of the group. We descended the mine down a steep twenty-five-foot slide. It went swiftly down another slide, and I knew then why the padding on the rear of our coal mining outfits was there. As we continued walking through the mines, we came to a boat we boarded that took us to the opposite side of still more. We saw the salt mines and samples on display and a movie on the processing of the mining of salt in English. It was a fun, heralding experience for all as we came away knowing a lot more about how salt was processed. None of the group would have missed that experience.

Returning to Salzburg that afternoon, we saw the world-famous Marionette Theatre. The performance was *The Magic Flute*. The story opera was about the concealed allusions of the rights and doctrines of free revelry, which the music had the power to transcend human fear and hatred. Men and women were equal. The voices, scenery, and staging of marionettes was superb! Afterward we returned by bus to the hotel. It was an extraordinary day, and all in the group retired to their rooms.

A TURBULENT LIFE ? ? ?

On August 1, we were on our own as it was a free day. Some shopped, and others rested in the group to enjoy the nightlife of the city. Kitty, Suzie, and I participated with the group in joining in the nightlife of the city. We stopped in Alpina Inn for happy hour. It was Salzburg Nights, which was a native folk festival of nonprofessionals featuring them in the original costumes, music, yodeling, dances, and songs representing the community. They were farmers, doctors, and people from every walk of life. The one hundred and fifty-two acts were unbelievable and exciting to watch. The waiters were generous with the beer, and it closed at 11:30 p.m. Needless to say, we heard it was always crowded with the natives. The group felt privileged to stumble upon it and have an exciting, unforgettable experience!

We returned to the hotel in a couple of cabs as we could not all fit in one. Some were stumbling out the door and could not walk back to the hotel. We all returned safely and immediately went to our rooms. It was a night to remember for all those that joined the group in going nightclubbing. Kitty, Suzie, and I were glad we had joined in the fun.

Munich, Germany

From August 2 to 6, we checked out of hotel and departed to Munich, Germany, and checked in to the Hotel Bayerischer Hof.

On August 3, the group was taken to Deutsch's Technological Museum in Munich, Germany. The museum gave demonstrations of casting metals, which was the works used in high voltage electrical plants (which was like lightning striking). A model railroad, the planetarium, was closed while we were there, which disappointed many in the group. They were able to see submarines, mines, and would take days to see it all. What they were able to see was impressive to most all on the tour.

On August 4, the group saw the world-famous Glockenspiel Clock with which dancers dance at 11:00 a.m. daily. The clock showed how the medieval mind worked and in pictures and images. That night was party time when the group went to the famous Hofbräuhaus, which was built in 1589 by Duke Maximilian in the middle of Munich. It opens at 11:00 a.m. to midnight year-round. They walked the stairs to the third floor as it was packed on the first two floors and sat on benches at the long wooden tables and ordered beer, pretzels, a plate of sausages, with grain bread and rolls accompanied with mustard and pickles. I like the others who consumed a lot of beer, which ended up being a good thing.

As I was walking down the stairs, the heel of my high-heel shoe came off, and I fell down several of the steps. I began limping, and some of the boys on the tour and my friends let me lean on them as we walked to a Catholic hospital run by nuns. I was put into an old wooden, rackety wheelchair, and the nuns wrapped my ankle and sent me to another hospital down the street for x-rays. Arriving at the more modern hospital, the doctor looked at the x-rays and found

A TURBULENT LIFE ? ? ?

I had a badly sprained ankle. They rewrapped it and gave me a set of wooden crutches. The doctor adjusted them to my height and showed me how to walk with them. It could not have been a worst time for me to have done that.

On August 5 and 6, I stayed in hotel room and rested, which was quite a hard task for me to do as I didn't want to miss a minute of my time in seeing Munich, but I listened to the tour director and his wife and followed there instructions.

West Berlin and East Berlin When Wall Was Up in Germany

From August 6 to 9, we checked in to Hotel Palace Berlin, West Germany, and I hated walking with the crutches, but if I didn't, I endured pain, and so I learned to get proficient in walking with them.

East Berlin When Wall Was Up in Germany

On August 7, we toured East Berlin by bus. Going through the checkpoint, the border patrol searched under the bus with flashlights and slid mirrors under the bus, checking for safety against smuggling people and concealed objects. They entered the bus giving instructions to the students as an East Berliner tour guide proceeded as our tour guide to enter the communist side of Germany. Our West Berlin Guide was not allowed to enter. It was no simple matter getting through "Checkpoint Charley." West Berliners were allowed in to visit their families at the time.

Most of the buildings in East Germany face the wall. Our guide told us they have free enterprise, but I knew their definition was different than that known in the United States. The hotel we were able to enter was small and was operated in an unorganized manner.

On August 8, we toured the Berlin Aquarium and Zoo. The aquarium had fish from every part of the world. They were of different sizes, colors, and species, and were amazing to watch swimming around in their aquariums. We entered into the insectarium with many different species of insects (such as bees, poisonous and nonpoisonous varieties of spiders and snakes) and birds. The zoo

A TURBULENT LIFE ? ? ?

appeared to have every type of animal in the world from hippopotamuses to various types of monkeys and apes. It would take days to have covered the whole aquarium as it was huge! We had breakfast at hotel and checked out and traveled by bus.

Copenhagen, Denmark

From August 9 to 11, we arrived and checked in to the Egmont Hotel. By August 10, we had a bus tour of charming Copenhagen. Passed the Amalienburg Palace, the residence of the king and queen. Their son, the prince, the tour director's told us, had an entire section of his own. All the group, except me, exited the bus for a short stop to take pictures. I handed my camera for Kitty to take pictures for me of the Shakespeare's *Little Mermaid* sitting on a rock, and the statue replaced the original one that had been stolen. We next saw Friedrich burg Castle, which is a national museum built in the sixteenth century and housed a collection of paintings. Portraits, Danish furniture, and other fine art, I managed to see it and sat on benches when the opportunity arose. It was onward to Tivoli Gardens Amusement Park, and the grounds were spectacular, and praise God I purchased a raincoat with a hood as I could not hold an umbrella while using crutches. The main entrance to the gardens were of Renaissance architecture, and the cafeteria was where we had lunch, and more elegant restaurants were on the grounds. Due to the rain, the group missed the pantomime ballet as we returned to the bus. All had a great time in spite of the rain.

On August 11, we checked out of the hotel, and some were taken to the airport as they didn't participate in the add-on countries for the extra charge. We made our goodbyes to those leaving and wished them safe travels back home.

Madrid, Spain

From August 12 to 15, those who remained on the tour flew to Madrid, Spain. My papa and mother paid for me to continue on with the tour. We took a short tour while on the bus of the grounds of the University of Spain, and we covered a lot of ground. One had to have a car, motorbike, or bicycle to get around campus. There were colleges of almost every field of study.

We toured the Royal Palace with 2,335 rooms. The small group was able to see thirty-five of the rooms open to the public, and most were sitting rooms, and all the palaces I had seen throughout the tour, this was her favorite. It was expertly preserved and still used for receptions. Every October 1, the guide told us the king has a banquet for his ministers and cabinet. The Arms Hall had exquisitely preserved oriental rugs, Spanish tiles, lovely chandeliers, and furnishings. The gala dining room, where the king hosted his banquets, could easily seat a hundred guest at the dining table. I counted six chandeliers in that one room with gold and blue marble, and Spanish tiles were a craftsman's dream. It would have been easy to disappear in the grand halls.

We returned to the bus and stopped for lunch in which they had paella and red wine sangria with different fruits in it. The meal was enjoyed by all. After lunch, we checked into Hotel Plaza. The room was spacious and had a private porch garden with beautiful hanging baskets of flowers. We had a siesta as it was the tradition to have a nap before working again.

On August 13, we arrived in Toledo, Spain. The approach into the city was of old brick streets dating back to the eleventh-century architecture. The hill overlooked the Tegus River with farmlands that had a panoramic view. The Saint Silesia Cathedral was pretty with its big A and low Capella (was a chapel). Toledo vendors, with their donkeys, had ceramics, clay pictures, and some fruit with hay on them to sell to visitors and those that lived nearby. They wore Spanish sombreros and costumes that were picturesque, and many in the tour group had pictures taken with them.

On August 14, we toured the Prado Museum on our return to Madrid. Hatamos Bosch, 1450–1516, painted *Lasteneaciones de San Antonio* that depicted San Antonio's temptation and reflected many thoughts and impressions. We saw many of Goya's paintings before and after his insanity. You could see his change vividly through his works and felt relieved he only lived two years after his illness.

Lisbon, Portugal

From August 15 to 18, we arrived in Lisbon, Portugal, by plane. I was still on crutches and getting tired of them but kept using them as the doctor had ordered. The Bettys checked us into the Hotel Estoril Sol in the capital city of Lisbon. The guide had a great sense of humor. The buildings were close together, and the native would sell fish in open markets and in the old town streets. They walked many flights of steps, which was challenging and exhausting for me with my crutches. We were also dodging clothes lines hanging from one home to another. Everyone in that area knew each other. Subtropical vegetation was exotic plants, and the main attraction was the butterfly greenhouse. I did it without complaining.

On the sixteenth, I purchased the national symbol of Portugal colorful nest of wooden roosters and had them packaged and mailed to my parents' home in Dunedin, Florida, USA. The Portuguese were known for centuries for making ceramic goods with artistic motifs found in bowls, dishes, plates, as well as many other ceramic items could be purchased.

On the seventeenth, it was a day of rest and having breakfast and lunch at hotel. I skipped dinner to pack with help from my friend staying in the room with me. It was a happy and sad day to leave Europe. I had seen and learned so much in each country that we visited and friends along the way. I had to keep a diary of the travels and relieved that I did. I wrote with a paper of my choice, comparing governments in order to get the six hours of credits from Spring Hill College when I returned home and sent it to Professor Betty. It was a trip of a lifetime, and one that I would ever forget and was grateful Mom and Papa who afforded me the opportunity of understanding Europe in a way I would have never been able if I did it a different approach. Seeing Madrid and Spain was unique to see that I would have never wanted to miss! As a group, we made our goodbyes as we were departing from home the next day.

Flight to New York and Home to Dunedin, Florida

On the eighteenth, struggling through the airport on my crutches, I presented my passport, and a porter gave me a ride in a wheelchair through customs with which I had little to declare as I had shipped most of it to my mother's home. The porter continued pushing me in the wheelchair to my gate. I thanked him and gave him a tip.

I left, secure in the knowledge that the treasures of the past were being preserved in the present times, for many generations in the future to be able to see and enjoy. My eternal thanks were given to the most wonderful, understanding, tireless tour guides, Professor Sam and Mrs. Betty.

I arrived at the Tampa Airport with Papa and my mother anxiously waiting at the gate to see me. As one of the last passengers off the plane, I entered the terminal where Mother and Papa were surprised that I was walking with crutches.

They asked, "What happened to you?"

I replied, "It's a long story and will tell you later."

My mother could not stop hugging me, and finally Papa had his chance to hug me. Loading my luggage in the car for the ride home, they wanted to hear every detail of my trip, and they thanked me for the purchases they received at their home.

I could not stop thanking them for the trip of a lifetime. I told them I took notes and had to author a paper from my diary of what I saw and learned to receive the college credit as well as I selected to draft a paper on comparing the governments in each country we visited to the USA.

On the way home, my mom asked, "Are you hungry?"

I answered, "No. I just want to get home and soak in a bathe and to sleep."

We arrived home, and Papa bought my trunk inside and said, "You can unpack tomorrow or when you feel like it."

I entered my clean bedroom and bathroom. My bed had fresh sheets, and I could not wait to crawl into bed, say my prayers, and fall asleep.

Kitty and I saw each other after the trip with both of us living in Florida. She had told me Suzie was traveling the world, selling Avon. What a great way to see the destinations one has not seen. It was sad as we never heard from one another again. I would return home on long weekends and vacation time to Dunedin, Florida, to see Mom and Papa who was like a second loving father to me.

Clearwater, Florida, was home to Clearwater Marine Aquarium and is a nonprofit marine hospital, marine life rescue, rehabilitation, and release center. They had sea turtles, otters, and later a movie was made called *Winter*, who became a famous bottlenose dolphin because of his prosthetic tail, he would wear a few hours a day. Several shows scheduled throughout the day featuring *Winter* in front of paying guest with his playmate. He would paint a picture with a paintbrush in his mouth, and they would be sold in gift shop with which I would purchase one as I loved dolphins. I would visit the aquarium to show visitors that stayed with my mom and Papa the aquarium. Visiting the aquarium often and watching it expand and change over the years was a thrill for me. I would attend charity events to benefit the aquarium. Over the years, it was my favorite place to visit. My best-loved event was walking toward a commotion on Sand Key Beach on a scorching hot day in June. Walking the beach, the marine rescue team with nets in the water were trying to save a dying marine life in the Gulf of Mexico. That day, a loggerhead sea turtle was in stress and floundering in the water.

I asked, "Can I help?"

A trained marine biologist replied, "No! Please step back."

The loggerhead turtle had laid eggs in the nest they made, and it was struggling to get offshore and to deeper water in the gulf. As a crowd gathered to watch the struggling turtle unable to swim, learn-

A TURBULENT LIFE ? ? ?

ing over harvesting of sea turtles for meat, eggs, leather, and tortoise shells, as well as coastal development and pollution, humans are driving them to extinction. All marine turtles in the state of Florida are protected under the Florida Protection Act.

Grace Boykin while making Debut in Mobile, Alabama with parties through the year and culminated on Fat Tuesday in Mobile, Alabama.

Debut while Attending the Private Flagler College in St. Augustine, Florida

Making my debut in Mobile, Alabama, in 1972 and 1973 at the ages of nineteen and twenty, while attending college on the east coast of Florida was one of the finest times of my life! My boyfriend would often keep my car for me as he attended college in Jacksonville, Florida. I felt like I owned the airline that year, while flying to attend many private parties.

Thanksgiving officially coming out to society at the Camellia Ball and escorted by my fourth stepfather, who was like a savior and real father to me. The celebration of the coronation of the king and queen and attending the numerous Mardi Gras Balls and parades throughout the year culminated with sitting in the prime reserved seats in sitting stands for VIPs in front of a private club in Downtown Mobile, Alabama, seeing many of the weeklong parades. The antics played by some of the knights of the court would be considered comical to those witnessing it in attendance of the numerous functions held that year.

The knights were unable to parade on the floats as traditionally done in a parade, as it was cancelled because it was raining, as the expression goes like "cats and dogs." Many attendees attending the traditional queen's luncheon held at a private club witnessed the funniest event held that year. It was when the king and the knights entered the queen's luncheon dressed in their costumes with large boxes and placed them in front of the queen and ladies-in-waiting asking to wait for all to open the boxes at the same time.

A TURBULENT LIFE ? ? ?

The king in his alto voice asked the queen and ladies-in-waiting to open the boxes all at one time on his count of one, two, three, open your boxes. The laughter resounded through the room as the attendees were in a frenzy in gathering the bunnies hopping around on the tables. Attendees and knights assisted in gathering the rabbits and placing them back in their boxes. Laughter resounded throughout the room for around thirty minutes as attendees tried to regain poseur in trying to contain themselves from laughing so hard.

It was a wonderful surprise to many of the debutantes and queen as it was so unexpected. One was heard saying, "It livened the room and waking all up as it gave many in attendance a great deal to talk about."

While enjoying the event, we learned the knights were going to throw them from the parade float to the queen and her ladies in the court, which many praised God, for the thunder and rain showers cancelled the parade that day. Many found the thought of throwing the boxes off the float to be inhumane to the bunnies.

If the parade wasn't cancelled, the king and knights of the court were a lively group! With many of them thinking outside the box but not of the consequences of their actions! People watching the parade and local TV news cameras could have recorded the commotion in the reserved sitting areas and showed it on the nightly local news channels. Witnessing the commotion of those in the reserved sitting area, it could have been considered an act of cruelty to animals if they had thrown them off the floats.

After the queen's luncheon, the queen and ladies-in-waiting returned to their downtown hotel rooms to dress and get ready for the ball they would attend that night. With many of the events, the king and queen and their knights were often never seen without a drink in hand. Friends and family would often hand them an alcoholic beverage, which they purchased for them. As not to offend them, one would drink the beverage. Many would get drunk after drinking and often with not much food to consume to lessen the effects of the alcohol. So many drinks handed to us, many of the knights and ladies would become drunk at many of the functions.

At one of the local country clubs in Mobile, Alabama, some of the knights got on the bus as the event was ending, and one knight drove the bus, taking the awning off the country club and dragged it around two hundred feet. All that saw it thought it was funny. The knight that drove the bus had to pay for a new canopy to the club as it was so mangled.

The knights on Mardi Gras day were able to parade on their original float. The float driver drove and stopped in front of the viewing stand, where the debutants and queen were sitting to receive the special throws in long white stockings filled with goodies and thrown to their queen and ladies-in-waiting sitting in the stands.

My dad was a member of the Infant of Mystics Organization, and he had his friend call me out that year, and it was an honor to have done so. I received a lovely gift at the ball as they were in costume with a mask after parading and never knew who it was until later in life. As a debutante with all the activities, parties, balls, etcetera lasting for a year, I enjoyed life at its best, met strangers, friends, and family being wined, dined, and entertained at Thanksgiving and culminating with a week of Mardi Gras. It was a whirlwind experience, and Papa and Mom were there to allow me the opportunity of a lifetime. Those were the good ole days!

At the end of the week of all the festivities and balls, many could have used oxygen as they had consumed so much alcohol. I, with my mother and Papa, found it to be a fun time and the only other celebration like Mobile, Alabama, was in New Orleans, Louisiana.

My mom explained to me, "New Orleans Mardi Gras was for tourist, and Mobiles was for visitors, and Mobile had the first Mardi Gras revelry on 'Fat Tuesday,' and New Orleans had the first parade."

I found that to be a good description of the differences in the two original states that celebrated Mardi Gras.

The king and queen and attending events with my chosen knight, I would never forget the festivities and wonderful time had by all. Many a picture was taken and captured for prosperity in which my mother put in two large photo albums for me. There is a Mardi Gras Museum in Downtown Mobile, where you can visit and see the kings and queens train and other Mardi Gras displays of past years of the many celebrations. Life continues with a sense of normality after Mardi Gras and getting back into the routine of attending college classes again.

I carried my bunny in a crate and flew back to Jacksonville, where my boyfriend picked us up. I kept the bunny in my dorm room. Friends would play with it, and I named it Bugs Bunny. It started to become a chore to clean up after the bunny, and I gave it to a maid at the college who lived in a house with a yard and was a good home for Bugs. It was a sad day for me as I loved Bugs but realized he would be in a home with children that would love him more. I had a sense of routine again, feeling refreshed to have a nice, clean room without bunny droppings.

Papa and Mother Hosted Debut Party in Dunedin, Florida

1972

Papa and Mom hosted debutants and knights or whomever they wanted as a date for a weekend in Palm Harbor, Florida, during summer break from college or universities. At Innisbrook Golf and Spa Resort, fun was had by all in attendance. A party by the pool, dined on delicious food, and alcohol beverages were enjoyed by all. Papa and Mother, on one beautiful full moon evening, with which most of those in attendance were thrown in the pool fully clothed. Everyone jumping out all at once with no towels to dry off with, put an end to that night as all retired to their rooms. There was a lot of happy faces, and a few angry ones as well as they didn't want the fun to end.

At 6:00 A.M., it was rise and shine as Mom called each room, telling them to come to breakfast. After breakfast, many found it hard to say goodbye as they had such a wonderful time. They thanked Mom and Papa and me profusely for having them.

They loaded into a large van and a hired driver who drove them back to Mobile, which was around five hundred miles and, depending on traffic, was about an eight-hour drive. Many memories of the event were captured on camera and placed in photo albums. I lost touch with those that made their debut then as all went our separate ways and never to be heard from again by me.

My knight fell in love with another out-of-towner who was quite a party girl. They were marrying, and the night before her wedding, she was missing. Early the next morning, the phone woke me up.

A TURBULENT LIFE ? ? ?

"Where is Sissy as I and my friend Avril had driven home?"
I said, "I don't know."

She took off by herself. Jackie was suspicious of me. He found out I was telling the truth as he found she was in jail. She had been belligerent to the police officer as they arrested her. He bailed her out, and they proceeded to get married. I was a bridesmaid, and Jackie was very cold to me, but his mother and his dad loved me.

I later heard they divorced a year or so later. I saw Jackie for the last time when I was in Mobile, visiting my dad. Jackie was with a girl and actually apologized to me for his accusations and anger toward me.

Flagler College as a Sophomore

I studied hard and left time for fun. I was able to have my car parked on campus and traveled to the beach quite often with friends. I studied hard and made some As, Bs, and Cs with economics being my best subject. St. Augustine was full of history that I found quite fun to learn as I soaked up the knowledge to share with friends and family who came to visit.

When the summer came that year, I flew to Buffalo, New York, with my daughter, and Dede picked us up and drove us to Lake Chautauqua Institution. We checked into the beautiful old Athenian Hotel for two weeks. The open amphitheater at night on weekends would have wonderful guest singers and lecturers. We saw Miranda Lambert as she was making her start as a country singer, and we found her voice and songs delightful to listen to. The Treft family and Dede walked us around the community so we would know where our classes were held. The shops and eateries were in the small area. Anna and I walked around the grounds with beautiful Victorian homes in the community and around the lake. During the day, I attended writing classes, and Anna would go to the classes she chose. The lake had sailboats galore as they sailed in some of the fiercest winds. Dede's family were so gracious and hospitable to us. A trip that would never be forgotten.

Flagler College My Junior Year

1973

This is a picture of myself & Robert Boykin (Dad) on Ted Turner's ranch in Montana.

I was a student council representative as I had bought my grade up and was on the president's list from when I was on probation my first year of college. I was able to keep my car on campus and would drive it to the beach to soak up the sun and have some fun as friends, and I would throw Frisbee around. My good friend Dede, who I considered my summer best friend, visited me on the small campus at Flagler College as it has expanded over the years. We would see the town and enter many of the attractions. Also, we rode the trolley around town, and we had a great time! We took turns with my camera, taking picture of us sitting on the lions and was named the Bridge of Lions. I hated seeing her fly away as I dropped her off at the airport.

Toward the end of the year, I woke up from a sound sleep around 2:00 a.m. with a massive headache and in pain. My roommate woke up and panicked when she saw me.

"What's wrong?" she asked. "Look at your face."

I entered the bathroom in the room and saw my face swelling, and it was huge!

She said, "We need to get you to the emergency room of the hospital!"

When we arrived, the door was locked, and they were closed. She drove me back to college as I was so miserable. I didn't want to go to Jacksonville or to a hospital. With no sleep for either of us that night, we immediately went to the school's clinic. A nurse saw me and called the doctor to immediately come see the patient. She put me on a bed until the doctor arrived.

He asked, "What bit you?"

I replied, "I don't know as I woke up at 2:00 a.m. with a pounding headache, and my roommate woke up and took me to the emergency room at St. Augustine Hospital, and they were closed as the doors were locked."

The doctor examined me and felt I could had been bitten by a spider, but neither of us knew what kind. He put me on antibiotics and kept me in the clinic for two weeks as the bite was too close to my brain to release me. He saw the bite was in my nose. It was finals week, and I needed to study for them. My roommate bought me my books and checked on me throughout the days.

I tried to study but was in pain and unable to at times as I would try to sleep. The doctor came in the mornings to see me like clockwork. The swelling was gradually going down. My mother was hysterical when I told her about it, and she wanted to come get me. I told her no, and that I would be fine.

My professors allowed me to take the finals in the clinic, and I did okay with them. I didn't get put on probation, praise God. With two days left of schooling, I was released from clinic and began packing my car to drive home.

My brother was home and stayed in the apartment over the garage, and he made it his man cave. He and I would sail my Scorpion sailboat together, and a few times, he took it out by himself. Whenever he was home, he or both of us would sail the high seas.

Roommate from Hell Senior Year and Graduation Day at Flagler College

In 1974, I had a roommate Betsy from Albany, New York. She was an early education major and would have projects all over the room. I would have to step over and around them as I entered as well as her mountain-high dirty clothes. Praise God I had a friend who lived off campus and was lucky to spend time at her rental house with her.

My roommate was a junior and got a job at a topless bar across the Bridge of Lions on the way to the beach. She had me pick her up one night in her old car that was a stick shift, which I had only driven stick shift once or twice before. Getting out of first gear was a challenge, but I did it. I entered the club and felt uncomfortable as I told her I would wait in the car for her. She drove her car back to the college.

I went to the room with two weeks left for me to graduate. Betsy got a box out of her closet and said a girl was having me hold this for her. In astonishment, she showed me a box full of illegal drugs. I had never done any sort of illegal drugs, and I told her to get rid of it as my papa was an attorney, and that would reflect on him and could hurt his career!

My education professor and head of the education department was my favorite instructor. After graduation, he hosted a party at his home with his father for me and one other student. He had observed me at Dunedin Junior High School in Dunedin, Florida, student teaching seventh graders, where I taught in an open classroom with one hundred and twenty students for an hour. I was on the world geography team in the afternoon when we would teach.

A TURBULENT LIFE ? ? ?

One teacher would teach the culture of a country, another would do locations on the map and shipping ports and goods, and the other recipe for the worldview. On the fourth day, students returned to their homeroom teacher and review for a test that would be given on Friday. For my sixth-period class, I was in a self-contained classroom, which was great as I learned to teach in both types of classrooms. I liked the self-contained classroom the best as I could get to know the twenty-five students with their individual personalities, and it was a better way for the students to learn. They threw me a party when I was leaving to go back to college. They presented me with a book that all had signed, and I still cherish it.

Graduation Party

For this day, I received an A for my student teaching. Later I became a full-time teacher at Dunedin Junior High School. With two weeks left, I was busy studying in the school library located on the upper floor and had a beautiful view of the city. I didn't check to see if the roommate from hell had gotten rid of the box or not. I did go to the dean of women and told her about it, but she was Betsy's friend, and I later find out she did nothing about it.

In May of 1974, I received a double major and obtained a bachelor of arts degree in secondary education and liberal arts. Our class was honored to be the first graduating class from the college when it received the Southern Association of Colleges and Schools regional accreditation boards. That day, I learned perhaps my most valuable lesson, and that was to believe in myself.

After the ceremony, Dr. Boise hosted a graduation party for me and Sue, another student, at his home with his father. My boyfriend was from Cuba. Luis was adopted by parents in Tampa, Florida, and we often go on dates, loved watching and betting at the Jai alai arena in Tampa. Mother, Papa, Dad, and Mimi all attended. It was a memorable day for those who participated in graduation day and witnessing those throwing their hats high up in the air.

Many commented as it was the first time they had seen champagne kept on ice in a wash machine.

Browder said, "That is a brilliant idea, and we will implement in our own home when we entertain a large number of people in the house."

They thanked him and his dad for the wonderful time and returned to the school, getting my packed belongings, and my par-

A TURBULENT LIFE ? ? ?

ents helped me load the car for home. Luis and I drove my car back. We kept in touch with Dr. Boise, and the calls and letters stopped, and I knew not why.

Visited Flagler College
1975

I returned to visit my alma mater and learned from Dr. Proctor, the president of the college. Dr. Boise had died from a massive headache and learned it was caused by an acute bacterial sinus infection that went untreated as doctor's misdiagnosed him and told him it was his imagination. If that was the case, he was going to take a trip around the world.

I asked, "How could that happen?"

He continued to explain that Dr. Boise visited his cousin who was a scientist and asked him if he had x-rays of his sinuses. He responded no. The scientist took him to get an x-ray, and through a rhinoscopy, they exposed a foul-smelling pus discharge and narrowed nasal cavities. Doctors drew out seven cubic centimeters (cc's) of pus, and they were too late. He died shortly after the diagnosis was rendered. He left behind his elderly father who outlived him, but he died shortly after he buried him out of loneliness from his son and, of course, his elderly age.

He also talked about my roommate Betsy from my previous year in 1974. He clarified how she had stolen a two-year-old boy and took him to Gainesville, Florida. He showed me the newspaper clipping and explained the authorities caught her and returned the child home safely. Her picture was in the St. Augustine and Gainesville, Florida, papers and left a terrible blemish on the college.

I proceeded to apologize to the president for my not coming to him directly about the box of drugs that Betsy had showed me, and I told the dean of women, who I had thought would have handled it. Dr. Proctor explained that in 1974, nothing was shared with him about Betsy from the young dean, and Betsy was made a resident advisor in the 1975 school year. She never should have been! I also told him how I called her the roommate from hell as I had to walk through a minefield with her laundry five foot high and her projects on the rest of the floor! I spent most of my time off campus at a friend's house. I expressed my regret to him again for not coming directly to him about her. He told me it was okay. Betsy was taken by authorities and returned home state to Albany, New York. We said goodbye, and that was the last I heard of her as she was unable to return to Florida after that kidnapping.

Working at Walt Disney World Orlando, Florida

1974, 1975, and 1976

I first lived in an apartment on Thirty-third Street with my black Labrador retriever named Zeke. The address can be found on old maps of the area from 1974 and earlier. The area became Lake Buena Vista with hotels and restaurants that had taken its place as the area had grown so much because of Walt Disney World and the many developments it has made over the years in the region to accommodate the many visitors. With the other parks, it has created such as Magic Kingdom, Epcot, Disney's Hollywood Studio's, Animal Kingdom, Golf Resort, Fort Wilderness Campground, and the continued growth throughout the area. Cirque du Soleil is an exciting live show and has its own building at Disney Springs and the continued growth throughout the area with numerous hotels and restaurants. Disney Cruise Line has buses taking guest that are sailing on one of their ships out of Port Canaveral, and other plans that are still on the drawing board.

I had worked twelve hours one day as they gave over time. When I returned home, I observed my headphones were out of place and by the sliding glass door. There were no accidents from Zeke (black Labrador retriever) in the house, and the sliding glass door was broken. I called the police, and my neighbor next door gave me his handgun to sleep with. The police arrived and observed it appeared to them to have broken from the inside to the outside. It was hard to believe the dog would have gone outside and then come back to the inside. He was a well-trained dog but still puzzled them as to

A TURBULENT LIFE ? ? ?

how he did it. My neighbor came back over and explained there had been cars broken into that day. It still didn't explain how Zeke could have done it, and the only thing on the inside out of place was a set of headphones that appeared to have bite marks. There were no accidents from Zeke in the apartment either.

One day in 1974, while I was working at Walt Disney World, at Mr. Toads Wild Ride in Fantasy Land, I recognized my old neighbors from Mobile, who's house had burned to its embers, and nothing was recovered. As they were in line and only knew me as a young child, they didn't recognize me, and I quickly explained I was there neighbor in Spring Hill. The light bulb turned on in their heads, and they asked me to have dinner with them after my workday at the Polynesian Hotel main dining room.

It was nice to be reacquainted with them and to get to know their young children as we talked about my mother, and they were genuinely interested in her welfare. I told them she was with her fourth husband, who was a successful attorney in Clearwater, Florida. He was a fine man and like my second father. They were glad to hear that as they felt Browder needed to find a respectable man. Reminiscing of the past over the delicious dinner and conversation at the Polynesian Hotel Restaurant, I was stuffed and thanked them profusely. How happy they were to get caught up on the latest of the families adventures. They invited me to visit them in Virginia, but I never had the time and regret I never went.

When my lease was up, I moved in with Ann who was looking for a roommate at Carlton Arms Apartments in Orlando, Florida. Ann worked with me at It's a Small World in Fantasy Land, and we became roommates from 1975 to 1976. One day, Ann came home before I did, and Zeke had left the carcass of a turkey. They were going to have for Thanksgiving dinner. Ann was furious as she had to clean it up. When I got home from work, she had some choice words to say to me.

I apologized and said, "I will make it up to you and take you and your date for a Thanksgiving dinner or just let the two of you go."

She was still unhappy about it. I totally understood as I would have been upset as well if I had to clean it up! We lived together for a year, and she attended my wedding in Clearwater with our coworker Ed at the Presbyterian Church, and the reception was held in Papa's large office building reception hall, and his partner converted it from a hotel to a workplace in Clearwater, Florida. It was later sold to the cult scientologist that made Clearwater one of its headquarters. Ann was from Hickory, North Carolina, and unfortunately, we lost touch over the years. I also lost touch with my friend Al. After attending my wedding and reception, they drove back to Orlando to work the next day. She is a principal in a school in Winter Park, Florida, and would like to reconnect with her.

I had a nineteen-foot Chaparral boat with a sixty-five Johnson horsepower motor that Papa gave me. Before leaving for work, some of the residents I knew at the complex and fellow workers at Walt Disney World would water ski in the mornings and then get cleaned up and go to work. I worked in Magic Kingdom Fantasyland operations at Peter Pan's Flight, Dumbo the Flying Elephant ride, Mad Tea Party ride, Snow White's Scary Adventures, Mr. Toad's Wild Ride, Cinderella's Golden Carousel, and my favorite to work was the Mickey Mouse Review, an indoor audio animatronic stage show, which later closed and moved to Tokyo Disneyland.

I gave my two weeks' notice to my Fort Wilderness Campgrounds supervisor, where I checked guest in and out and also sold tickets at the outpost. I told him I was getting married. He accepted my resignation and welcomed me back at any time. I was being trained at River Country for when it first opened up and would sell tickets, but the supervisor moved me back to checking guest in and out at the outpost entrance as I had been trained to do it.

In 2022, I still stay in touch with three of my Disney Family of Friends on Facebook. We hope to gather for a reunion soon. Rita considered me as her mentor, and she currently lives in Colorado, and John Homer remains in Orlando, Florida. The Knowlton's worked together at Fort Wilderness Campgrounds at Walt Disney World and currently lives in Melbourne, Florida.

John McCown worked on the monorail system and was from Mobile, Alabama. He became successful in the shipping and cargo container business and has several patents and well-known in the

A TURBULENT LIFE ? ? ?

industry, as well as authoring a book on cargo shipping *Giants of the Sea*, a captivating history and development of the modern shipping industry and those that developed it to what it has become today. The many other workers I worked with, I lost touch over the years.

With the growth of Disney Parks came Universal and Sea World and swimming with the dolphin adventures, many other developments that are still being developed or on the drawing boards in California in renovating Disney Land and the Magic Kingdom constantly trying to stay current with the times. The animated, nature, princesses movies, action, and true stories in existence that are streaming on Walt Disney Plus and feature films in movie theaters after opening up as the covid pandemic closed them, and many had to get better ventilation systems in the theaters.

My Wedding in 1976

I attended the Dunedin Presbyterian Church for several years as Papa was a Sunday school teacher. I came to know the children's minister, Mr. Amory, well as his daughter and I were friends. One day, his daughter and I were driving in my car, and I was behind the wheel. I noticed men in a truck began following us. I knew to give them the runaround and drove to the front of a neighbor's house, and they stopped a block away and watched us. I sped away and drove into the local police station, and the harassers drove away and left us for good. I felt safe to drive her home and dropped her off and waited to make sure she got in safely. I proceeded to my house and felt safe as I told my mother, brother, and Papa what happened.

Papa asked, "Did y'all get the license plate?"

I replied, "We were too scared to have thought of doing that."

He said, "Now you know what to do if it ever occurs again."

The family was happy to see me safe and sound.

Endy and I got engaged in a dark restaurant with no ring presented in Orlando, Florida. The sad thing is I don't remember much about it. He and I later picked a wedding set together as I had received a proposal from Ed after I graduated from college and remember every last detail of that one. It was romantic as he proposed to me at my apartment, getting on one knee, handing me a beautiful ring, and telling me it was love at first sight. At that time in my life, I did not know what being in love was and perhaps never have known it. I told Ed I would think about it. When he called to come see me, I informed him I was engaged. That was the mistake of my life, and the coldest thing I could have done to anyone. Not saying yes to Ed was perhaps the biggest regret in my life as he genuinely loved me and knew me to the depths of my soul.

A TURBULENT LIFE ? ? ?

The after-dinner rehearsal party given by close friends of Mother and Papa in the home of the Charbonnet's who introduced me to Ed (who, in hindsight, I should be with) was done to a tee with bartender and succulent hors d'oeuvres and a sit-down dinner. The wedding party and guest had a lot of fun with the laughter, good conversations, and background music.

At home, I was woken up by Papa at 2:18 a.m. As I looked at my bedroom clock, he was drunk and had his hands around my neck because he was told by my mother that I was not a virgin at age twenty-four. My mother rushed in and said that she lied that I was a virgin. Confused at the event that took place that night throughout my entire life. Why would Papa try to strangle me? I never had an answer other than it was the alcohol he consumed.

My brother was a groomsman in our wedding and bought a model with him from New York, where he was living at that time and had done modeling himself. He met my fiancé Endy for the first time. Later, Robby told me he felt he was gay but never told me that before I married him. Endy's brother was his best man, and his sister was a bridesmaid. Endy worked for a railroad as my grandfather did and worked himself up to a station manager.

On June 19, the wedding day, Pastor Amory married us. I made it down the aisle without a tear, but when it came time to say the vows, I was crying, and my dad was giving me away and gave me his handkerchief as he always carried one with him and was prepared for anything.

From the tears and sniffling, I never said the words *I do*. We were considered married anyway. The wedding photographer took many pictures of the afternoon and evening at the reception.

We were escorted out of the church into a limousine, and a car passing by mooned us (showing a naked bottom), and we laughed at it. The limousine driver drove us to the reception in the lobby of an old hotel that was converted to Papa and his partner's law office, where I worked for a summer, working the old phone switchboard and elevator for their clients. The band was playing music as we entered, and the lobby that was beautifully decorated by my mother and was full of guest greeting us with claps like thunder.

The guest book was signed with Dad and Cora's daughters greeting the guest and having them sign it. Their two boys attended as well. Endy and I danced to our chosen wedding song, "You Are the Sunshine of My Life" by Stevie Wonder. Dancing and fun was had by all. The time came we went up in the elevator and changed clothes to leave for our honeymoon. We came down together in the elevator with Endy exiting first, and as usual, I was last. I came to realize later I was the last in his life.

When we left, rose petals were thrown, and we ran to the yellow Volkswagen pop-up campervan my dad and Cora gave us as a wedding present that we loved! We named it the Yellow Submarine after the Beatles's song. While Endy was driving, the cans dragging in the back with the just married sign was noisy. Then a foul smell permeated the van, making us both cough. He pulled over, and after continuously looking throughout the van, he finally took the cover off inside the van and found a fish that his groomsman had put in it, and praise God, my brother had not participated in that as he had just met the groomsmen the day before. Endy also took the cans off the van. He continued driving to the port for our sailing on Carnival Cruise Line as we entered our state room, and I unpacked and saw my birth control pills were not there. I used the ship to shore radio and told my mother, and she had a fit. She called our good friends, the Stromires, whose daughter Anne was one of my bridesmaids. He had a plane, and she had him fly to the ship and drop them to the captain on board. It was insane for her to do that!

We were sailing to the Virgin Islands with stops along the way in Puerto Rico, and we bought rum to take back as gifts. While in Saint Thomas, we rented scooters with, and we drove most of the small island on the right side of the road. It was beautiful and boarded the ship to return back to the home port.

Upon our return, we moved to a two-story apartment in Melbourne, Florida, and he was from St. Augustine, Florida. He went into transportation with Harris Corporation. One night, we were skinny-dipping in the apartment pool, and the lights suddenly went on. Endy hopped out and grabbed the towels and handed me one, so we were covered. No one came outside, and that was the last time for doing that. Another time, he had taken me to Orlando, Florida, and unexpectedly it was a nudist camp. We entered his friend's home, and I, being very modest, did not participate in the nudity and was insulted that he would not tell me beforehand. He knew I would not have gone. Henneth felt right at home in doing it as they rode around in a golf cart to the beach.

First Child Arrival

We purchased a three-bedroom house in Melbourne, and shortly after our marriage, Endy would be out with male friends to the wee hours of the morning. He told me he didn't want a child. He was too late in telling me as I told him I was pregnant. Later I realized when it was too late that I should have lived with him for two years. I told my children before they married to live with their partners, but none of them listened to my advice.

The obstetrics gynecologist (OB-GYN) and nurse in the office told me I was going to have a girl as I was carrying it like a girl. The ultrasounds used today was not used then, and I had the baby two weeks late. The doctor had me take one Clomid under the tongue at the hospital to have the baby come. Shortly after taking it in the hospital, labor pains started, and I asked for an epidural, which didn't take effect until after my baby was born as he entered the world in two hours on a Friday afternoon. Endy and I had taken Lamaze classes to prepare for the baby's arrival. Endy helped calm me down in the delivery room and gave me ice chips from the nurses.

"Breathe in and out, take deep breaths." The contractions got stronger, and we continued the process until "push one last time" was said.

Weslee James Was Born on September 7, 1979, at 4:44 p.m., and he had a loud set of lungs. He was eight pounds and two ounces with a few strands of dark hair. I was given a room in the maternity section near the babies' nursery. In the private room, the epidural took effect, and I was unable to walk for twelve hours. It was an easy delivery, but I had morning sickness the entire nine months. The epidural was worthless when I was having labor pains! I was finally able to walk, and I could feed him. I breastfed him, but he was losing weight and not getting enough to eat, and the doctor put him on formula for me to feed him with a bottle. He sucked his thumb immediately as an infant.

It was time to take him home, and the doctor told Endy and me that Wes was jaundiced with a yellow coloring of skin and eyes. Doctor explained he had too much bilirubin in his blood, and he was put under the bilirubin light, which was an ultraviolet light for two days before we were able to go home together. Endy came by after work to visit Wes and I. My mother and Papa drove over to see him and immediately melted at his cuteness. Endy's parents visited him in the hospital as well.

The day came, and we took him home to the house we purchased in a neighborhood across the street from Florida Institute of Technology in Melbourne. When he was older, it was a great place to stroll him through the gardens. He was colicky, and to get him to sleep, we often had to drive him in the car with his thumb in his mouth or his bottle or rock and walk him to sleep. I would gently lay him in his crib as not to wake him night after night.

At fourteen months old, Wes started climbing out of his crib, and it was time to put him in his own bed. At age one, he had a square with different shaped holes he had to match the shape pieces to put them in the holes. When he couldn't do it, he would get frustrated and hit his head on the floor. I would put him in a shower, and it didn't get him to stop. He was a head beater, and we tried every method possible to get him to stop.

One day, we left him in his room for a while, and when I entered, his forehead was red, and he had a rug burn. That was the last time he did that. He finally outgrew it. Praise God! I told him I was pregnant with another child.

Wes said, "No, I want to be an only child!"

I had a miscarriage and didn't even know I was pregnant as my period was so irregular. I could have one every three or four months, making it harder to know if I was pregnant or not. I was bleeding and taken to the hospital by a neighbor, where I learned I was pregnant and had to have a D&C to remove tissue from my uterus. We were having a party that night, and Henneth didn't want to cancel it, and

I had a few hours to prepare for it. My reactions were running across the board with a two-year-old under my feet.

Guest arrived and could not believe we didn't cancel it, but Endy paid no attention to my feelings. The evening was short as the guest recognized from my face and lack of conversation knew how sad I was and stressed by the events of the day and left early. I put Wes to bed and then went to bed myself.

I was substitute teaching in Melbourne Junior High School and had gone to the bathroom and saw I was bleeding, and I knew what that meant, and they had to get a substitute for me. I left and went to an older female military OB-GYN, who told me, "I could have told you this was going to happen. You don't get pregnant right after you have a miscarriage." Just what I didn't want to hear!

"Don't lift anything heavy, don't vacuum, do any teaching, and have plenty of bedrest!" She wrote on her prescription pad. If I bleed again, I needed to go to the hospital and give a note to the hospital staff. I went home so upset, so I called Endy, crying and telling him what she said. He calmed me down. I rested and took it easy for the rest of the months and had terrible morning sickness.

Second Child Arrives

I woke up around 5:40 a.m. on October 14, 1981, at age twenty-five. I heard mother raising her voice as she wringed water from her nightgown and threw it off. Immediately, putting on a roomy moo to cross the threshold of the hospital.

"My water broke! The baby is coming. These labor pains are excruciating. Get me to the hospital!" I said.

Taking his time, he brushed his teeth and dressed while I was screaming. He called the neighbor across the street and had her come watch Wes while he was sleeping and when he woke up. Finally, we were in the van.

At the emergency room, a nurse ran out and asked if I could walk.

I said, "Hell no, the head is coming out! Get me a stretcher with my legs far apart!"

She put me in a wheelchair and ran me immediately to a delivery room. The doctor was called, and he couldn't make it in time.

Head nurse said, "I have delivered babies, and I shall deliver yours."

The contractions were coming fast and furiously as I was breathing heavily. Nurse told me to take deep breaths and held my hand while the contractions were intense, and the head was coming out. "Push!"

Henneth had cleaned his hands and put on the hospital attire as the head was out. The nurse continued telling me when to push, and it came out in a total of forty-five minutes from home to hospital. Praise God we didn't live in a large city with a lot of traffic, or he would have been born in the van.

Bevo Brevard was born at 6:14 a.m. on a Tuesday. He was eight pounds and fourteen ounces and was a big boy who was bald at birth. With time, he grew thick blond hair. He had a healthy Apgar score, and we were able to go home after two days.

Weslee came to the hospital with Endy to see his baby brother. He blamed me for at least two to three weeks for bringing another child into the household and had nothing to say to me.

He said, "How dare you bring someone else to share my space." He held me responsible, but as his baby brother played with him, he began to forgive me and had fun with leading his brother around.

Bevo was easy to care for, and at nine months, he crawled out of his crib, and we had to put him in his own bed. It was summertime, and an instructor taught them to swim in a pool another parent had. When Bevo played with Wes, he was glad to have Bevo as a playmate. Bevo swam before he walked. He began walking at eleven months to keep up with his brother. They both took to the water like fish. The instructor had mothers get in the water with our children and count to five teaching them to blow and dip them in the water. Time after time and then, they caught on. We had a pool at our new home, and Weslee, at age five, was riding a motorized vehicle around the pool, and with me watching, he fell in the pool with the vehicle that floated, and he swam to the side of the pool. Participating in the instruction of my children as infants to swim was the best thing I did as a mother. Wes and Bevo wanted to swim every day as they both loved it! I swam as well as it is the best exercise at any age for one to do! My mother was visiting in Melbourne and taught the boys to march around the pool as soldiers, "Hup one, two, three, march on," and repeated it several times until all jumped in the pool to swim. They had fun with their grandmother Browder.

I had an appointment with another OB-GYN who told me I was pregnant and would have an ultrasound done in a few months to determine the sex of the baby. The time came, and Endy and I found out it was a girl. We immediately chose her name to be Anna Grace. I was so excited to have a girl! Weslee and Bevo were happy to hear it was a girl as well.

A TURBULENT LIFE ? ? ?

The day arrived, and Endy was out of town for work as it was again hard to determine a date as I was so irregular. I called Mrs. King bright and early in the morning and told her it was time, and my little girl was coming. She lived right down the street and arrived quick as lightning to the door. Judy, across the street, came to watch the boys as they were still sleeping. Arriving at the hospital, I was immediately taken to a delivery room as the staff remembered how quickly Bevo had come. Mrs. King was coaching me to breathe as I was having strong contractions. She held my hand and put cool washcloth on forehead.

Then the Doctor said, "Push, push one more time!"

Anna was delivered at 6:24 a.m. on February 26, 1985. The OB-GYN took her immediately to suction meconium from her lungs. He cut the umbilical cord before she was placed on my stomach. Mrs. King kept me calm, saying, "Everything is all right." As with my other two babies, they were placed on my stomach immediately. She was seven pounds and thirteen ounces with a few strands of dark hair. We immediately counted her five toes and five fingers on each side. Mrs. King was a great calming voice through the birth. It was a thrill for her to do it, and I would enter her home as she would be cooking seaweed with a distinct odor. It was known to help people with various types of cancer, especially with her type. Endy immediately got the quickest flight home.

The Nightmare of Abuse of My Daughter

One night, while in my daughter's room at age four, she was asleep around midnight, and I fell asleep with her. Endy waking me up, saying, "I shall stay with her."

At the time, I had no idea why, and so groggy from being woken up from a sound sleep, I went to our bed to fall asleep again. I never dreamed of what I learned from my daughter in later years and also from a friend she told at a younger age. My friend had told me, and somehow I didn't hear her, or I totally blocked it out. How could I do something as detrimental to a young child as that? Why? It haunted me until I started writing this story as my autobiography. What was wrong with me in not recognizing and facing the truth?

My dad demanded to come in, and a big fight arose. Mom taped it, and Dad made us stay in the room and listen to the anger displayed. We left for the keys for a little over two weeks. When we were driving back from the keys, Mom called and spoke to each of us on the phone and said she had bought a new house and taken some of her things and the antiques that had stayed in her family from generation to generation. She left the majority of furniture and belongings behind. Dad was furious!

When we returned, Mom, with her dad and two brothers, came to get us and showed us the new house on the water that led to the river! It was the only way. Mom thought she could get out, as she was scared of him at the end.

Wes said, "My things are at the other house." Bevo went with his brother. The boys were returned to Dad's house. Remembering the eleven-year-old daughter that raised her voice and stood up to her grandfather Boykin, "I will live with Mom! You are the strongest person I know and even with the mistakes you and I have made, you consistently get stronger! I loved you that day and never felt I could love you more than then, but it just continues growing more and more as each day goes by."

Only to find out it being confirmed to me when my daughter was older, and she came to live with me at age eleven. I was called by a pastor to come, and he gave me directions to their home. The pastor, wife, and boyfriend proceeded to tell me how she was abused by her father and did not feel she could tell me alone. We prayed, and I was so angry. I felt bewildered that I was unable to see the abuse and to deal with it at the time. It was by far the most turbulent awareness of the depth of the sexual abuse, and numerous times I waited until I had the courage to divorce him and move out.

In a letter to Henneth, I wrote the following:

> What loving father would have their daughter break and enter into her mother's home through a small second-story bathroom window when you knew her mother was out of town and on her way back home? You broke the court order and had Anna, Bevo, and Wes involved in breaking and entering into my home. I would have prosecuted in reflection, and I wish I did! Did you ever even think about Anna's emotions and how she could have broken a bone and been injured enough not to open the door for you and the boys? Then I enter my home and trip over luggage in the front door with no children at home. I saw where you had gone through my home as you left your business card. You are so thoughtless and completely out for your own needs to snoop through my house. I was home before the court order an hour within the time you broke and entered my house in Palm Bay, Florida. You have never learned how to love anyone! Do you even know what the word

like or *love* means? Have you ever apologized for teaching your children how to break and enter and not teaching them right from wrong? I hope one day you realize the trauma you continue to inflict on our daughter. Have you ever taken responsibility for your actions?

You go through life thinking everyone owes you something for nothing. A perfect example among others is your going after the cash value of my stepmother's life insurance policy during the divorce proceedings that I and her children were paying. Praise God, the court saw through your lies, greediness, deceit, and deceptions. One major regret I have in life was not leaving you within the first two years of our relationship. I only wish I had called the police when you abused Wes in the keys, having him on the floor for thirty minutes with a hammer in your hand. Also, throwing him many times against the wall at the house, and it was always with Anna and Bevo present. I realize now you set Wes up many times. I will never forget his working in the garage on a project, and he was not hurting anyone, but you insisted upon him dropping what he was doing to help you with something minor. When he was in the house, you kept throwing him against the wall. I can't believe how weak I was not to have called the police. You have dodged jail, but you continue on the path you are currently on. You will get your jailbird wish.

Quit abusing your children verbally and with your negative actions. Learn how to respect your children and others! Look up the words *respect, lies, like, love, trust* in the dictionary as you obviously don't know the meaning of them. Stop taking advantage of others! Learn to like and love yourself so you can love and like others! Until you do these, please leave me alone and stop ringing my doorbell once and then leaving every day for months! The only reason we have to talk is if there is an emergency with our children. Please stay away from Anna and don't introduce her to any of your young lovers and friends unless she wants to be with you, and it should be with whomever she can trust.

I listened to your put-downs for thirteen years and hope you will listen as well as take the advice I offer you for once in your life. Seek professional help as we all know from your telling us that you have enough money to do anything, so don't walk but run to get help, especially with your identity crisis you have dealt with, but have you really dealt with it? I applaud you now for coming out of the closet and admitting to be gay.

Sincerely,
Grace

I believe the events of her father is what led to the following. In 2009, Anna had a boyfriend named Jess who moved into my home for six months, and they found an apartment together. It was shortly after those events transpired that I slowly began to realize the magnitude of his crimes and that he was con. Besides stealing more than an estimated 111,800 dollars in items and money, he disrupted every aspect of my life. I moved from my home and hired a credit-monitoring service for both my daughter and me in an attempt to regain a little sense of safety and peace of mind. However, neither of those were much consolation, and I am still emotionally scarred from the situation. He was sentenced to seven years in prison.

Anna's two brothers with their wives and police moved her from the apartment as Jess became violent. I obtained a permanent restraining order from the judge as he tried to shut the car door on my hand among other things. Anna went to live with her older brother and wife on the east coast of Florida. Years later, she met her husband, and they are happily married for seven years and having their first baby together.

Memories of My Daughter as Flashbacks

Some of my daughter's adventures began when she went hunting for the first time at age ten in full camouflage with her aunt. They set up in the tiger hole field when five deer suddenly appeared: three bucks—a four point, an eight point, and a ten point—plus a yearling and a large doe. The doe was blocking the shot from the ten-point buck before it finally moved, and Anna was able to get a shot off. Using her aunt's .243 rifle, she shot the deer, and it dropped to the ground. Her aunt and Anna ran to the deer, made sure it was dead, and began counting the points. Anna's heart was racing as her adrenalin flowed with the thrill of her first kill. The caretaker helped take the deer to the lodge and hung it on the skinning rack. Her aunt put blood on Anna's nose and cheeks, and her dad smeared it all around her forehead and face as my daughter officially joined the bloody ranks of first-time buck killers. Many pictures were taken of Anna holding the deer's head up to display its horns as it hung from the deer rack and was taken to taxidermist to mount.

Anna was especially excited to tell another story, this one describing an adventure she'd had in the woods with her grandfather in the hunting house one afternoon. They were comfortably arranged, waiting for deer when they fell asleep. Suddenly a loud noise in the brush woke them up. Wide-eyed and bushy-tailed, looking into the field directly in front of them, a mere twenty yards away, was a large eight-point buck with horns outside of the ears.

Granddad said, "Shoot it, shoot it!"

Anna shot once but missed with the older semiautomatic thirty-thirty rifle she was using. Lining up her sights, she fired again, and this time the deer fell down with a broken leg. As he tried to get up, she shot him again, and this time it was a bull's-eye, but just to make sure, she fired one time until the deer was still as the dusky night air was falling.

Together she and her grandfather called on the CB radio to get help drag the large 165-pound deer out and back to the skinning rack at the lodge.

Bevo answered the radio and said, "It sounded like World War II out there."

Robert said, "Send help, Bevo. Anna just shot a huge buck."

Within minutes, help arrived. Anna ran to them, smiling from head to toe with the second buck she'd ever killed, actually being larger than her first. Happily, she sang, "It just gets better and better!"

Returning to the lodge, they were surrounded by an ecstatic crowd who gathered around, taking pictures of Anna and her granddad with the largest deer killed on the grounds that year. Excitement was in the air throughout the plantation.

A highlight of hunting was when we took a trip of London and saw the sights. I rented a car and drove to the countryside, where we stayed in a hotel and had a hunt. Our guide first had her shoot a cone and then a rabbit with a .243 rifle that blew it to smithereens. He felt she was ready to shoot a roe. Buck one appeared, and she took aim and fired with a perfect shot as she downed her roe buck. Our guide took the roe buck to a pub for them to prepare it for dinner that evening. It was cooked to perfection and melted in our mouths. The guide told Anna she should be a hunting guide in Africa as she was an excellent shot, and he liked women hunters because they listen as he had found men not to listen as well as they feel they know it all. Unfortunately, Anna never followed his advice as she liked staying close to home.

Family's Favorite Vacation Spot

Anna wrote the following: I've been to Breckinridge and Vail, Colorado, and the majority of my experiences in Colorado have been good and memorable ones. Colorado is my favorite place to visit because it has good slopes to snowboard on, has a lot of action-packed activities, and beautiful resorts.

The mountains in Colorado are gorgeous. There is one mountain in Colorado that has snow on the tip-top of it year-round. There are many ski and snowboarding slopes in Colorado, and many of the slopes are challenging. The four different difficulty levels of the ski and snowboarding slopes are labeled as follows: bunny slope, green circle, blue square, black diamond, and double black diamond. I don't like going on the beginner slopes that much because there's a lot of people who don't know how to ski or snowboard. My favorite activity is snowboarding. Some slopes have ramps and rails to do tricks on. I don't know how to do many tricks, but I take classes every time I go to learn more. The best trick I can do is a switch, which is when I go up a ramp with my right foot forward and switch to land with my left foot forward. Keeping control of the board or ski's tough, so I don't run into anyone.

My second favorite activity with my brothers is rock climbing at the recreation center in Breckenridge. We enjoyed swimming at the recreation center after a hard day on the slope. The majority of the resorts my family and I have stayed in are immaculate. My favorite resort was right on the ski slopes, so we could snowboard straight from our room and get on the lift that takes you to the top of the mountain and snowboard down. They offer many other activities at the resort like tennis and racquet ball. We found the arcade to be fun, but it took all our spending money. The pool is big and beautiful, and the spa is nice and steamy, hot springs, and river rafting are just a few of the summer activities we enjoyed the most. Overall, Colorado is a wonderful family-oriented place to live or visit in winter or all year round! Mom, in her later years, was looking to purchase a home in Breckenridge, but it did not pan out for her.

Cora's Death

The family made their goodbyes when Dad's wife Cora was at the Dauphin Island house, and her death was imminent. I was there when she said something special to each of us lined up at her bed as we made our goodbyes, but I knew I would see her in heaven one day. Cora died July 14, 2000, at the age of sixty-three from lung cancer, and she had a lot more life to live. Dad was devastated, and some of the immediate family seemed not to move on as part of themselves died with her.

Children in Our Home in Little Torch Key, Florida

Before they left to the Keys, their father and I had a big fight with the kids present in the guest bedroom downstairs where I was staying. They were saying goodbye before leaving. Henneth entered as I had the tape recorder on, and again we fought with the kids in the room. He told me to turn the tape recorder off, but in the same breath, he said leave it on. It was admissible in court as he had given his permission to keep it on and was heard on the recording.

My father and his two boys drove from Mobile, Alabama, to help me move into a home in Palm Bay, Florida. My best friend was a realtor and helped me find what came to be my favorite home. My sister in Christ Helen and her then husband helped me pack up to move, taking only what furniture belonged to me. Yet in court, Henneth said some of the antiques were his. My mother had given me a list of things she had given me in our home, including the antiques, and written when we were first married. It was used in court as Henneth was going for the jugular. He even wanted to go after my interest in the family land and timber company in Mobile, Alabama, which he was unable to do as things were set up in the 1963 irrevocable trust Frank and Other had, and it was ironclad as written only direct descendants could receive the benefits from the company. The divorce was finalized, yet he pursued, taking it to the higher circuit court where it was upheld. I believe if he could have taken to the Supreme Court and had the money to do so, he would have.

A TURBULENT LIFE ? ? ?

The children were in our home on Little Torch Key not far from Marathon and Key West. It was purchased with money that had come directly from the family-owned business to me. My dad and Cora started with their children a land investment company of their own and asked me to join in, but praise God I didn't and invested it in the house in Keys. Henneth was awarded it in the divorce decree along with the house near Brevard, North Carolina. I received the land in interest in Gulf Hammock, Florida, as Papa had a major interest in it, and I knew he didn't want to have Henneth a part, so I settled for that property and was not going to bicker for the other. I paid child support for the two boys until age eighteen and one lump sum as alimony. Then he paid a pittance to me for Anna as he didn't earn that much money at Harris Corporation.

Later Anna's brother Bevo was using the French provincial furniture with headboard, dresser, and two side tables in the design of a dollhouse with thatched roof and rooms to display items. Given to his daughter Veda, she had the rooms filled with horses she loves and owned her own kept in a stable with her trainer. She participated in small local rodeo, doing the barrel racing. Till one day, a Japanese Akita-ken dog, around fifty-five pounds, was powerful, dominant, and not good for younger children. The hunting dog mauled her. Having almost two hundred stitches to her face and some on her hands surgery, which was about five hours. A week in the hospital, she was such a brave girl at age nine. She had gone through two divorces with her mother and managed to smile and be alert. She will have to receive more plastic surgery through years of her life to have her look herself once more.

I thought about my extended family's hunting adventures and misadventures. I also started to think about my own and about my immediate family in general. Weslee was nicknamed Moonbeam in 1979; he eventually became the second in the fourth generation to become a board member of the land and timber company at age twenty-six. He was a public relations graduate of the University of Florida and was married in 2006 to his auburn-haired wife, Jen, nicknamed Red by my dad. She was a math teacher. Just before my son's wedding, I wrote the following and shared it with Jen and Weslee at the rehearsal party dinner:

> Let's raise our glasses together in this wish for my moonbeam and his sunshine. Watching you grow into the great man you have been is the greatest joy I've ever had, and I wish for you all the joy one life can hold with your sunshine to light up all your days, on and off the flag football field, and in and out of hospitals, in complete togetherness! May these be the happiest days of your life, as you share many smiles, laughter, and although I don't know who's the best hunter and will not venture to guess who's the best at cleaning all the game and fish you catch! I hope in your togetherness, you will always share your challenges, strife, visions, and dreams forever in everlasting happiness. Wes, I just wish you and your sunshine all the love your heart can hold as you continue to walk hand in hand in perfect harmony.

I taught my sons and daughter to take many pictures, and that they can never laugh too much, and to love as if they'd never been hurt because every second spent upset is a minute of happiness one can never get back.

Wes's new wife, Jen, enjoyed hunting to the depths of her heart. She was first of the fourth generation of women to have dressed her own deer, and she became a die-hard hunter within the first year. Bevo dropped Wes off to walk into the field, where Wes set up his blind in the lowland. He was joking with his cousin, Mary Francis, that he didn't think he would see a large buck and was really not interested in doing so, as he didn't have room for a trophy in his new house with his new wife.

He told her he wanted to wait 'til he had a larger house, but his teasing proved ironic when after sitting for twenty minutes, Wes looked out and saw a doe. Then as he put his binoculars to his eyes, he spotted a larger deer on the edge of the field. He focused long and hard, counting each point several times, not believing he actually had an eleven-point buck in his sights at last.

Pondered to himself, *When will I ever see another deer such as this?* Not knowing where he would ever fit such a trophy, he decided not to worry about that and pulled the trigger, not even sure his scope was properly sighted. After the loud shot, the deer just stood there, looked at Wes's stand, circled around, and then fell dead to the ground. In total surprise, Wes looked at the large buck with an eleven-point, nontypical rack outside his ears, and immediately called Granddad to come get him and his trophy.

As the crowd saw him drive up in Granddad's truck, onlookers were heard, saying, "I don't believe it. That deer is beautiful!"

On another hunting trip at the lodge with his wife, Wes heard *gobble, gobble, gobble*, which, from the mere volume alone, indicated he must be huge. Extremely excited, Wes instantly leaned forward his gun, but Hubby (the caretaker) put his hand upon him, pushing him gently back against the cypress tree. Then they sat motionless and silent, until Wes saw Hubby cup his hands before his lips. He heard him swallow, and then there came from his cupped hands the soft yelp of a turkey hen. Instantly the gobbler answered, and his gobble was heard throughout the swamp. Two hours later, they were still waiting for the gobbler to come, and at long intervals, Hubby would softly call to him, and each time, the turkey answered. Then they also heard the high-pitched rasping bark of a dozen deer. A doe ran within twenty-five feet of them, along with an eight-point buck close behind her.

As if mocking them, three redbirds began to play in the bushes, showing off their courtship rituals, while directly overhead a fox squirrel chattered, as if inviting them to play. But Hubby just sat motionless, waiting for the gobbler to come. Finally, he did, with a great big neck and a head high and white as cotton, his wings unbending beside him, and his tail spread like a golden fan as the sun glazed upon it. Every so often, he thrust down his long snout, then raised, and thrust it down again. The bird would suddenly run forward a step or two in full strut.

Hubby and Wes were close enough to hear his wings scratching over the ground. Closer and closer, he came until he was in range of Wes's shaking gun. *Pow!* came the shot, and by a lucky chance, it caught the turkey square in the neck, and it rolled over instantly, dead. Then it was Wes's turn to hold his head up high; he was so proud and excited after killing his first turkey.

He said, "Hubby told me of the hundreds of turkey that he's seen on the preserve, and the hundreds that are still there. As we walked back through the woods, we even disturbed three coveys of quail, so it was obvious how plentiful game birds were all around."

When they returned to the lodge, everyone was waiting to see the beautiful three-year-old bird. Wes had the tail feathers prepared and put in a shadow box frame that he hung on the wall at the foot of his bed throughout his college years.

Ringing through halls were feet scattering rapidly through the wings to arrive at class. One of the most important days of the year for juniors and seniors had sweat and tears streaming down some drawn faces taking the SAT test to enter into college. Concentrating on one question at a time as the clock ticked. Wes engrossed with lights shining on the paper with specks shimmering in his eyes, he doubled over in pain with a massive headache. Wes could not finish SAT and later found out he scored only ten, and we knew why.

I was teaching at the Christian school when Pastor Mark entered the room and called me outside.

He said, "I shall take over your class as Wes has a major headache and seeing bright lights."

I immediately took him to his doctor who ordered x-rays and said, "He must go to a brain surgeon immediately as he has a tumor."

A TURBULENT LIFE ? ? ?

Remembrances of Firstborn Son Weslee

Standing with you on September 7, 1979, and facing the days before you
I trust you may meet all life has in store. With composure, one lifts their heads.
I hope this will be your most gratifying year in trying to do the greatest good.
Exasperatingly, we are doing work for you to succeed in doing your quest
The largest number of people as you work in the public school system as a teacher.
Working with disabled children, coaching swimming, teaching women in jail,
And your favorite, of course, teaching physical education but only for a short period of time.
You were suddenly taken away from us as you fought your battle with cancer
Not with just one but three different types of brain cancer from age sixteen to thirty-two
Oh, so young for you to depart life on earth.
God soared to greet you in the dawn of day, you came to face your Maker
Standing by God in the grace of heaven!
The life you endured with cancer was not for the faint at heart
Leaving all that knew you blessed to know your caring heart
You handled in stride but leaving tears along the way
As custodians with vast acres of God's beautiful land,
You were able to take great pride in his wild creatures with your wife.
You loved the beautiful sheen of sunlight, the leaves, and multicolored changes in the
Fall season!
You left behind beautiful drawings, a cartoon drawing as a comic book you wrote, and letters
You would leave in your bed to your mom to find,

We started chain letters throughout the years, and it caught on to your brother and sister to join in the Fun!

The natural things to me are the beautiful things said as words are a vehicle of one's expressions.

The perfect inscriptions and forming of phrases is a special gift of God, which you delivered so eloquently

They are the heartstrings we echo, with inspiration of laughter, tears, and compassion and producing

Feelings of anxiety, hurt, and pain can be found, especially from one's own illness.

With triple multihued rainbows with something drawn of its loveliest aspects of color

As seen through the eyes of a mother in Kauai, Hawaii, on many days and, oh, what a beautiful sight it was.

You were taken to see God and your relatives to greet you on March 7, 2012. On earth today, twelve years later, you would be age forty-four, and as I reflect on you, your wisdom and strength and beautiful smile are never forgotten to those you left behind that had the good fortune of knowing you on earth!

—Written by your loving mom

Not many hard-hearted words were said, but one I heard that had to be said from Dr. Parker Mickle, "We must do major surgery right away." We scheduled it for Monday morning as we had time to get clothes packed as we lived several hours away only to return to Shands Hospital at the University of Florida in Gainesville. Weslee didn't have time to digest just what was going on as everything was moving so fast.

I landed on the floor in a sitting position, crying as I heard the words *you have medulloblastoma, brain tumor*. I had researched and read from the Internet, and it was life-threatening. That was one of the most tragic and turbulent days in my life! Yet there were many more excruciating painful and turbulent days for our family moving

A TURBULENT LIFE ? ? ?

forward. As a mother, I prayed to God many times to let it be me, but that was not to be.

*****

The doctor performed surgery, and you lived for another sixteen years. You had chemotherapy in the hospital for two days as they flushed you out with water and then administered the chemo drugs and again washed you out the next day after the drugs entered your system. It was done several times over a period of months. You had the strength of many that carried you through the days. After chemotherapy came time for radiation, which was the hardest treatment of all to carry you through to many more days on earth. Praise God!

The treatment was the most grueling thing to see you through as you were five foot eleven and lost so much weight. You were skin and bones, weighing eighty pounds. I was desperate and would try anything for you to eat. At the hospital, I purchased some gel caps and filled them with weight gainer powder, but you were so smart you would not take them as you knew they were not prescribed. You made it through radiation and were able to eat all your favorite foods to gain the weight you desperately needed. You graduated high school and junior college, then onward and upward to University of Florida as you retook the SATs and scored high, and you were accepted to the colleges of your choice.

One day while you were in Shands Hospital in Gainesville, surprise visitors walked in, and Coach Steve Spurrier and Danny Wuerffel entered your room with your eyes big and bright, and they handed you a football signed by all the National Championship players in 1993. Then Coach Spurrier handed you a framed signed photo of the Gator stadium. When you were well, you never missed the Gators play. Through the years, they remain your immediate family's favorite team. Bevo's son named Boykin wanted to attend your alma mater as he loves the Florida Gators because of stories about you.

When you were playing flag football, it was a hazard to you as you had your finger dangling as it got caught in a pocket of a player.

You were rushed to the hospital by your soon-to-be wife. Once married, she took care of all your medical needs.

*****

Later came another surgery for a meningioma benign tumor caused by radiation. He had it successfully removed at Shands, and my daughter and I were at his side with his fiancée for a week. They had cut through his skull above the ear and put a plate in, and a week later, he had surgery to remove the skull plate and infection. He survived his second surgery with his fiancée taking care of his every need, and what a strong man he was. We were at his side praying for his health and successful surgery. Anna (his sister) stayed with him in the hospital during the night as he had some focal seizures. Four months later, he returned to Shands for surgery to have a prosthetic skull piece put in. Two months later, he was back to Shands to have a shunt put in. He had four brain surgeries in less than ten months.

Every time he went to Shands, my heart and mind were there as I held his hand. Anna was also sick at Shands Hospital in the emergency room while Wes was having surgery. Anna had a bad kidney and urinary infection. Anna became a wonderful caretaker taking care of me as I recently became a diabetic. I also had an infliction of kidney stones for many years. I have had three lithotripsies, and my daughter was like having a nurse as she cared for me at our home. Wes was married and doing quite well. Anna moved in with Wes and Jen and helped them around the house. Our prayers have been answered with a wonderful wife who teaches math in Jenson Beach, Florida. Weslee worked with autistic children in the Palm Beach elementary school system.

"Say what you must as long as it's what you really think." With his mom, he could breathe easily and freely. And like me, everyone could share their innermost thoughts with him. Wes had vanities, envies, hates, likes, dislikes, and no one ever had to be careful while he was suffering with cancer. His last surgery and tumor was a glioblastoma, and he was given a terminal diagnosis, crying on the phone as he told me and friends, a call one would never forget as tears came across the phone lines. Weslee took his final breath at age thirty-two with his immediate family gathered around, and hospice was there as he said his final goodbye.

The following words were said to my two remaining children: "Our hearts are broken with your loving brother's death, and I hope now that you, in your adolescence, always remember how this feels because your heart will be broken in the future many times. You'll fight with your friends. You'll blame a new love for things an old one did. You'll cry because time is passing too fast as you watch your children grow, and you'll eventually lose someone else you love," I told my children sincerely. "Bevo and Anna, despite these trials, turbulences, and tribulations, always hold your heads up high and continue on your life's destiny."

Bevo had his children, Boykin and Veda, with biodegradable ingredients, sticks for legs, and painted a Florida lobster and added some of his ashes to have ceremony in the sea. Friends and family gathered at the Key's house and got in several boats. Bevo, his wife, and kids were around as we took to lower the lobster into the Atlantic Ocean just south of Lou Key and said a prayer. It floated and began to sink as we were snorkeling to watch it land on the ocean floor. Wes enjoyed tickling with a tickle stick to capture and eat for dinner. On the cookbook he made for friends and family with his favorite, *Wes's Recipe Book,* he was on the front with his prize lobster he would consume.

On his sister's birthday, his wittiness shined through as Bevo, and he would do a puppet show. Behind a backdrop, they created a show of laughter and smiles from Anna's friends, displaying talents of Wes and Bevo's abilities and creativity. Bevo did not talk much, but the expressions on his face communicated what he needed to say.

Wes often talked for Bevo as I would drive him on many days after school to a speech pathologist that helped him speak clearly and understandably to others. His brother needed not to speak for him ever again as he talked with gladness in his heart.

Dealing with the sorrow of losing a child and brother was painful to us all. As we walked, there were reminders of him almost daily with words he might have said and visions we behold. We carry on living life to the fullest and never forgetting the loving and fun times we shared. He often lived by the following words: With small challenges give you the opportunity to build strength. The big challenges give you the opportunity to make valuable use of force that gets you through other days.

He said, "I am glad I have this as perhaps it saves Bevo and Anna from a tragic event." He was always thinking of others! He fought a long hard battle as he was not ready to die and worried if his wife, he loved dearly, would be all right. In his last breaths, he knew not what was going on but was holding out for a shot that would help him, and it never came.

His celebration of life was held at an indoor pavilion as he loved the beach. Family flew in, and friends of his brother came to support Bevo through the devastating time. Many students, friends, and teachers he worked with and taught were in attendance. ROTC students marched in, and as he was not in the service, they presented him with a dive flag as he loved to see what was under the sea. His immediate family with each saying a few words. A video of him was showed on a screen, and when it showed his picture of skin and bones, I had to get out, and with the overflow of people in attendance, I walked into the arms of Pastor Mark who I worked with and said, "I want him back," as the tears flowed from my eyes. He entered heaven where my brother and other relatives are. I prayed they greeted him at the door of paradise by God, his Maker.

In his last days, I read the book *Heaven Is for Real* to him and didn't get to finish it as God needed him sooner. He had a thirst to know what heaven was like in his last days on earth as no one has come back for him to know what it was like. The book I was reading to him was the closest account of heaven I had read. The account of my eldest son is the hardest words I have written to date as tears still flow from my thought of him.

Shared Memories of Other 1980

After Frank died, family members would look after his wife. She lived in the Mobile house near Downtown Mobile. She had massive antique oriental furniture and player piano when Dad and Cora would take her to visit our grandmother. Other would share about her membership to the Colonial Dames, whose mission was to promote the historic preservation of sites and objects, award scholarships, educating the public on American history, inspire patriotism, and promote fellowship among its members. Its motto is to "gain, retain, train." To be a member, one must be over the age of eighteen or over, who are lineal descendants of an ancestor who lived and served prior to 1701 in one of the original colonies in the geographical area of the USA. It was established in 1915 and is a nonprofit organization in which she was proud to be a member and enjoyed seeing her friends when she was able to attend meetings when she wasn't in Washington, DC.

"My dad taught us all, including my sister, how to shoot and kill the different game living on the plantation fifty miles north of Mobile. We loved tagging through the woods with Dad on the hunting preserve, where he taught us to shoot straight and tell the truth. He took us coon hunting with his dogs as soon as it was dark. We would bring back at least five of the furry little fellows with the feathery tails. He would allow his children to earn forty cents apiece for each coon we killed and then handed us the money. Then she smiled, secured in the wisdom of her own beautiful mother "Blondie," who'd often told her throughout the years, "If one doesn't resolve or learn from the opportunities placed before him, then God will put the prospect before you again." Dad shared the good time he had with his father to his mother.

Another turbulent day arose when James and Fran broke the news to their mother before she read it in the Mobile *Press-Register* newspaper as she would read the paper every morning. Martha, their maid and nanny, was in tears when they told her in the kitchen that Jack died at age fifty-eight on June 26, 1980, from his battle with lung cancer. Martha entered the room when they broke the news to their mother. It was devastating to Other in her elder years and almost turning ninety. She never thought she would outlive another child.

"How can this be? A mother is not supposed to outlive her children!" She broke down in tears of the news.

James went into her medicine cabinet and found a tranquilizer prescribed by her doctor to calm her down as Fran had her drink water to relax her and gave her a pill as her breathing was becoming labored. James called the doctor to come see her, and he made a house call. When the doctor arrived, the tranquilizer had taken affect, and she was sleeping. They woke her up, and the doctor took her blood pressure and pulse as she had pale coloring in her face.

She asked the doctor, "Why are you here?"

"I just wanted to check on you and tell you in person how sorry I am for your loss."

She responded, "That is not supposed to happen as mothers are supposed to go first. I am heartbroken!"

Doctor said, "While I am here, I am going to take your blood pressure and pulse."

She responded, "Okay."

When he read the monitor, her blood pressure was high. He said, "I think James and Fran should take you to the hospital."

She was agitated and said, "No! I want to stay home! Martha is here, and she will take care of me."

Dick (her youngest son) arrived, and she favored and adored him as my father would tell me that. He lived the furthest away in the country near their hunting lodge. He was able to calm her down, and the doctor took her blood pressure again before he left, and it had dropped some but was still high.

Martha listened to what the doctor said and entered the room. "I will set up a cot and sleep with her in her room for the next few nights."

A TURBULENT LIFE ? ? ?

The family agreed and believed she would be better off at home. The doctor left, and they thanked him for coming and wrote a prescription for some sleeping pills to give her an hour before bedtime. James took the prescription and left the house with Dick and Fran still looking after her. He returned to her home with the pills. Martha had set up the cot in her room.

It was getting late, and Dick said, "I will stay with her tonight."

Martha had a room in the back of the house and said, "Oh, all right then, and if you need me, I will be in my back room." Fran and James left for their homes.

At the turn of the year in 1979, Robert's twin brother Jack tragically died of lung cancer. As he grew up, Jack learned that many people couldn't be trusted, and sadly he was betrayed many times in his life. His heart was broken more than once, and it became harder to bear each time, so he turned to smoking as a release of his tension and anxiety. Robert spoke of his twin brother fondly and missed him terribly.

Jack was laid to rest at the family plot in a Mobile cemetery with other family members. James, along with his mother, little brother, and sister, grieved for his loved ones he had lost. All the family realized Jack was in a far better place, believing he was in heaven, and he was young again and was free of any pain that he suffered on earth and reunited with his older brother in heaven and his relatives he had never met. Jack's son and daughter were consoled by my dad James and his wife, Cora, and Aunt Fran; they knew that was what their brother wanted them to do until his children became of adult age.

I recall Other's many stories of her travels to the Orient, Europe, and other countries showing us the pictures and postcards she collected of each country and of her fascinating life with Frank and the nobility she had met along the way. They had seen the world and shared happiness, grief, and sorrows together. I loved hearing about her travels and hoped to journey to those places one day. My grandmother stood by Frank's side through thick and thin.

She said, "It was not always easy, but my belief in God, faith, and teachings from my father as a minister, I learned to cope with all the upheavals and turbulences throughout my married life to Frank. Washington, DC, was a beautiful city, and I would often visit the

Daughters of the American Revolution building with the museum displays from the States. There was never a dull moment in my life."

It was a sad day when Other died in April 1985 at the age of ninety-four. She outlived Frank by eleven years and is buried in the family plot in Mobile, Alabama, with her husband. She never remarried after he died.

Other was remembered by James when she said, "You will be heard by family members and her telling their dad, 'If you're exhausted, rest. Your endless energy is exhausting to me!" She would tell her children, "If you don't like talking and saying something nice, then just be quiet. Time does not have to be filled with endless energy like your dad has. You are enough and just be yourselves."

James tried to follow his mother's advice but was not always able to. Dick was always her favorite child being the youngest, but on her deathbed, she told James, "You and my daughter, I am the proudest of!" James told his sister what she said, and they both smiled in joy for her telling him that.

I was unable to attend as I was married and had young children in school, and my husband was not at home very much. I told my father over the phone the following poem that she loved.

> Count your garden by flowers,
> Never by leaves that fall.
> Count your days by golden hours,
> Don't remember clouds at all.
> Count your nights by stars, not shadows,
> Count your life by smiles, not tears,
> And with joy, count your age by friends, not years.

He told me thank you and found it to be an appropriate statement as he told me that was what my mother would say. Yes, and we both echoed the sentiment "I love you" and proceeded to hang up the phone.

My Recalling Visits to Uncle Brevard's and Aunt Betty's

1983

Robby and I with our mother visited Uncle Brevard's home in Spring Hill that had a gully in the backyard. Robby, his youngest son, and I—and on a few occasions, his oldest son—would play in the gully. We would have a blast climbing and running in it. We would come into their house with mud all over us. Our mother had Robby and I stayed outside while Mom made our goodbyes and took us home in Spring Hill to get cleaned up. We enjoyed playing with our cousins. They moved over the bay to Fairhope, Alabama, where they had a beautiful gray house with a barn, which became Aunt Betty's painting studio. She was talented and would enter art shows with some of her paintings winning awards.

  One day while I was visiting them at their bay house, I rode a bike in their unpaved driveway, and I started screaming, "A snake!" Aunt Betty ran outside to the rescue with a shovel in hand and coached me away from the snake. She explained to me it was a garden snake, and there was nothing to be afraid of as they were not poisonous. When inside, she showed me in the encyclopedia pictures of nonvenomous snakes like the one we saw with a rounded head, but when they flatten their head, they can look like a venomous snake. The venomous snake has a triangular-shape head, and in Alabama and throughout the southern states, we have rattlesnakes, copperheads, cottonmouths (also known as water moccasins), and coral snakes.

"Look at the color of the snake and the pupils of their eyes in this picture, it might give you the answer of rather it is poisonous or not," said Aunt Betty.

I said, "I hate snakes! I never want to get that close to one again!"

Eph was the oldest of our cousins, and his younger sister Francis was a lot younger than her two older brothers. I didn't get to know their daughter well because of the age difference. I had learned that Francis loved to ride horses and would go to horse shows. The oldest son Eph graduated from Vanderbilt University and was on the tennis team and became a masterful tennis instructor at a resort in Gulf Shores, Alabama. The younger son was his mother's favorite known by all that witnessed their interactions together. He was fun and a bit of a jokester and loved asking questions as if he was genuinely interested in the replies.

I recall that my uncle Brevard died in 1983 at the age of sixty-four, which many family members believed he died from the boat motor explosion on the ski, fishing, and leisure boat he owned. He suffered third- to fifth- and eight-degree burns to his face and other areas of his body. He was in excruciating pain on his body from the burns. He and his wife traveled to many doctors to see if they could help him with the horrific pain he suffered from the burns. They visited his sister Browder and Papa in Clearwater, Florida, and saw the best burn doctor in that area. They stayed at the Safety Harbor Spa.

Many in his family believed his dying at age of sixty-four was from the intense pain he endured from the burns. He was too young to die! His wife never remarried. What was interesting to many that noticed the reversed numbers was when his dad died, and when Brevard, my only uncle on mother's side, pondered as to what the numbers meant and how Uncle Brevard died in 1983 and his father's birth was in 1893. Many pondered with the numbers and what they symbolized, or did they symbolize anything? Many family members questioned for years and were unable to produce an answer, other than it was coincidental.

Memories of My Brother Robby

1988

I recall the short time of life's memories with Robby as an adult. Living in Dunedin with Mother and Papa, he had the apartment over the garage. It was fixed up to his liking. Robby was a favorite child to James and Browder as that was evident to all that watched him grow up. One story I remembered was when my brother, a strapping handsome boy of ten, was from the third generation of the family like me. We were staying in the bullpen with ten cousins. We were fast asleep when a howling wind whirled about, waking them all up. In a frenzy, we ran to close all the windows, although the air seemed still and calm outside.

Staying at the lodge, Robby ran down the many flights of stairs to check all the doors below and then ran to check the outside perimeter, where he could not hear a sound except for a slight breeze rustling the trees. Then running back to the bullpen, he told all those who were awake that everyone on the other floors was sleeping and dead to the world.

Robby told them, "Go back to sleep, as all is well."

He told me he could not sleep, as chills ran up and down his spine. Suddenly, it felt as if I am being tickled, and he started giggling, saying, "Stop it, stop it!"

This woke me up, and I asked, "What's wrong?"

He replied, "Stop tickling me!"

I, sleeping next to him, said indignantly, "I'm not."

Robby said, "Who *is?*"

I sat up and shrugged my shoulders, "I don't know." Gas heat kept everyone warm in the cold upstairs room despite the drafty old windows that surrounded the room on all sides. As many as twenty young cousins, boys and girls, slept in the same room at night during the 1950s and 1970s, and pillow fights were a customary ritual everyone loved. As soon as the lights went out, the first pillow would be thrown, and another would be thrown back and another and another until everyone joined in, screaming and laughing.

"Stop it now before someone gets hurt! Stop it!" said Robby, finally out of breath and tired of the game.

No one ceased fire until someone heard the footsteps of an adult coming up the stairs.

"What's this noise and ruckus going on?" asked Aunt Fran.

Soft-spoken and feeling shy, I murmured, "Nothing's happening, Aunt Fran. I was trying to sleep, but everyone else is just pretending to be sleeping."

Returning to Dunedin, Florida

Robby's friends came over often, and they would party in his studio apartment. One day, I was in his apartment and found a letter about the methadone drug to treat pain and narcotic drug addiction. I took the letter and showed it to Mother and Papa. What a mistake that was, and I had no business doing that, but perhaps later I find out there was a silver lining to my doing so.

Papa and Mother confronted my brother with the letter and arranged for him to be in a drug rehabilitation center in New Orleans, Louisiana, and closer proximity to our father and Cora. He reunited with Dad as when we moved out of state and had seen a lot less of. Being near and around Dad more, their bond drew stronger, and he pulled further away from Mother and Papa.

Our dad and Cora visited him often and felt he should have never been placed in that facility. After a short time in the facility, he was released. Dad and Cora were proud of his having a high IQ quotient at that time of being 156. Dad paid for him to attend Tulane University, where he received a bachelor of science degree in foreign languages.

After graduating from Tulane, he obtained a job with *American Horseman* magazine and *American Dog* magazine as a photographer and also did some modeling for other magazines. He moved to New York City. Dad assisted in purchasing a large apartment on the West Side of Manhattan for him to live in as rent was so high, and it was a good investment.

While living in New York, he made many friends. He, with a partner, opened Hurrah nightclub in 1976 on Thirty-Six West and Sixty-Second Street. It featured punk, new wave, and industrial music and served aphrodisiacs and other beverages. Studio 54 was its competition. Both clubs would have lines around the block, and their bouncers stayed busy as many nights they had to turn away people. Robby closed the club in 1980.

He was living with a clothes designer who he was so proud of, and when I visited them in his apartment, he told me he would be famous one day. His prediction was right. Mark became a famous fashion designer and has socialized with many of the rich and famous. He donates a lot of his money to the AIDS foundation.

My brother asked me to give him away when they got married. I said, "Of course, I will."

The day was never to happen as he became ill with AIDS, and at that time, there was no cure for it. He did enjoy life and lived it his way.

My father and Cora brought him from New York to their home when he was still able to travel. They gave him the best care he could have in their home in Mobile, Alabama. They rented a bed that looked like a coffin so he would not get bedsores as he was dying a painful death. Along with Cora's many talents, she could have been a nurse as she knew the right thing to do when administering his medicine.

I left my home and children with their dad to visit my brother for the last time. It was good to see my dad. Robby told me he saw our mother on a stagecoach in the days of cowboys and Indians, and she worked as a saloon girl as he gazed out the window. I told the story to Cora who I called Mimi.

She said, "That must have been the strong medicine he is taking as he must be hallucinating."

"I am sure, Mimi."

My dad and their family added more time to his life on earth as the wonderful caretakers of him. It was so heart-wrenching to me to see him in the state he was in. When I had a problem in my marriage after I was married in 1976, he was the first I called, which was many times, to hear his advice to me.

It haunts me to this day as I ponder the thought of that incident at Gaga's home and my reaction to what happened. Did it contribute to his becoming gay and Hudy and the rumor of the boy violating him, or was it my mom being so strong-willed and dominant to us

A TURBULENT LIFE ? ? ?

growing up? A question I will never have an answer to, but hopefully in heaven, I will get the resolve.

He died on December 20, 1988, at the age of thirty-nine, and it was way too young to die of such a tragic death. It was a devastating and turbulent day when my brother was laid to rest in the family plot in Mobile, Alabama.

I flew into Mobile Airport to attend his memorial service and burial at the family plot in the cemetery. Many family and friends were in attendance. His partner Mark was unable to attend as he was devastated of hearing about his death. He lived in their apartment on the West Side of Manhattan, and Robby left it to him in his will.

My mother and Papa at a later date traveled to Mobile in their motor home and had their own graveside service with friends at a later time. I didn't understand why my mother would not attend his service with other family members. Who was I to question it? There are many days I find myself in 2022 thinking of him, and I still see his face not in photos but in my many memories of the days we shared together. The good advice he would communicate with me. When I visited him in New York, I would stay with my good friend Dede who lived on the East Side of Manhattan.

He is always in my heart, and I know he is with my son Wes who I lost when he was thirty-two. Robby visited my children and family in Melbourne, Florida, while I was married, and they were young. We often look at the picture of him with them at a local restaurant as he had fun teaching them to wave their napkins and using them as bandanas. My son, Bevo, and I can be walking or see a reminder of him online as he remains close in our hearts and is never forgotten.

Ski Trip in North Carolina

1989

I yelled to now my ex-husband, "I told you to let me go in the ambulance, and you and the kids could finish your day of skiing." As usual, you would have no part of that nor listen to me as he only liked to hear his tone and affliction of his voice as a dictator. I began to cry as a sign of shock, shaking, confused, and started hyperventilating. My children Wes was ten years of age, Bevo was eight, Anna was almost six, and they were scared and afraid for their mom as they have never seen me like that before and in such intense pain! It was as if they felt my pain and told their dad, "Hurry and get Mom to the hospital!"

Wes said, "You should have let Mom go in an ambulance!"

After the hour-long drive, we arrived at the emergency room of the hospital. I was unable to walk, and Wes ran and got a wheelchair. I was immediately taken to triage for my vitals, temperature, and blood pressure that had dropped to an unhealthy level. I was taken to an ER room, and the doctor came in and ordered x rays stat. They gave me through intravenous fluids through a needle and tube to deliver the fluid needed as I was dehydrated.

After my x-rays were read, the doctor enters my room and said, "You have a broken tibia bone, which is the larger of the two bones in your lower leg. It is a stable closed fracture."

I asked, "What does that mean?"

Doctor responded, "The broken ends of the tibia line up correctly, and the bone did not break through the skin. Your internal soft tissues such as tendons and blood vessels may be affected by your type of break. They should stay in place during the healing. You are fortunate as it is one of the most common bones to be broken in the lower leg. It confirms that you broke it at the ski boot."

I was relieved when the doctor said, "You don't need surgery. We will cast it, and later you will need physical therapy and at-home exercises. For pain, you should take an anti-inflammatory, or if you like, I can prescribe a narcotic for you."

I opted for the anti-inflammatory and a pain reliever. Endy continued complaining the whole time, even in the hospital. He had to be in control of everything, and his behavior was one of a dictator. The ER doctor ordered stat and medicine for the nurse to give me for pain. Doctor entered and had nurse cast the leg from the knee down. The nurse adjusted crutches for me to use. She bought papers to sign, and I would be released.

Married to a Dictator

1989

Nurse told me to make an appointment with orthopedist when I return home. Endy had no sympathy at all, and I had to manage on my own with my older children helping me.

I later thought he wanted me to die as I learned how heartless and callous he was. My mother had claimed he was stalking me while at college and while working at Walt Disney World. I didn't believe her but later realized my mother was telling the truth. He understood I was from a family that had money and class with which he wanted to become a part of. He had told me he had no friends.

That was the start of the collapse of the marriage and lack of communication to one another as well as the criticism to me becoming more prevalent! I began to realize he was heartless and cold as a fish! I deducted and finally reasoned and understood why he had no friends! It was as if ice ran through his veins. He would constantly put people down as he was so insecure in not knowing himself or his identity. Putting people, especially his wife, down made him feel better about himself as he would bully others. He was living with an identity crisis in never knowing who he really was until two years into the marriage. That was when I started to believe people should live together for two years before getting married.

I wanted to have children and had trouble at first, but after seeing my gynecologist, I learned I could have children even though I had an irregular period as it didn't come every month, and it could be two or three months or longer. When I became pregnant, it was awfully hard for the doctor to determine the due date.

A TURBULENT LIFE ? ? ?

As a Rotary district governor, entertaining other district governors that stayed in our home, we attended local rotary clubs and functions. It was customary to buy drinks for the visiting dignitary and his wife. Unfortunately, Ken had not done that, and his wife, observing the custom, would do it as not to be embarrassed her husband's lack of gentlemanly manners. He would find himself to busy, gabbing to other people. I would come to pity and feel sorry for him as he had never learned how to be a gentleman.

The next day, he brought the boys with him to see Anna. The boys climbed on top of the small hospital bed while I was holding her, and it got crowded quickly.

Wes said, "She has hazel eyes like mine."

Bevo struggled to say, "Me too."

We were able to take her to our new two-story house with each having their own room. The boys helped build by carrying the two-by-fours from the rental house down the street to the new house. It was built with a lot of sweat and tears.

Each child had their own room, and Anna had a crib in hers for the first eighteen months as she was in no hurry to climb out as the boys were. The day had come, and we were in our cabin near Brevard, North Carolina. Endy and I and the children were walking through an old furniture store in downtown Brevard. We were upstairs and saw a one-of-a-kind beautiful Singer French provincial furniture set as a dollhouse with thatched roof on double bed and large six-drawer dresser with mirror, and two bedside tables. She would put miniature dollhouse pieces in each room of the furniture and loved to play in her room. My three children would fight for me to put them to bed and stay until they were fell asleep. I said prayers with all three and stayed in bed until they were fast asleep. Some nights would take longer than others.

Bevo, everyday once he was school-age, loved swimming, and I immediately placed him on a swim team. They would practice in the morning and evening in order to keep body and soul together in the heat of the day with respiration weighing heavily on the heart and soul. Water relieving pressures of the day running in and out. The coolness of the water swiftly rolling by as the jets as his feet would propel him through with tensions in school were washed away. Relieving the stress, emotions sounding the beat of the heart to rise had him prepared for many swim races, earning many metals and ribbons. He was a formidable competitor who came in first place in the heats and overall winner.

Bevo once placed number 6 in the state of Florida for the butterfly stroke in a junior Olympic swim meet held in Orlando, Florida. He could easily outswim any competitor, man or beast. He had a 102 temperature and chills; he laid in a corner wrapped in a towel until it was time for him to swim. It was "ready, get set," the gun was fired, and all dove in from six platforms to swim the fifty-yard butterfly, which was two lengths of the Olympic-size pool. Bevo's best stroke!

After several heats swam, the family waited for the results before returning to hotel. Toward the end of the day, the results were posted, and Bevo, eagerly looking at the sheets hung up, saw he came in sixth place with swimmers from all over the state. Being sick and if he had no fever, the family and his coach felt he would have placed higher and possibly had been the first-place winner. The coolness of the water swiftly rolled by as the jets pound the skin and tensions of the day away. Relieving the stress, emotions sounding the beat of the heart to rise swim in order to keep body and soul together in the heat of the day with respiration weighing heavily on the heart and soul was Bevo's motto. Returning to the hotel, he was exhausted and fell straight to sleep.

"Bevo like his granddad has always been a friend to everyone, a true friend, one with whom you could dare to be yourself." He was also an adventurer as a daredevil like Dad's older brother Frank Junior. Praise God he has outgrown that time as he is a father of my grandson turning thirteen and a daughter who is nine.

Turner Classic Movie (TCM)

Late 1990s

The Walt Disney Cruise Line from Port Canaveral, Florida, is where my roommate of almost a century worked. At Port Canaveral, she would greet and check in guest into their staterooms as the guest boarded, and she would wish the bon voyage. The newest Disney Wish's ship will dock there as well. The Disney ships have their own terminal with characters greeting you as you enter the ship. Bellman greet you at the curb, taking your luggage to be delivered to your stateroom before parking in an empty space. I enjoyed my cruises with the Disney Cruise Line, and it felt like I was traveling first-class. A most memorable experience for all that have the pleasure of taking a Disney Cruise, especially those with children as they had their own area to play in and were treated as VIP guest.

I was on a Turner Classic Movie Disney Cruise (TCM) with celebrities such as the host Ben Mankiewicz, as well as others that were with the TCM movie company. Lucie Arnaz was the daughter of Lucille Ball and Desi Arnaz, who acted on stage and owned her touring show. *Jeopardy!* host Alex Trebek had a full house as he would play the game jeopardy with participants aboard the ship. It was his last cruise with TCM as he died in 2020 from stage 4 pancreatic cancer. He lives in the memories of many guest from his cruising days as well as *Jeopardy!* honoring him the way he deserved as he died in 2020 and never to be forgotten as he lives in the hearts of many watchers of the famed game show host.

Guest host took his place until two were named as his replacements, *Jeopardy!* all-time champion, Ken Jennings was a software engineer, is a consulting producer of *Jeopardy!*, has written several books, and appears as an expert on the game show called the *Chase*, and very intelligent. Mayim Bialik, PhD brain scientist, and known for her appearances on the show *Big Bang Theory*, *Call Me Kat*, and other television shows. She was the child who played Bette Midler in one of my favorite movies, *Beaches* in 1988. She obtained her doctorate degree in neuroscience, and she is a neurobiologist, and as the saying goes, "Smart as a whip!"

Other celebrities were Kim Novak, an American retired actress who was popular in her forties until she retired and started painting. On the Disney Cruise, she sold some of her beautiful paintings. Her real name was Marilyn Pauline Novak from Chicago, Illinois, and was a delight to talk to. *Dick Cavett* was the title of several talk shows he hosted and a comedian on various television shows taped in New York City, occasionally in Los Angeles, New Orleans, and London in the 1960s through the 2000s and hosted many actors and actresses and appeared in movies as well.

Jerry Lewis was an American comedian, actor, singer, director, producer, and was in a wheelchair on board ship and started in one of my favorite movies *The Nutty Professor* and could make any one laugh. Michael York, an English film, television, and stage actor, and my favorite was seeing him in *Cabaret*, and he had a battle with amyloidosis, a rare disease caused by abnormal deposits of proteins called amyloids in various tissues of the body, and he was having fun on the last cruise he would take. He lived in Minnesota, receiving treatment at Mayo clinic for his disease.

The Lawsuits That Changed the Family Dynamics of the Family-Owned Land and Timber Company

1987, 1988, 1993

The years 1987 to 1988 were turbulent years for the family-owned corporation as well as the family members. My father and Aunt Fran's youngest brother Dick along with their deceased brother Jack's wife and children joined as plaintiffs in the lawsuit.

They reached an agreement in 1993. Dick and Jack's wife entered into an agreement of hunting lands of 2,100 acres and hunting leases. Dick and Jack's wife gave up 27,000 acres of land and a $40,000.00 hunting lodge in consideration of $75,000.00. They also received approximately forty million dollars in assets they split between the two families. Sadly, it took extraordinarily little time for them to spend the money with which they became broke. It took little time for them to squander it.

Dick and his two boys are dead today. They played hard, and the boys died too young. Jack's children spent their money like wildfire, and his children didn't have any of the money they received either. Working became a way of life for them.

An opinion of a lawsuit of deficiency of $5,496,674 in the federal estate tax of the estate of Frank. The case involved stock in the family-owned land and timber company in Alabama and was sued in 1987 and 1988. The lawsuit of the Dick and Jack's wife's families as Jack had deceased. Dick talked Jack's wife, and they together filed a lawsuit against the company. People believe if Jack were alive, the lawsuit would not have occurred with his family joining in with Dick's lawsuit.

Another suit involved a dispute over hunting rights. The plaintiffs stated because of the way the hunting was done in the fall of 1992, it was unsafe to hunt the land. The trial court ruled failure to properly post the property, as well as their dumping garbage, building tree stands, and planting inappropriately. The two trust that changed the dynamics of the company came to an agreement designated as a "hunting lease" of approximately 2,100 acres in Clarke County, Alabama. The agreement provided, among other things, that his licensees and his invitees had the right "to enter upon the lands held by Lesser and hereby leased to Lessee;" that they had the right to hunt or fish on the leased property; that they would not do any act that would become hazardous to the growing of timber; they would comply with state laws; not construct any plantings, food plots, roads, structures, and so forth without the written consent of the owner; that they would keep the property clean; that they would keep all gates closed and locked; and that, if requested, they would post the land with black-on-yellow signs containing the names of the owner; and the hunter. The agreement provided for annual rent, beginning at $840.00 per year. The agreement was for hunter's lifetime.

It was unfortunate after a few years that the agreement was not upheld. They lost their money, and the boys died at what would be considered a young age in today's times. Some family members believed the lawsuit contributed to their mother's death, worry, and her heart to give out. James said, "Her youngest son was his mom's favorite, and it was obvious to those watching him grow up. It was so sad to witness him sue the family-owned company, and ultimately he was her greatest disappointment."

In the settlement, ultimately Aunt Fran's side and James's family retained the commerce. Her only son is currently president of the company, and his side has future generations offering suggestions to maintain the holdings and initiate and innovative ideas. The vice president and accountant keep impeccable accounting for the company taxes. She knows the numbers backwards and forwards and a great asset, especially to the titled secretary and treasurer of the company that deals with hunting clubs. Also, shopping, providing food for family and judges hunts. Those in heaven are looking down upon them and smiling!

Food plots were not breaches of the lease; therefore, the lease was valid. The trial court upheld the hunters' rights under the lease needed not to be addressed in the courtroom. Dick and Jack's wife after he had died sued with Dick and his two sons the family company. After several years, they squandered their money and didn't maintain the property in the agreement. Dick and his oldest son moved away after several years to another state.

The younger son remained with his family in the area and tried to maintain the property but found he had little help. Dick's children passed away at a relatively young age.

Some of Jack's children are still alive, and little is known about them today. Aunt Fran and James's family, other than through lawsuits, never had anything to do with Dick's side of the family nor Jack's side of the family because of the expense, frustration, tensions, and sorrow of the lawsuit.

Bevo in 2004 DEKE Fraternity Brothers

Three fraternity brothers from the University of South Alabama were visiting the lodge. The visitors and Bevo brought along his dog, a young lean and frisky Boykin spaniel, were staying by themselves in the expansive lodge, which contained within it more than seven thousand square feet, fourteen rooms, and eight bathrooms. It was a late pitch-dark, summery night when they all decided to retire to the upstairs rooms to sleep. As they closed their eyes, however, doors began opening and closing with a bang.

The athletic, well-built young men came out of their rooms and asked each other, "What was that?"

Bevo was frightened as they replied, "I don't know, but let's go and look."

Everyone, including Roxy, Bevo's dog, went downstairs, yelling, "Is anyone here?"

There was no reply as they inspected each and every room of the lodge. Suddenly they noticed Roxy had disappeared and was nowhere to be found. They yelled and yelled for her, but Bevo's devoted and usually faithful dog would not answer his desperate call. Meanwhile, the doors and windows continued to open and shut as the strong breeze blew through the house. Every one of them was terrified and shaking in his boots, not knowing what to do next. Despite their fears, however, the boys continued to hunt for Roxy, fearing for her safety, and stuck close together as they searched with no weapons in hand, except for their own brawn. Finally, after almost two hours, they found her in the wee hours of the morn, shivering in her hiding place under a bed. They left and vowed never to stay there again by themselves.

A TURBULENT LIFE ? ? ?

Boykin and Veda, my son's children, called me Gaga, and at times Grandmother. Some of their favorite memories are of fishing from my dad's cabin on his own man-made lake. Young and old would sit in rockers, fishing with cane poles and using live crickets as bait to catch small, medium, and large perch right off the front porch. Dad taught all his grandchildren to bass fish, using a rod, a reel and a black squiggly rubber worm with a hook. The children loved it and caught all sorts of fish this way.

At night, with bright lights, Boykin and Veda in their dad's truck would look up high into the sky and trees above to see if they saw eyes of a coon to shoot. They would give their kills to Lizzy the maid at the lodge to take home and consume.

When not catching fish in the lake from the porch of Granddad's log cabin, the kids would jump into Bevo's truck and head to another fishing hole on his property. There they would catch loads of fish for breakfast at Dad's log cabin, that James his houseman would clean and fried up for breakfast. He would serve up the succulent fish with cheese grits and eggs, one of the finest breakfasts one could ever choose. James would also cut tenderloins of a deer and wrap in bacon to serve as appetizers. Oh, how delicious they were and consumed until there were no more. Later the kids and adults headed to the berry patch near the lodge that was filled with luscious, ripened blackberries. They would fill large bags, and with smiles and lots of laughter, they would sneak a berry or two to eat straight from the bush. Even without washing the wild fruit, they all survived childhood without getting sick. Fun was had by all as an adult would tell them stories from the recent books she'd read while they picked the juicy berries.

At the hunting lodge, Boykin and Veda enjoyed feeding apples to the donkey and horse in the fenced in area near the lodge, and they enjoyed their treats and would often ask for more with heehaws, and the horse would sound like he was sneezing.

I recall my special times with Grandmother Other when the pecans flourished on trees in front of the lodge. Collecting enough for pecan pies to be made for desert and be eaten by all. It is sad to say the pecan trees are there no more as freezes and hurricanes had them die and taken away to have no more.

While Bevo Was Living in Mobile with His Granddad

He attended a junior college and enjoyed doing homework which his granddad could help him and being just hanging out with him. He loved going hunting on weekends during the different hunting seasons. Unfortunately, the wetlands along the gulf coast have suffered extensive loss of food sources and nesting habitats for waterfowl. The suffering has been made worse by declines in acorns and aquatic invertebrates such as amphipods on the hunting lands in Alabama.

Despite this, Bevo, with his gun, often set out in his aluminum Jon boat with Roxy and his waterproof boots and waders on the Tombigbee River. He hauls his new ultrarealistic decoys and spreads them out wherever he felt the ducks may land. He had ten full-bodied mallard decoys that he placed not too close to one another, and two bigger and darker goose decoys to help attract any birds that may be farther away. Once with the decoys floating about fifteen yards from his boat, Bevo turned into a blind and waited with his automatic twelve-gauge shotgun and Roxy for the birds to come. Anxious to jump into the water, Roxy was restless but sat still as some ducks landed nearby. Bevo raised his gun, fired, and killed one duck on the water and another two on the wing as they flew away. Roxy immediately plunged into the water, gently fetching the first bird in her mouth and bringing it back to the boat. Then Bevo sent her back for another and another until Roxy had returned all the beautiful wood ducks in perfect condition. With not one torn or tattered, Bevo's training of her had paid off. Bevo and Roxy proudly returned to the lodge with their ducks in time for them to be cleaned and prepared for dinner. Sadly, Roxy died and was buried in the woods; she was loved so dearly.

Bevo found a new Boykin spaniel he named Rubie. She is a house dog and friendly to everyone having never met a stranger. She is afraid of lightning and not the hunting dog he had hoped, but Ruby stole his heart and his families as well.

Bevo would often live by the word to follow to teach his son and daughter the following: "As a toddler, I could not speak as my brother did my talking for me. The way out of disappointment is through effort. The way out of worry and anxiety is through energy to seek new things to fill your mind with happiness! The way to get beyond the obstacles of unfairness and anxiety standing in your path is with determination and looking ahead, blocking out the memories that may be holding you back. At school, positive work can energize your spirit for the best outcome. Keep your mind free of any rumors and staying a straight course with a positive frame of mind. Sticks and stones may hurt you, but words never have to hurt you."

While attending college, Bevo also had a job and went into the roofing business at age eighteen and in the summer worked on a lobster boat while in the Keys. He later married and had Boykin and Veda. He worked hard in providing for his children and his lovely Christian wife, Valery. They stayed in shape as they were involved with a gym. Each of them now do the triathlon and practice bright and early every Sunday before the rising sun and heat of the day as they prepare to enter competitions. Bevo and Valery are die-hards, and they work together in perfect harmony to stay young and in shape. They currently are in training once or twice a week preparing for triathlon competitions. Living a healthy lifestyle, keeping them young.

The Family-Owned Land and Timber Company from 1988 to 2022

Power lines and food plots for the game. Audubon indemnity through the Alabama Wildlife Federation, tree stands, posting the property signs as dealing with trespassers became an ordinary occurrence. The language and yelling from trespassers that would become so agitated, while the owners and caretakers had to maintain their composure. Posted no trespassing signs were throughout the property. Hunting trespassers would pay no attention to them. Caretakers of the land would find dumped garbage, tree stands, and planted food plots. Families learned it is no easy task to preserve and maintain leased hunting land as well as the owned land, only to be used by family and guest throughout the years. Each year goes by, more money is needed to maintain the hunting lodge, acreage, caretakers, and cooks and cleaning staff and newer buildings added to accommodate the increased size of the families.

    I have learned there is a lot to know about maintaining hunting lands and keeping families happy. Learning how to deal with power lines, easements, and throughout the year's lawsuits. Dealing with the hunting rights, trespassers, and hunters infringing on the hunting land have been a common plague to the company. Aunt Fran's and James's side of the family have maintained through the company a team of attorneys throughout the years to deal with the legal issues in preserving the land.

    Some frivolous lawsuits have been before judges about preserving the hunting lands, poachers, leases, hunting rights, boundary lines, and mundane land issues. Attorneys have made a lot of money from the family and lawsuits throughout the years. Many of the third

A TURBULENT LIFE ? ? ?

and fourth and future generations know, from participating, how hard it is to run a family-owned corporation, especially to benefit all concerned and maintain peace with family conflicts and through the mounting pressures of upkeep and retaining land revenue. The turbulent life gets more prevalent throughout the years in dealing with numerous family members that don't always agree or agree completely on pressing issues. Through Frank's motto, "Everything is made for love." It seems to melt people's hearts, and all is well as love flourishes.

Suggestions often go unheard as to the direction the company should go to grow for future generations. The mundane issues, the president and staff of the company have to deal with, can cause them a waste of time that they could be using in solving and negotiating more pressing issues.

The president and many of the family members realize the vice president and financial manager is one of the greatest assets to the company. She is the one who keeps impeccable accounting and knows the numbers better than anyone in the company. She has stayed with the company for around thirty years or more and has seen it through its difficulties and always comes out on top with her numbers.

Many family members are thankful for the leadership of the president and staff of the family-owned company, which has changed over the years but always passed on to future generations. Onward and upward to the future generations with the company. Aunt Fran's side of the family and the president of the company have maintained, negotiated, and continued to leave a legacy to future generations. Many of the third generation have not had to work as the president and a small staff have increased the earnings of the company to support many with monthly sums of money.

The oldest Tarasee has worked in the company, maintaining hunting clubs, the lodge, and family hunts. Her degrees were in physical education. She would purchase the food and unable to delegate to people who offered to help. She would carry the food herself for the cooks to prepare and complain at times for having to do it. She also made the menus for the family hunts and worked with the full-time caretakers of the land.

The current president followed in his mother's footsteps as being the only female president of the company. As a grandson of Frank, founder of the family-owned business, Frank looks down from heaven proudly as does his mother and father of his many accomplishments and the advancements he has made with the company. Having a bachelor of science degree in commerce and business administration from the University of Alabama made him the perfect candidate for becoming the president of the company. He worked with his father's real estate development committee and has a real estate license. He served as secretary/treasurer of the company and, nine years later, became president in 1988.

The president has continued to grow the company for his only child and cousins of the third and fourth generations to continue to suggest and has implemented more ways for the company to grow for future generations. Many praise God as Frank, James, and Aunt Fran's side of the family with Will and Lee as board members continuing today to increase Frank's legacy. They have fourth generation learning to continue the tradition of leaving the company and interests to future generations. They realize the ingenuity and education in diverse fields of work will lead the company into the future with all sides hopefully in agreement and listening and digesting what others have to say in growing the company with open minds in hearing the entire suggestions with no interruptions.

He has negotiated and has the company moving into solar agreements as energy-saving methods are a way of preserving the future. No one would parlay the medium of hunting and tree acreage to their professional advantage than the president and staff of the family-owned company, which has changed over the years, but always passed on to future generations. He has given his time generously to many service organizations, hunting and fishing organizations, and has made contacts throughout the world in helping the family business diversify in many ways.

Technologies continuously help the direction of the company as it moves into the potential, earning power of vast opportunities! Major changes have occurred throughout the inception of the family-owned business to keep up with the current trends as it contin-

A TURBULENT LIFE ? ? ?

ues making advances in technology, energy, and what Frank loved the most was holding on to some of the land with trees, water, and the white antebellum home the families call the lodge. He wanted it to be enjoyed by the relatives and friends of the family until the end of time!

As the years pass by, it is expensive to maintain the lodge with constant upkeep and maintenance of appliances, windows, painting, fixing foundation issues, additions for the growing families, and what is needed in updates and recommendations are being offered for of the lodge to earn money to keep it up. Renting and advertising in magazines for the use of the lodge with a large nonrefundable deposit. If cancellation period has exceeded, its time has been recommended to the president and current board members of the company to pursue with advertising as well. The removal of artifacts and things of value were offered or sold to family members that would like them.

I feel pursuing oil and gas exploration around the head of the Tombigbee River as the geologist recommended to my grandfather in the 1930s, which an oil well has not been drilled in that area. Surrounding oil wells near that property have been producing a good income for the owners. Getting creative and going back in time to all the uses that Frank had created on the land in the past. Some were outdated, but others could still be useful.

As a past American history and geography teacher, researching current and ancient times, especially in learning the story of my grandfather's legacy, is a passion of mine. I am aware of history sometimes repeating itself and personally feel going back in time was a way to move forward into the current years and future.

I also feel looking into the future of the possibility of any of the acreage that could be used for a growing process of bringing nature indoors with Mother Nature helping in the ability to cultivate the soil. Growing indoors, hydroponics promotes a root system that is healthier in producing long-lasting plants. Having the plants in an indoor growing system can make the best conditions for growing food for future populations as well as those of today. Help in making a global food system and organically grown. May be an expensive endeavor but later could make many earnings for the future of Alabama as well as the family-owned company. The organic food industry would be beneficial for the family-owned business to look into. Most of all living beings cannot live without food and water as well as applying ingenuity from the past to the current year of 2022.

In teaching history, I discovered it hard for public schools to keep present with history schoolbooks as history changes so rapidly. In 1973, I found myself teaching in the history schoolbook that the Berlin Wall had not come down with, which it had, and I realized it is hard for school history books to stay current. Historiographers are often frustrated with the current times and changes of past times being told incorrectly. An example is how President Hoover, in his time, was considered a bad president, and in today's time, he is considered a good president by historians. It can be found in many areas where history can repeat itself.

President and staff of the family-owned company have changed over the years but always passed on to future generations. Technologies continuously help the direction of the company as it moves into the potential and earning power of vast opportunities! Major changes have occurred throughout the inception of the family-owned business to keep up with current trends as it continues making advances in technology, energy, innovative ideas, and what Frank loved the most was holding on to some of the land with trees and water close to the railroad tracks that he wanted to be enjoyed by the families until the end of time! Frank and Other with their large handworks and giving hearts would be appalled at the greed of the families that sued and departed the family-owned business. Most of them had died at early ages from neglect and not maintaining the agreement they had made with the company. He would also be thrilled at the way the two current families are maintaining the land and lodge for future generations for he and his wife's legacy to live on.

Moved to Fairhope, Alabama, in 1998 to Be Near with My Birth Father James

I moved to Southern Alabama to be near with my elderly father both in our older years. I bonded with my dad and learned about his favorite memories with his sharp long-term memory, and his short-term memory had dissipated when he was in his '80s and '90s. His most memorable years to talk about at that time was being in World War II. I loved hearing of my father's repeated World War II experiences time after time as they never got old to me. He had me read many times his copious letters he had written home to his family and were preserved in a scrapbook. James had learned from his father to write many letters. He wrote to his parents and twin brother and sister that was taking care of the family business and watching over his mother and father. Dad enjoyed serving his country, especially his love of flying even in those harrowing times.

Riding in the car with the youngest male driving, my dad was heard saying, "I wish I had taken your brother to live with us." I felt worse than insulted when he said that, which was more than a dozen times. Almost every time, he was in the car with his youngest son caring for him. On his sixteenth birthday, my father purchased a brand-new green mustang for Robby. I felt slighted and unwanted throughout my years of childhood to adulthood from my mother and father. My father purchased a five-year-old 1963 white Chevrolet impala automobile for my sixteenth birthday in 1968. That was proof to me I was just a secondhand person to them. It was confirmed to me in later years when I moved to in 1998 to Fairhope.

Learning of One's Phobias

As the author, I have found in living my life with nine broken bones and frequently associated with my impairment of gait and balance (my balance is zero) and association that it is medicated through cognitive and motor pathways have been found to help some people but not me.

Physical therapy and balance exercises, I have experienced it and found helpful and fun to do. One was putting signs on doors in a hallway and looking left to right as I walked. Another was outside and using a deck of cards looking straight, left, or right, turning my head as I walked and telling the physical therapist what card it was as she would hold it up, right or to the left or down. I was able to do that excise regularly at the condominium I had purchased in Fairhope, Alabama. Also, walking a white line in the road, she taught me a lot of tricks of her trade.

I have had a pin in my wrist, breaking my right ankle four times, fifth metatarsal bone on my right toe, and later on my left toe and broken leg. Learning it is common after a fall although it can occur in the absence of a fall. FOF has been described as a symptom rather than a diagnosis itself.

To stop my fear of falling, the orthopedist told me the things to do to diminish my fear and handed me instructions on a sheet of paper to follow.

"There are several things that would help you to stop or curve back your fear of falling. My diagnosis from research I have done on the subject that your many falls have caused you to have basophobia."

I asked, "What is that?"

"Basophobia is from your falling throughout adulthood." He helped me realize that living alone with my computer and keyboard was a way of releasing my life story and developed phobias in adulthood. He insisted I must have exercise other than sitting in front of my computer, writing my life story, only using my fingers and mind. I purchased a small treadmill and exercise bike desk, utilizing every space in the apartment. I found myself living and dealing with my fear of falling (FOF), which was a reasonable fear of mine from my anxiety toward walking alone in breaking over nine bones. My most recent fall, I had no balance and had muscle weakness in my legs and feet. I have broken a bone every time I walked by myself and would often fall as an adult. I broke my left thumb when I fell near a swimming pool while walking to the apartment rental office. I realized I fell because I was not focusing on my steps nor paying attention to my surroundings as I was depressed as I had been seized by the nicknamed, oldest and dictator of the three stooges Tarasee who convinced my son Bevo that he had to intercede in order to help his mother.

Orthopedist ordered an MRI, and the nurse scheduled my next appointment with the doctor. My son Bevo drove me to the appointment.

The orthopedist said, "You reinjured an old injury to your shoulder, causing you intense pain."

I recalled putting a Christmas tree away on New Year's Day in Melbourne, Florida, in our two-story home. As I got to the top of the stairwell with the seven-foot artificial tree, I fell six feet, and my wrist swelled up to the size of a baseball. My husband called the neighbor across the street, and she ran over and made a sling with a magazine, and she watched the kids as my husband drove me to the emergency room of the hospital in Melbourne, Florida, arriving there on apparently the busiest day of the year.

With ice on it continuously, they finally called me to the triage, taking my vitals and accessing the damage to the injury. It was in the late afternoon, and I was taken to a room, and the doctor had surgery scheduled so late I had to stay overnight in the hospital to put a pin into my small bone in the right wrist as it was broken.

The orthopedist replied, "As a way of your learning to live by yourself and to address your fear of falling (FOF), first, you need to identify why you are falling and take action to reduce the risk. Then you must have full concentration and looking down with each step you take. Second, devise a plan for getting help if you should fall. I suggest you carry your cell phone with you every time you walk alone. Share your thoughts to someone about your fears and anxiety of having a fall and then set small achievable goals to help you feel more confident again."

I interrupted him and said, "I have friends as well as acquaintances who have noticed I go from side to side as I walk. Thus, unable to walk a straight line. If I am stopped by a policeman, they might think I was drunk. I have found that looking down at each step, I don't see my surroundings fully if I am carrying boxes."

Orthopedist responded, "You need to keep active, and if not outside, do it inside. Practice relaxation techniques."

I declared to the orthopedist my main challenge was my unhelpful thoughts with having so many broken bones and reinjuring a shoulder to find out that I have a bone spur and was concerned my shoulder could freeze up, so I have to move it throughout the day.

He replied, "I want to see how you progress in two weeks."

My primary doctor in Milton, Florida, treated my osteoporosis with medicine. After my last fall carrying boxes to a dumpster and falling on the hard pavement, I was x-rayed and had no broken bones. Alleluia! The medicine was working.

In recalling my memories of the past, I understood that time does not heal everything or the turbulences and mishaps one endures during their life but through one's belief in God. I was able to have forgiveness in my heart as Jesus has showed with all he endured while he was on earth with which no one could ever compare what he suffered to their own!

I have never been perfect or thought myself to be. I have said things that have made no sense to others. I have misquoted words, not knowing there full meaning. I have battle scars from childhood and adult life of being bullied by other people, challenges, physical pain, hearing loss, and losses of loved ones. I had learned to grow up and love with all my heart, putting others before a quest of money, power, or fame.

A TURBULENT LIFE ? ? ?

I have matured from all my personal experiences rather good. Turbulent, bad, and losses of loved ones, it has helped me to deal with trauma and healing, which has enabled me to rebuild myself and live a fulfilled life with no remorse in the way I live on in my elderly years. As time has moved by slowly or swiftly, I learned what acquaintances said about me make no difference. It is the people who show their genuineness, caring, wisdom, and love of God as one should listen and pay attention to as my many Christian friends showed their love of self from smiling from their inner soul outwardly and how others would be attracted to the trait they displayed. With respect and liking the energy that is exhibited, therefore, wanting to be a friend and those observing want to implement the affection of self into their own lives!

If one is able to laugh and smile with friends or family and follow their dreams, you are blessed and able to have a full and complete life while visiting on earth and to encounter your next journey. A heart that is in tune with others and shows compassion, kindness, understanding, freedom with no expectations or limits to be themselves is perhaps the best way to show true love to yourself and therefore able to show to others.

Lies, Arrest, and a Family's Dirty Laundry

I have to achieve knowing myself in ways I had never known before and finding myself in a situation of drafting this book in isolation seemingly from the entire world for me to move on with my life. I asked myself the question: Did they remove me from reconnecting with my daughter because of money, or was it caused by families' jealousy and envy of one's life? Or God or the devil, who would be so devious in thinking they were helping a person by abducting them and putting them in an unknown city, not knowing anyone?

Suddenly I was left to recall life's soul in solitude of one's life in writing. I recall remembrances of the past flowing fast and furiously with sad and fun-filled reminders of life's doors opening to the soul.! Late in life, doors to the depths of the soul open in complete solitude is earth shattering to the one that experienced learning of all the lies and deceptions of my father's three stooges and oldest son that they had committed legally and illegally.

In my adult years, I moved to Fairhope, Alabama, and purchased a condominium in Southern Alabama, observing a family that had not learned right from wrong over the years. They continued living with blinders on and living in the past without moving forward through the years as the three stooges. They continued to abduct unwilling participants, lie, cheat, open marriages, having a child with a Black woman that others may or may not know about. They continued paying people off from not pursuing lawsuits and alcoholics that continue to get through life with pain pills and alcohol. They continued playing thousands and perhaps hundreds of thousands of dollars at Mississippi casinos and in New Orleans.

A TURBULENT LIFE ? ? ?

Tarasee was known as a high roller with her casino host and earning many chartered flites to Lake Tahoe, Reno, Las Vegas, and other destinations. Tarasee, oldest of the three stooges, would often brag about how good of a snow skier she was, and it was a good way to pry her away from the casino.

Tarasee would tell people of her horror story, being pulled over by police with their sirens roaring. Shortly after she left, the youngest brother of the three stooges, son's wedding, and reception with her partner, Tarasee found a place to pull over. She was given an alcohol analyzer test, and her number was over the legal limit. She was put into a police car and driven to a local jail. Her picture and fingerprints were taken as a routine by the booking officer. She was placed in a psychiatric area of the jail as the officer arrested her for a DUI (driving under the influence of alcohol). She described her story of staying in the psychiatric area of jail for DUIs until her bond was posted the next day.

I had a terrible arrest happen to me after attending to my oldest son's graduation at the University of Florida in Gainesville, Florida, where he received his degree in public relations and advertising. We drove to a restaurant to have a celebration lunch. While just sitting down to the table and being handed a menu, an officer entered the restaurant, asking for the owner of my car. The officer walked me over to the car. My thirty-two-pound black English Pomeranian named Bear had been placed in a pet officer's car. My two sons and daughter followed me out to the car with the officer. I was speechless as two pet officers were going to release me!

The policeman, as my sons told me, said, "They were showing off in a university town to a rookie cop and the pet policemen."

He arrested me for not having enough ventilation in the car on a hot day for a dog. Bear was known for his panting, and I had water and air from the windows cracked, and the window on top of the car was open, letting air in. My friends had their car and had driven back to their home in Clearwater as they could not do much to help.

I called my stepfather, Papa, who was like a loving father to me. The judge in Pinellas County, Florida, would like to speak with the office, but the officer would not talk to the judge under any circumstances! I was placed in the police car and arrested for cruelty of animals.

Riding in the back of the police car and transported to a local police station, I cried and sniffled with no Kleenex to wipe my nose, and tears were streaming down my face as I was being driven to jail. I was innocent and never experienced such an outlandish nightmare and perhaps the most horrible night of my life.

Entering, the booking officer took a picture and my fingerprints. The female officer booking me had me undress and put their black undergarments and a shirt and pants that were slipping off as I walked. The jail jumpsuit was way too large for me! The female officer opened the holding cell door to enter the cold, dark, cell near the lobby that appeared to be clean. I was able to hear others throughout the night being booked. The officer was stationed across the hall from the holding cell. I heard language I had never learned before, as officers were booking drunks and others for unknown reasons to me. I could hear the cussing and words I had never heard before as I could not stop crying and sniffling, wiping my tears and snot from my nose onto the jail shirt the female officer had me wear. I had never cried so much in my life, and it was when I was released from the jail as the sun was rising and was able to put my own clothes on.

My two sons and daughter were on the phone throughout the night, trying to find a bondsman that was open to obtain a $1,000 bond for me to be released. They were all closed, and the jail was also closed, except for those being booked for their arrest. At dawn, they sat on doorsteps of the jail, waiting for it to open. My sons and daughter were sitting on the front doorsteps of the bondsman's door when he opened his office. None of the family members were able to sleep that night as it was the most turbulent night for all involved. It was the most humiliating and turbulent episode in my immediate family's life series of sagas!

Upon my release, my children sat in front of the jail, waiting for it to open. My two sons and daughter embraced me like never before. It was as if we had not seen each other for what seemed to be an eternity. I shared my nightmare experience with my son's family as they shared theirs when I finally stopped talking!

A TURBULENT LIFE ? ? ?

They all huffed and puffed at what occurred and turned from a great day of watching my oldest son with friends from Clearwater as we watched my son's graduation from the University of Florida with a degree in journalism. It was in the early wee hours of the morning. I exited the door and felt I had seen sunshine for the first time in my life! It was an earth-shattering event that occurred to me and my immediate family's life. The day turned to turmoil and turbulence, which none of the immediate family had ever dealt with before!

My youngest son, Bevo, had left his Boykin spaniel dog in his truck, and he was not arrested. Understanding the events of that day and night would never be forgotten and everlasting in the immediate family's turbulent memories. Before leaving the area to return home, we had to pick up my dog Bear from the ASPCA (Society for the Prevention of Cruelty to Animals).

Arriving to the local dog ASPCA to pick up Bear, I had to pay the sum of $100 as a donation to the ASPCA for Bear to be released. The good thing was he obtained a chip by his ear to help in finding Bear if he was ever lost.

All were happy to return to some sort of normalcy being reunited together and were relieved to have the mentally, excruciatingly painful nightmare end. We were able to return to our perspective homes, living in different areas. My oldest son was living in Gainesville at the time. My daughter and I lived on the west coast of Florida in Palm Harbor, and my youngest son was living in Alabama with his grandfather on his father's side of the family.

Alphabet of Jail Thoughts

Anticipation of entering the police car with handcuffs on has your heart-racing.
Beguiled in the events and words of the officers. While in jail, the thought of bail is first and foremost on one's mind with hopes of getting out soon. Yet hours and hours go by as paperwork and people operate at a snail's pace with no sense of urgency.
Captivated in one's surroundings.

Disgraced in front of family, friends, and strangers are memories haunting one's mind.
Enthralled in graffiti, filth, and colors used in the jail cell.
Forgetting nothing that has happened within the time of being processed in.
Giving in to tears of emotion as if Noah's Ark were needed to carry you out.
Happiness is the last emotion to be felt in a jail cell as many of the words thought upon while sitting on the hard cold metal bench started with the letter H such as "This is *hell*. Who cares about *health* in here?" is in the mind of the one behind bars.
Integrity guides the mind through the events of knowing rather one is a criminal with intent and quest for expunging the incident.
Jail is where jealousy of others prevails.
Jail cell but not to be found in a holding cell.
Kings are what police would like you to believe they are as they march to the beat of a different drum.
Loving is not in the vocabulary of most standing in jail.
Mature behavior is hard to find in one serving time.
No is the word most often said under one's breath while sitting in jail.
Ostentatious colors are used throughout the jailhouse.
Police of all colors walk with heads in the air.
Questioning by officers makes one quite intimidated and inferior to the one carrying a gun.
Reflections of events haunt one's mind for eternity.
Satisfaction is never guaranteed, or no truer words can be said!
Temperaments of the individual are never considered while sitting in a jail cell.
Unilateral decisions are unheard of by police in our police state.
Victory is seeing one's family and friends on the outside.
Walking aimlessly among the four walls seems to make one's mind race.
Xenophobia is found foremost in a jailhouse and among police mentalities.
Yes, sir, and **yes**, ma'am is strictly adhered to while in jail.
Zany is the emotional feeling one has when leaving the jailhouse.

A TURBULENT LIFE ? ? ?

When one is released, a sense of euphoria engulfs you, being free as a bird away from captivity as emotions run rampant. You rejoice to the Lord for being with family and loved ones once more, and jubilation is had by all. I was wishing for a helpful hand, but it was not always found from a police officer of the law. It was hilariously ridiculous what you'd hear from other prisoners, resonating their voices throughout the jail to the ears of a refined, educated individual. Hate of people seems to be foremost in most officers' minds with no caring to the person. With one objective and purpose of arresting one to put in jail regardless of what they may have to say.

The question that haunts one's mind is how everyone knows all the laws of the state without becoming an attorney? Are even the simplest everyday laws posted in a paper? Why does an individual on a first offense for a law they didn't know with so many interpretations of that law pay such harsh consequences with which was not an open shut case? Yet knowing the police officer had the right to treat the offense civilly rather than criminally yet proceeded with the harsher of the two. A woman in her fifties gave no resistance and volunteered information to an overbearing authoritative police officer. The prisoner learned the hard way to get educated on all the laws of the land and state before one might end up on death row as so many innocent people have as seen in movies and read in books and newspapers.

Life Rolls on 2022

James would visit the gravesite of the people he loved for all the holidays, taking beautiful arrangements of flowers, and laying them by their gravesites. He always said a prayer while visiting the gravesites. As he grew in his senior years, he visited their graves in the cemetery often. That was where he would lay to rest with his family at age ninety-eight, and because of the covid epidemic, his wake was postponed. The family had prayed he would make it to one hundred years of age. God needed him sooner and called him to heaven after having a long-fulfilled life. He was cremated, and no wake was done because of the horrible covid pandemic.

My favorite time in the Grande on Sand Key Condo where I lived for several years was when my grandchildren Boykin and Veda would visit and would throw the frisbee on the beach and splash in the gulf water to retrieve it then go swimming in the pool.

As the years were going by so fast, I experienced problems with the Internal Revenue Service. It was a scary time for me. After a few years, the local bank with a female wealth management officer, who had a law degree, helped in getting my tax issues with IRS settled. I had been dealing with a California tax company that was taking me for a ride and their methods could have been considered scrupulous as they asked to pay my way to meet them in California.

The wealth management officer, Kat, recommended a tax accountant April in Mobile, Alabama, and both offer a considerable amount of time to resolve my tax issues and explained how I got taken for an exorbitant amount of money with the California group. The tax group in California ultimately did nothing other than accrue money from my account to pay to IRS, which they pocketed it.

A TURBULENT LIFE ? ? ?

Kat and April were called my miracle workers! They fixed my tax problem, which created smooth sailing from then on for resolving my tax challenges. For the time and expertise they put into resolving the issue of my tax debt, I am in their debt and for their proficiency of doing so! Working closely together after a considerable bit of time with their working with one another to resolve the Internal Revenue Service issues! I pray and thank God for them in my prayers every night!

Tarasee the stooge felt as though she should get involved with no one asking her to. She was in control of my father's estate and had April come to her office to pay taxes for me. It was appreciated but completely unsolicited. The accountant has been retained to continue doing my tax returns for many years to come as she has the knowledge of the complexities of them through the years since the family-owned company revenues change, so does the taxes.

A Legacy Left to Future Generations
Family-Owned Corporation

Many a time I would sit in meetings observing two of the nicknamed three stooges and the older brother biding their time by playing on their cell phones during the meetings. I was appalled as I sat and listened to what was being said and would ask questions.

Tarasee was often writing the minutes of the meetings. Her title in the company was secretary treasurer, and she would work the operations at McIntosh and hunting clubs. At times, you could notice distress over her brothers and sister playing with their cell phones, distracting those in attendance of the meetings.

Interested participants asked questions and paid attention as others in the meeting would participate and learn with open mind and ears. After several board meetings, I watched those in attendance; their facial expressions would show frustration and found it annoying and distracting to many in attendance, especially to those listening attentively, asking questions, and taking notes and letting what was said sink into their minds in hopes to benefit the company.

Praise God, a family member must have spoken to two of the stooges and their oldest brother playing with his as well. Whoever told them to stop distracting everyone in attendance at the meetings with their playing on their cell phones made sure they were not seen again doing it again.

Family members were pleasantly surprised in the next meeting to see no cell phones displayed, and those family members had to pay attention to what was being said, instead of exhibiting and showing others why they were known and nicknamed a part of the three stooges. It was embarrassing to many who attended the family-owned business meetings and witnessing the unprofessional, rude, destructive, inattentive behavior. It was as if they were playing the game *follow the leader.*

Many of the fourth generation have BA degrees and others with a BS as well as master and doctorate degrees. Two of the fourth generation were placed as board member on my father's side but unable to finish their terms as requested by the oldest nicknamed of the three stooges. Earning a good living, the two fourth-generation trustees had business backgrounds and was qualified to serve their terms. Were they removed because of a power struggle and deception? What was the oldest nicknamed as one of the three stooges trying to hide? That is a question that remains unanswered as it happened many years ago, but it remains on the mind of a few trustees today in the year 2022.

Several people often pray that the company continues to many generations, keeping an open mind and receptive to new and prosperous ideas. Many knowing, with God's help, it can be achieved, especially with qualified individuals rather it be family or hired qualified personnel!

The company will remain solvent with all questions being answered with truth, honesty, sincerity, integrity, and expertise with knowledge from highly qualified family or outside individuals. Recommendations for moving the company to future generations and hopefully into the next century with the next generation having business, real estate negotiation skills, finance skills, law, estimating and work backgrounds in their fields of expertise in one's perspective areas can drive the company into the next generation and beyond!

Those with impeccable credentials as experts in their noted fields to recommend the way to move the company forward nationally and into the future for upcoming generations to enjoy as the third, fourth, and fifth generations enjoy it today. Making memories of their own and into the future with many pictures documenting the successes. Each generation's memories are different as the years seem to pass by rapidly.

The current, phenomenally successful, and receptive president listens and is open to all new ideas and continues the tradition of the company as Frank did and the others before him. With his open mind listening to suggestions proposed from all whom propose them, he knows if it is a refreshingly new idea and rather to pursue it or not as it may have been tried and failed in the past.

His wife, quite smart, offers refreshingly new ideas to him. Their daughter and her husband are remarkably successful in business and fresh ideas in promoting the company forward. The president knows what to bring to a vote in a board meeting and what not to. He is attentive and listens with full attention to his family members as they suggest and implement their ideas for what's best to move the company forward. What will work for the existing or creating new accomplishments for the company to keep it moving forward should be up to the next generation.

With the president's knowledge of what should be implemented and what has failed, his side of the family want to make great efforts to move and implement effective ideas in making more money for future generations and for those that are qualified to run and develop as he and many of his families side of the board offer new ideas.

With new diverse ideas and expertise being initiated from his side of the family and promoting the newer generations into the company to recommend newer, effective, and more creative ways of expanding the company to the next generation and beyond. Also, learning how their great-grandfather had eighteen different businesses with millions of acres, he earned hefty returns with and the uses on the land that might be useful today to develop.

Family Sub-Trust Fund

I resigned from Tarasee's trust as a stooge with which I encouraged Tarasee to be on her own sub-trust. I believed one should be in control of what is done with their own interest of funds. In the original trust document from Other, it called for five trustees, which presently consist of two stooges, and Hint removed himself and appointed Bevo, and I appointed his son (which both were board members) as the oldest stooge immediately removed them from the board.

Often the truth was spoken when Tarasee the stooge was drunk or taking painkillers. Father, Tarasee, and youngest boy of the stooges would offer the prescription painkillers to others, not knowing if they were allergic or had reactions to the medicine, and their having no medical degree, they could have been sued. Praise God, I am unaware if they had ever been sued for doing so. Many of those they offered to me, and I had the good sense not to accept them and said, "No, thank you!" I have sensitivity and allergies to over thirty-five documented drugs by doctors, and I knew better than to accept them.

I regret my decision of resigning from her mini trust. Tarasee told a lie so detrimental to one's life by mentioning I was "diagnosed with mental issues." Those words changed my life forever! They removed me from a life of discovery to an unknown place to me at that time. Was the devil in control of Tarasee? Having the youngest brother and sister make demand on others as they follow and do whatever she asks. Heard from many, and it is like observing two people who are brain-dead.

Always keeping ears open and not prejudging or listening because it causes one more work and being judgmental does not help a company move forward for future generations into the next century! Many members of the family would like to see, especially those of the fourth generation being allowed to understand the workings of the company as it operated in the past to be preserved for future generations. In the upcoming years, the fifth generation should be put on the board to move the company forward and onward to the next century with new technology and motivations with fresh minds and ideas perhaps to be implemented. It has worked for three generations thus far why not continue the family tradition?

The company has moved forward as Frank did when he started the company with each one of his living children becoming presidents of the family-owned corporation. They handed it to the third generation, and now my cousins are starting to turn it over to the next generation as they have no fears. What does Tarasee and the two-stooges have to fear of letting other generations take their earned places on the board? Some ask, is it because she is a mother hen? No one has answered that question to date.

Those up-to-date with future technology and suggestions as industry, laws, taxes, climate change, and pandemics have changed how many companies are to move forward. To date and often following along party lines in Democratic states and Republican states that determine how companies move forward. Other people that knew Tarasee and her brothers and sisters from James's second marriage would ask me, "Why are the three stooges unable to move the company into the future for next generations to learn?"

It appears, to an outsider looking in, one side moves forward, and the other side steps back, and remains stagnate and unable to move the company to future generations. What are the three stooges hiding? They have been unable to answer questions posed to them in the past to other generation's satisfactions. Why? No reasonable explanation to date in 2022 have been given.

Aunt Fran's side and cousins moved forward being progressive in their suggestions. Also, moving the company into the future for generations to continue the company in the way Frank and past and current presidents have intended and implemented. Outsiders watching from near and afar are asking, "What are they covering up and trying to hide? Will the truth only be known to the three stooges, law enforcement, and documents with the company and in

A TURBULENT LIFE ? ? ?

courthouses throughout the state of Alabama, as well as being held in the Alabama State Archives?"

The oldest brother was never considered one of the three stooges as he graduated from the University of Alabama with a business degree as his father did. He ran a family business that was unable to sustain itself through the years. His love of family, not without some controversy, have maintained a family and children that remain close to one another. Even with separation from his wife, they always maintained their love of one another and getting back together. God and family remain the center of their lives. Like most people, they experienced some growing pains and did what it took to remain a happy family.

The sad thing is the family business is not a joke and should be taken seriously by all those that have an interest in it! I am sure that was Frank's intent as the current president makes the path for others to continue the tradition. Never to forget Frank's love of land that helped create his legacy to move forward to fourth, fifth generations, and hopefully beyond with God's help. Frank, Other, my dad, and Cora are all smiling at the work accomplished by the current president successes in the business.

Words heard from others spoken and observations of the three stooges joined at the hips, and some were unable to think for themselves as they echo the sentiments of the two girl stooges and whatever they have to say as written in text messages and emails. Makes some wonder, can he speak for himself and have an opinion of his own? He often sounds like a broken record! Many were unable to understand them as they follow the beat of a different drum.

They are also known as liars with their affairs and cheating on their partners in the community as heard from law enforcement officers and documents in the state of Alabama. The family remained passive and stagnant with not moving the family business forward to other generations and unwilling to give up control has some asking why. They seem to surround themselves in controversy.

Frank came from nothing to making himself highly respected among his peers with his drive, ingenuity, hard work, and love of people, animals (especially dogs), bees, flowers, and trees and surrounded in controversy. He stayed secure and knew who he was until his last breath. Never having a childhood and working with his blood, sweat, and tears! I considered myself so fortunate to be a part of his family and to have known and bonded with him, even with the controversies surrounding their dad through the years.

Her dad (James) and Sister Fran followed in their dad's footsteps with his hard work ethics, love of land, trees, and the railroad with their families appreciating and maintaining it. Like their father, they would buy and sell the land for their families or keep as an investment, or to live and enjoy the purchased property.

Always humble and knowing who they were and where they came from, they were known for being loveable, respected, and hardworking as their father and mother were as they followed them. Thankfully in their older years, they lived with less controversy as they stayed away from politics and only helped in their father's campaign office as he continued to run for congressman in his district. They managed to stay happy and away from the drama. They followed the beat of their own drum, working hard, maintaining their happiness with integrity, and putting God and their families above anything else! I consider myself extremely fortunate to have known them.

My dad James would always ask, "How I was doing?"

I would reply, "Okay, I guess."

We would reminisce of the lessons and times we had together. In the talks we had shared, he taught me how to appreciate the little things in life, to think of positives with no negativity. Dad would be silly but also show he was the adult and was to be heard if he said anything. When he spoke, it was often conveying inspiration to others. All things can be good if you listen to God! At bedtime, he would always say his prayers with Robby and me.

Abduction 2022

The *Webster* dictionary definition of *abduction* is "to seize or take away a person either by force or compels a person to go from any place that is said to abduct a person." Then two worlds were shattered by unforeseen abduction occurring from acquaintances that instigated it, and their nicknames throughout their lives were the three stooges and oldest son of my dad's second marriage.

Why would one mention in a board meeting where they were asking for money for themselves and bring up another person who was not present nor a trustee on her trust? Was it just to spread rumors and a lie? The nerve of Tarasee telling a lie about me being diagnosed with mental issues and having it written in the minutes of a board meeting for her to obtain money from her trust by a wealth management officer taking the minutes of the meeting. As the author, I am looking into a lawsuit for deformation of character of Tarasee spreading a life-changing lie about me.

Tarasee had my son to contact the realtor, and he lied telling her they were coming to help his mother with her bugs. Tarasee talked to my son into driving to Palm City on the east coast of Florida to get his mother. Tarasee flew down. Why was she so compelled to get so involved in my life? I can only guess. Instead of helping me, they seized me to a life with which I never wanted! With me in such shock and unable to think quick enough as I was in a mental fog that was so life changing! It hurt two people to the inner core of their souls.

Bevo entered my hotel room, and then Tarasee sneaked in, and the oldest stooge plopped herself on the couch in the room with her crossed hands and tone and affliction in raising her voice, saying, "Get packed! You are coming with us!"

Her authoritarian voice sent shivers through my body. Bevo accompanied her and gave no notice to me of their coming or thinking of my needs! Was it the devil working in the oldest stooge to tell a falsehood that would change one's life forever? It affected my friend of over thirty years life as well. We have traveled long and short trips together for over three and a half decades. With our children playing together from third grade on to adulthood, and we met as public school co-room mothers of our children in third grade. The question arises, Was the devil responsible for changing two lives so drastically by abduction of one adult with no heads-up or warning of their coming? Who else would do such a tragic thing to a person they say they loved and were helping? It is yet to be determined. The oldest and dictator of the three stooges who wasn't happy with her own life that she must get involved and take over others as she did with the other two stooges and the oldest boy!

I showed them my parasite bites, and Tarasee immediately showed off her red bugbites she obtained in the woods, which is quite common to get. Once again, she displayed her ignorance to me! There was no comparison in red bugs, and one diagnosed with parasites and was going to be tested to confirm the diagnosis, which was detected by a dermatologist (specialized skin doctor) and primary care physician.

I just shook my head and said, "Wow. Tarasee must do one up on everybody, but she didn't have a clue about scabies!"

Scabies is highly contagious and not that common to get in the United States but frequently found in third world countries, which I had not traveled to in years. If a person has ever had scabies, mites, they know it is highly contagious, and they can remain in your body and return at any time to feed on your blood. Red bug bites are not transferrable. The most obvious difference is red bugs don't burrow under your skin the way scabies does. I could only shake my head at the ignorance of Tarasee.

I realized she probably didn't even read about them nor cared when I texted or emailed pictures of the bites on my skin from scalp to toes and articles about scabies to my entire family. Anyone that has had scabies or an infestation of parasites from bites head to toes is familiar or learns from the internet about them and knows there is no comparison in red bug bites to parasites of head and body lice or scabies as the oldest nicknamed stooge was implying. Why would she put my son who has two young children in harm's way?

A dermatologist and a medical doctor treated and confirmed the diagnosis of parasites to me, and he took pictures. My female doctor retired from the military and opened an angels to care center.

She explained, "Gracie Lu, I am prescribing another dose of what the dermatologist ordered for you, and you ran out of and an antibiotic and another dose of shampoo like a lotion to rub from your scalp to your toes, and prednisone [steroid] to help treat your skin and was prescribed by the dermatologist and I have ordered an antibiotic for you. If its scabies, it is very contagious and caused by a female mite that burrows under your skin to lay her eggs. The redness, blisters, bite pattern rash on your skin, and configurations are all over your body, and they are sucking on your blood, which is why you are itching so intensely. Like dogs, cats, and other animals, scratch or lick trying to get the flees off their fur or bodies. Gracie Lu, you must have willpower, strength, and the most important thing is you do not scratch when you are itching! Pray to God the Supreme Healer to give you the strength to conquer the burrowing mites without scratching where you itch! It is not helpful in eradicating them! You must not scratch!"

She handed me her cell phone number.

"If you need me, call this number."

I replied, "Thank you."

Doctor said, "Before you leave my office, I want you to realize from the pictures I am showing you that contact with other people could make you responsible for spreading it to a whole community! This is what you look for if the infestation continues to get worse! They are so contagious that you need to isolate yourself from other people in your community. Wash on the hottest setting your clothes or buy new clothes." The doctor emphatically expressed how important it was. "You do not get near people or animals and isolate yourself while the infestation is active."

I was in isolation for around two weeks, and if the parasites were scabies, they could spread like wildfire over your body and onto others. Through physical contact, the mites can expand like gangbusters to anyone you are near! No hugging, shaking hands, sharing washcloths or towels as skin-to-skin contact can have them move like the speed of light on to others. Using a lot of willpower, concentration, try to put mind over matter, praying to God, and discipline as not to scratch and try to get some sleep. I was constantly wanting to scratch as the itching became intense from my head to my toes. I had lent rollers and could roll different colored specks that were the mites from my body.

The doctor saw the bite patterns and heard my being unable to sleep from wanting to scratch, which was the worst thing I could do. She diagnosed and recognized the importance of scabies but needed further testing to confirm the diagnosis. It is not normally found in the US but in poor countries.

"If it gets worse, as your doctor, I will refer you to a dermatologist in this area to confirm my diagnosis."

I felt like Tarasee enjoyed comparing herself to others as she must hate herself and her own life. Many people feel sorry for her, especially when she displays in public her ass when drunk or taking pain pills or both at the same time. Her gambling with the high rollers and spending thousands of dollars were customary for her. I thought of her as an acquaintance as it was mainly through the company for meetings and to sign papers of the family-owned corporation and not a close friend. On occasions, we would have lunch with our dad together! A couple of times, her partner would join us for lunch. Once or twice, she and I would just have lunch together. We saw a concert at a casino in Biloxi, Mississippi, as she bought drinks for the strangers behind us. After the concert, she continued gambling, and I did as well. I walked the casino floor but didn't see her and went on the elevator to the room she got for us. I fell asleep, and early in the morning, she had ordered a delicious breakfast to the room. She had stayed in the casino to the wee hours of the morning. She checked us out of the room. As we drove separately, I drove my car to Fairhope, and she drove home.

While I lived across Mobile Bay, Tarasee and her partner visited one time because of the party I had for family and some condominium friends on the terrace. I would have lunch with my dad, her, and the youngest stooge that echoes everything the girl stooges say. It was as if they had control of him like a robot, and he would tell you the youngest girl stooge raised him. He would come to echo whatever words they said. Some friends thought he was mindless and could not read anything but comic books. His lust for women was childlike, and like that was all about which he could think!

It was none of her business as only a half-sister acquaintance. She and I only saw each other slightly, and neither considered each other as a close friend. She only knew me on a casual basis, never knowing my likes and dislikes and my knowing her love of fishing. We shared the same wonderful, smart father, and that was all we really shared. Tarasee didn't know my heart, feelings, life experiences, and losses, or all that I had accomplished in my life as a teacher and the places I had traveled and what I accomplished when living in Southwest Florida.

When my oldest son was first diagnosed with medulloblastoma brain cancer, she came to the hospital to see us and consoled us as it was so hard to see a loved one so young at the age of sixteen to go through major surgery. I appreciated her being there.

Tarasee and Bevo, with no notice of any type, checked me out of a hotel to an unknown city. I was in shock at the boldness of Tarasee the control freak, removing me from just getting reacquainted with my daughter as we had not seen each other for around nine years. If I had not been in such shock of their surprise arrival, I would have stayed and let them waste their gas driving and Tarasee's flying from Mobile to the area and her time! The real reason for their coming was the root of all evil, taking my money and power to control another individual! How sad and sick that was to me. Currently unable to trust my son and the three stooges with the oldest as the leader and the youngest male playing "follow the leader" as told by some that knew him and have observed his childlike behavior! Tarasee involved Bevo, and what they did was at the root of all evil! Tarasee had mentioned the biggest falsehood and lie written in the minutes by the investment banker recorded in writing as she was chosen by the three stooges and the older boy that followed along with them at a board meeting held in a local bank that I had been diagnosed with mental problems taken on February 16, 2022.

I had asked to borrow some money a few times and would pay them back the following month so I could put a down payment on house to be near my daughter. Tarasee, at another time as the dictator, had the nerve to ask me for bank statements I had and asked what she considered to be a large amount of money went to. It was quite puzzling, and what business was it of hers? Tarasee was asking to know every aspect of my life. I decided to oblige her with her insatiable curiosity of how I spent my money with sending her statements as I had nothing to hide. Also, if she worked for the company, was she doing it on her time or on the company's time at work, and did she involve others in doing so? It was because of jealousy, envy of her and her pal, and that all they really wanted was to control my money and get me away from my roommate and traveling friend who I had given proceeds from the sale of my condo and that she could have helped me, and perhaps they were right, but she had it invested and felt unable to help. They also felt she should not have accepted it if she was a good friend. The nerve and gall of family members taking control of one's life was all because of money and power wanting to control my life. It was as if they gave me a prison sentence and no longer in control of living my own life. How devious, conniving the three stooges were! How does one in their senior years learn to deal with people like that, and why would one even want to?

Shortly after that meeting, Tarasee the oldest and most controlling stooge proceeded to drive my new car back to Mobile, Alabama. As I was not given much of a chance, I did choose to ride back with my son in his truck. They gave no consideration of my feelings, anger, disgust, and being unable to trust anyone again, especially in that family. He drove his mother to the panhandle of Florida. They must have known if they took me across state lines, the FBI would get involved if I had told them of the abduction. Tarasee had taken control as the dictator that she was with the two other stooges and with my son. I was under a doctor's care, who gave me her cell phone to call when I was in need.

A TURBULENT LIFE ? ? ?

Also, under the care of a dermatologist care for parasites that my childhood best friend Dede had immediately set for me on the same day. My son and the eldest controlling stooge had other ideas to disrupt my life forever. I shortly learned all they wanted was to control me and my money and put my son Bevo in charge. Also, to get me away from my friend that the two stooges and oldest male son wanted to be with for themselves. It was like watching a horror film as it was their way to control and have power over me keeping me under their hand and foot.

What was sad it was for money, power, and control over Bevo's mother. Their attempt to have me declared mentally incompetent failed miserably, and they could not succeed with their total plan to control the money. Ultimately perhaps they wished it out of the hands of Bevo and my daughter. The three stooges and eldest son worship money and not God! The oldest stooge claimed to love the Lord, but the Lord would never condone abduction and what they did. It was evil, greed, and the worship of money the three stooges love.

I question often, were the three stooges trying to get control of the trust money for themselves and not leave anything to Bevo and my daughter? Did they want a major lawsuit where all their dirty laundry would come out in court? They are just foolish enough to do that for their love and worship of money! They are heartless and don't care how they come to get money. They could obtain it by growing marijuana illegally on the property owned by some members of their family or dispensing painkillers to people and perhaps charging them or cheating with an elected male official and the lies they have told.

In the process, they hurt my traveling buddy and gave no thought nor care of how disruptive it was. Jealousy? Tarasee the eldest stooge had said, "I want your life," on a telephone call. She must have meant it literally as she put an abduction plan together in disrupting my life forever!

Two of the stooges will not get anything off my trust as they need to report everything back to Tarasee to implement their next plan. Another was from the youngest male stooge and the youngest girl stooge taking orders from their supreme leader to do whatever she needed them to do. They were demanding me to go to my sub-trust meeting with the bank in person, or they would not approve anything I asked for from the trust. I called for a Zoom meeting on the phone with my son, and praise God, I didn't have to go in person for them to abduct me again. The sad thing is to watch how the youngest boy had chosen to follow the girl stooges as if he had no thoughts or brain of his own like the scarecrow in the movie *Wizard of Oz*, echoing their every word in text, emails, and phone calls.

I can never trust them, their lies and illegal deeds! They collectively still try to demand to see me in person. Why? If Tarasee had abducted me to Alabama, I could have called the FBI for taking me across state lines. Praise God I rode back with my son. They stopped just short of doing that. How evil and destructive minds that love and worship money primarily can be? The oldest stooge pretends to love God, or is she worshiping Satan with her controlling ways?

They use money to control other people's lives and to ruin other subsists as if they are dictators! They can never be trusted by honest, caring, believers of God that died for our sins on earth. He is an all-forgiving Lord who teaches lessons to those that genuinely believe in him and listen and read the Bible and scriptures. Acts of prayer to communicate directly to him. I taught his scripture and verses throughout my years of teaching in private Christian schools. With all the documented illegal actions by law enforcement, who knows what other corrupt dirty deeds they do as they have managed to keep it from law enforcement, or they pay them off.

Tarasee, not having any children, became the mother hen and leader of the clan who would often tell them what to do as they would go running to her with their predicaments they would find themselves in. She was a strong-willed controller of her younger sister and brothers, as well as their children when they allowed her too. She had some big shoes to follow. In some observers, eyes she never quite lived up to her father nor her mother. The youngest daughter and son also had a great sense of relief as not to have to ever speak to them or have anything to do with them or hear their lies and deceitful deeds they continued to do! They may try to abduct me again as the oldest stooge Tarasee did, and if given the opportunity, I learned they may have tried to pay doctors to have me committed to a mental institution. It was all about my money habits and their selfish power to control how one spent their own money.

Tarasee wanted to take me across state lines to her house with her partner.

I said, "I am not going anywhere with you two, especially your house."

They probably wanted me to cross the state line so they could pay a doctor to institutionalize me and get control of the trust and money.

The three stooges and oldest son are corrupt liars, stealers, kleptomaniacs, sex fiends, cheaters, deceitful, and will do anything for sex and money. They would try to control other people's lives and getting into things that are none of their business or concern! Their way of life was beyond my imagination!

I was abducted by my son and Tarasee who complained of her flying from Mobile to seize me with my son who drove. He obtained an apartment in Pensacola, Florida, for me. First, I stayed in a hotel for a week or so with him living in Milton, Florida, about thirty to forty minutes away from an apartment he rented in his name.

First, he took me to a hospital, saying, "I had a mental problem." I was placed in a mental area of an ER department at a hospital and was seen by an emergency room doctor. I was not seen by a psychologist or psychiatrist. I was placed in the filthiest room I had ever been in, especially at a hospital. They took any jewelry or possessions I had on me, except my hearing aids, and the other items were placed in plastic bags and labeled. It was the most humiliating thing anyone could do to a mother for no good reason! Other than wanting control of my money and to shorten his mother's life and pretending he was helping her. He had quit his job, which I believed initially from the events that transpired was to live off his mother.

My relationship with my son was strained for quite some time! He did not even have the common courtesy or trust in his mother to tell me he was coming to get me. His mother of seventy years was bought to a hotel for a week and a half and later to an apartment he chose and rented in his name. He took over the money arrangements at my bank. How could I ever trust him again? It was as if he was in control of my life, and it sickened me! He could have at least told me he was coming, instead he was devious with Tarasee in her plot to abduct me. They must have been planning it for a while.

I didn't think of my son in the same way I once did until I learned the truth and the plan Dad and Cora's children had plotted. He has made it up to me by taking care of my every need and felt guilty as he knew he was wrong and apologized several times for not telling me they were coming. He also felt he was protecting me from the grips of Tarasee and the stooges who wanted to put me in a mental institution. He did what he felt was best, and that was all a mother could ask for at her age in life.

I would never see the oldest stooge or any of them as I only considered them to be acquaintances as I slightly knew them, and they were never known to be close friends. With over nine years living close to Mobile in the area, Tarasee only came once to my condominium for a party that my roommate and I gave.

The oldest son was infatuated with her and told me when they first met her at a restaurant with his kids and wife if he weren't married, he would give the youngest brother a run for his money as he found her to be smart and beautiful. Another time at their dad's Dauphin Island house with just me and their dad present, he said, "I am having withdrawal pains from your roommate!" Tarasee had asked my roommate to work for her and to take care of our elderly dad. I came to believe because she was gay and has a partner that she wanted to know my friend better.

My friend said, "She felt like it was lust on the youngest male stooge to babysit me and show her around town. When you were out of town, she told me he offered to get her an apartment near him, and he would pay for everything. She would not be a kept woman and bought by anyone! She realized he was thinking of one thing—sex! She had no part of that! She also told him and Tarasee she was there for Gracie Lu and not for them as she and Gracie Lu were like sisters and had known each other since we were room mothers with our sons in third grade, and they played with one another."

When asked why she was there, she replied again, "I am here for Gracie Lu! Gracie Lu was abducted and moved to an area she was unfamiliar with and away from friends and family. South Florida real estate values could not be compared to Alabama or another southern state where she wanted to purchase a home to be near her only daughter."

Was it power and wanting control over people that were happy, and the oldest of the three stooges Tarasee could not cope with seeing other's happiness because she was so miserable? The oldest son was in the meeting as well and must have voted and agreed with the others as a follower. Was the devil working in Tarasee's life as well as the others in the meeting with the wealth management team at the small local bank as they discussed about me being "diagnosed with mental issues"? That was written in minutes a wealth management officer was selected to take, which I have seen no documentation of. That is because there is none unless they bribed a doctor in Alabama to say so, as they needed to ruin and control a family member's joyful life as well as others. How sad and pitiful is that? What is worse is they had the money and contacts to do so.

I had purchased for my son and his wife a home and paid it completely off for them so they would not have a mortgage as my son had brain cancer. I had received money from the land and timber company. The president had negotiated with the state and German Company TK steel company to build a mill in offering inducements, and the state of Alabama offered cash and other incentives to come to the state of Alabama. With the money I received from the steel mill to be built on the company's land that was sold to TK, I paid my taxes and bills off with enough money to buy the home for my son who asked if I would. I was unable to say no as I did not want them to have to worry about anything other than beating his brain cancer!

The youngest son of my dad and Cora visited my daughter-in-law on his way to Sarasota, Florida, to have his comic book collection appraised as that was all he read growing up. He visited her and had said things to make her angry at me such as I didn't like her appearance with all the tattoos and whatever else he conjured up to say to ruin my relationship with my son in heaven Wes's wife.

My friend and roommate had heard her trying to console someone on the phone from the TV room. After thirty or so minutes of hearing it, she entered the room, asking, "Is everything okay?"

I shook my head as if to say no. She heard the other person crying on the other end, saying, "I thought I was family to you."

Then I said, "I don't want to hear from you again." I hung up the phone after saying goodbye.

Discussing the conversation with my roommate, we deducted the youngest male was in love with my roommate and friend, and because she didn't reciprocate his feelings, he took it out on me. He destroyed a loving friendship. It was evil, deceitful, and wrong in every way!

Years before Wes, my first son, died, his wife had taken such wonderful care of him. Keeping his medical records, taking him to the doctor, seeing him through surgeries, and witnessing his pain, she always managed to maintain a smile and kept him moving through it all, sharing happiness, love, and togetherness through all their aches and pains as young adults. I had bonded with her and had made a promise to my son on his deathbed to take her to Japan, a country he visited, and he loved the people. That would not happen as she didn't want to hear from me ever again. It was a turbulent moment in time as I would not be able to fulfill my promise to my son, and it broke my heart!

Taken from a blissful life of traveling all the states and traveling to foreign places never visited before, fulfilling a life of dreams, traveling to parts unknown to me, I had been an exceptionally good travel agent in my married life. I knew where to go rather by boat, train, plane, car, or hiking, and best of all was to get the deals traveling first or in second class to visit the exotic wonders of the world.

The journey on the path of seeing my last state from my years on earth was to finally visit Rhode Island. My traveling friend and I saw Newport with all the historic homes along the waterfront. We took turns driving my Acura MDX SUV from Fairhope, Alabama, and on the first road trip, we drove from Fairhope, Alabama, to Washington State to visit my friend's son who lived there and to check on him as he had Dirksen's disease.

A TURBULENT LIFE ? ? ?

Bevo removed me to live in a rented apartment as a senior citizen with not knowing anyone or ever living in the city or surroundings in helping me to get out of the grips of Tarasee. I found myself placed in front of my new keyboard and computer, recalling thoughts from memories of the past, being written fast and furiously in hopes of fulfilling a lifetime dream of becoming a best-selling author.

Do the three stooges have anything better to do than conjuring up ways to ruin people's lives and to control them for their trust money? The reader will need to decide the answer to that question. Why does the eldest of the sons go along with them as he professes to love God and attends church regularly? The question is, does he really have the Lord in his heart as he is known to cheat on his wife? Does anyone have the right to destroy a life of one who taught Christianity for the Lord and worshiped God not for money and power or to ruin another person's life? Was it revenge because they could not have my roommate? How pitiful and sad is that? Is Satan in control of their lives? What is sad is with their free time, they conjure up ways to destroy a family's life for the worship of love of money! To one who has taught the scriptures in schools and read the Bible twice in its entirety, I had never seen the likes of such deviousness and controlling ways. Never wanting to deal with such vengeful people again. Their parents and relatives are watching from heaven and could possibly be ashamed of their behaviors. They don't live by the words of their grandfather Frank who trademarked the slogan: "Everything is made for love!"

It is sad to watch and observe such unchristianlike behaviors. My dad would be appalled at their childlike actions. He told many people he spoiled his children way too much! That was a regret he had before going to heaven, seeing the Lord who he loved dearly and followed his scriptures throughout his life! A respectable, hardworking man like his father who he admitted him to get the job with the local paper mill, and he did his father proud.

My dad was loved by all who were lucky enough to know him! He loved his daughter from his first marriage and wanted me to author a book about him as he was so proud of my writing *The Southern Hunt*. He was sorry I did not name the real people in the book. I explained to him I was afraid to be sued. He had me print the names of each person and printed them out on a computer to insert in the book with which I immediately did.

He, with the youngest male stooge, attended several book signings with me. The oldest and youngest stooge attended one with him in Clearwater, Florida, as they felt he could not travel alone. They were introduced to the crowd, and those in attendance that new Browder were so glad to meet my dad, that they heard all good things from my mother and I about him. James was quite proud of the book and felt honored to see the crowd gathered for my book signing. He encouraged me to write about his World War II stories. This book currently being written is as much about him, as his father, Other, Browder, Cora, his second-family children and Robby, me, and my children.

He and Cora were a team, and now they have no pain, sorrows, or disappointments that life held on earth. My belief is they are reunited, rejoicing and singing in heaven, youthful as they stand with God, and their relatives are reunited in heaven and having no pain or suffering. They lived their lives to the fullest on earth and now standing in the kingdom of heaven. Unfortunately, because of the covid epidemic, he has not had the proper send-off he deserved on earth for going to see his maker. I know there was much rejoicing when he entered and was with the Holy Trinity and archangels.

My father is not happy with the three stooges and how they acted to his daughter from his first marriage who he genuinely loved and was proud of!

I found myself apologizing to my travel buddy and friend who found my father's family to be toxic to her. I have learned the hard way never to involve anyone in my life. So they won't be involved with a dark-sided family that people can't trust, respect, or admire, and qualities that bring out the worst in people. If a person reads this story, you will know why I am this way. Being placed in an environment where I pray, this is God's plan for me. I am back in a world that was foreign to me for many years and happy to be with my son, his wife, and grandchildren with my daughter nearby and having her first child at age thirty-seven to be a little girl soon to enter this world, and her name-to-be is Hannah. Oh, what a glorious day that should be.

I reached into the depths of my mind with many departmentalized moments like a file cabinet being opened for the first time in my life! Learning how I have accepted things, I thought that I could not change! I have found those few words is what I grew up thinking my entire life. How wrong I was, and they were perhaps the most detrimental words in my life! I am learning the life I have led would be damaging to many individuals. It is an eye-opener as I reach into the depths of my mind, opening records and now believing those were lies and words I was bought up believing my entire life. Now I know they are lies as I have lived by them. If anything has helped me to find the real me, it is what I have learned from my traveling with others and in authoring this book. The words should have been, "Accept the changes that enables one to make changes!"

Working on learning my genuine self when I complete my story, I should finally know what makes me tick. A wise friend who has saved my life through recognizing sickness and withdrawals from strong pain medications encouraged me to write my autobiography. Telling my experiences in a book are therapeutic, and I pray it helps others. I knew that to move on with life, I had to finish what I started to get to the next chapter of life.

I have felt like a misfit and second fiddle to many as I saw events differently than others. I could not ignore that sentiment as I had taken a back seat to friends and family. I made enemies and bullies, I was lied to, cried, hated, had negative and positive reactions, have been happy and joyful, wrong and right with my beliefs, hurt from illnesses, people, pets, and peacocks as they flew with a toe close to my eye leaving a scar, and fishhook in my eye. I am amazed how lucky I am to never have lost my sight in my childhood. One may consider life as a double-edged sword. We pray to have a better and more complete life and understanding with those that enter and leave during one's lifetime on earth.

Individuals enter one's life as pages in a book and helps construct meaningful chapters in one's volume. A heart for others is carried with me throughout my life. Nothing or anything can ever break one's true heart, not even a dysfunctional family. If I get in trouble, I fall and break bones, and perhaps that is a way of showing me that has been what my life in the past and today had been all about. A traveling buddy opened closed doors to finally living one's own life as a step to finding and believing in myself.

Through writing, whether good or bad, is all in one's opinion. That has been the only way I have been able to express myself as others never paid attention to what I had to say. It only takes one person to open the doors to the unknown self. Mutual respect in supporting an individual with trust, boundaries, and growing with acceptance of others. A roommate showed love in a way one could actually understand through simplicity. I believe in knowing the Holy Spirit and watching miracles from all forms of media and churches ministries as well as prayers to God and healing of people that have had life-threatening diseases, epidemics, cancer throughout the beginning of time. With that knowledge, I had learned to deal with all forms of my turbulent life.

How Native Americans dealt with climate change with nature rituals have worked at times. Perhaps we could learn much from the Indian tribes, natives, as well as scientist or a combination of all three. Learning to deal with parasites in one's body that could be life-threatening was a turbulent experience for me as I wanted to scratch my severe itches and thought of how Native Americans dealt with pain in the past and how they may have helped me.

I went to an urgent care doctor who became my physician in Stuart, Florida, while in the area who had treated me with an at-home nebulizer and albuterol twice daily as I had a hard time breathing, and I had explained I tested positive for covid in Arkansas on the way back to Florida from Colorado, and the emergency room doctor saw the parasites on my hand and did nothing about it.

My treatment was an experience that I have learned to deal with since January 1, 2022. I got rid of my clothes and suitcases as I could see the white specks of parasites in them. I stayed in hotels on the way back as well as in Clearwater, Florida, and in Stuart, Florida. I did not have access to the hottest cycle in a dryer that would kill the infestation. I had to tell the hotel I was staying in that I saw lice, and they gave me another room. The maintenance crew came in and took the mattress off and used vacuums and heaters in the room to get rid of the nits and bugs. I developed a short-lived paranoia in seeing any specks in car or anywhere. Praise God I dealt with the paranoia myself and shortly returned to what professionals considered to be a normal reaction to what I dealt with.

Lessons Learned and Experienced 2022

Live life to the fullest as it is too short to have any regrets! I loved the people who had been good to me and treated me as a whole person and forget those who tried to control me. I had learned through all my travels and personal experiences to believe that everything happens for a reason. Learning life was not easy, but one should challenge themselves and follow through with your individual hopes and dreams. If others want to come along, I know that two is always better than one. Together, more could be accomplished as well as having a greater understanding and meanings of what is to be seen moving forward.

    I, through telling my story, have come out feeling I could face anything life presents to me with the newfound confidence I have in myself! I had plan to fulfill all my hopes and dreams of traveling to the continents I had not been. That has remained my ultimate vision, but if it is not meant to be, there are many other visions in my life. Being a grandmother to a newborn baby girl named Hannah, my daughter is having her first baby at age thirty-seven. Living near me to nurture and spoil as grandmothers have the prerogative to do so.

    I know that if there is a will, there is a way, and it can be done! Through prayer to our Maker, all hopes and dreams are possible! I can accomplish anything I want to achieve and do with determination and knowledge of how to fulfill my own desires. I follow the path to doing them with God leading me to the way as he led me to come to the closing and healing of writing my autobiography. I was able to accept and listen to my own needs for once in my life. Love myself, and through my emotional history, I understood to follow

A TURBULENT LIFE ? ? ?

my own intuition. I can pursue my hopes and dreams as I have seen beautiful scenery and adventures in all the states, including Hawaii and Alaska, if only once or several times as well as the twenty-five foreign countries and terrains I have been blessed to see. Moving through life as I ponder all the beauty surrounding me, there are many more countries I have not seen, but the good thing to me is seeing scenes in photos, magazines such as *National Geographic* or specials on TV is not like having your own firsthand experiences, but it comes a close second as showing animals, areas, and scenes I may not have been able to see on my own.

A true friend has Christ in their heart, I have found is one you can abuse, neglect, tolerate, and best of all, just keep still with you. No matter what, a true friend will love you unconditionally like one of your family. A friendship that cleanses the damaging words or actions that have been seen or heard calms you by listening and witnessing your impurities of body and soul. A discussion ensues with me in front of a fire I love so dearly as the flames open innermost thoughts in the patterns that warms me to my inner soul with one who listens intently. Sharing blessings and travels on road trips together with all the hazards set before us with much laughter in seeing all the states not once but some twice with our road trips.

Trafficked roads in large cities, she saw me frozen behind the wheel, telling me to go with horns honking, and I did realize the miracle as I drove, not to have any accidents. Then I drove following the GPS as it told me to turn into oncoming traffic stopped at the light as people stared in our car motioning to back up and go straight on our way. I didn't believe I had ever laughed so hard with my eyes closed not to watch the drama unfold.

We rode on dirt roads, collecting rocks as they were free in hoping to get on the highway. Alleluia! We did, and the adventures we shared shall never be forgotten as it is some of the greatest highlights in my life. I shared it with a friend and learned what sisterhood was like, even with ups and downs. As she had written a poem to me when we first met, we found ourselves as friends and room mothers with our sons growing up as playmates. Friendships taken lightly often come to abrupt endings. Leaving behind the generosity of others and owing multiple depts. In later years, we became roommates, and the blessing best to me was learning sistership and the fun I had missed.

Faithful friends, children, and grandchildren understands you as a sister or mother and as a believer in Christ with only acknowledging my abilities to see beauty and harmony throughout my journey on earth. I have love in my heart with every step I take. Jesus, from afar, is calling me and saying, "Love oneself, but also be guarded as not to put myself in a situation to be controlled by others! Rely on yourself and faith to guide you!" With every beat of my heart, I come to know who I truly am. My every step forward is a cleansing of negativity and only of positiveness with a smile warming others' hearts in visiting earth. My ultimate destiny is with God calling me one day to **HEAVENLY PARADISE!**

About the Author

Grace Boykin is a native of Mobile, Alabama, but she moved to Clearwater, Florida. She received a BA degree in social science and secondary education from Flagler College in St. Augustine, Florida. She studied art in Europe with Spring Hill College, Mobile, Alabama. She made her debut in Mobile and was a member of the Mardi Gras Court. For several years, she was employed in Walt Disney World and resided in Orlando, Florida.

Boykin taught geography in Dunedin Junior High School and taught history in several schools throughout Melbourne, Florida. She tutored braille at the Florida School of Deaf and Blind for four years in St. Augustine. Also, she taught and created a mass media curriculum for high school students and directed the high school play *To Serve a Higher King* in Palm Bay, Florida.

She was an active member of the Clearwater/Tampa Bay Chapter of the National Society of Arts and Letters and served as president, chairman of "Career Award Luncheon," program chairman, and member of the board.

As a longtime member of the Clearwater Chapter DAR, she served as a scholarship and junior membership chairman and as a personal page to the Florida State Regent, National Page at the Eighty-Fifth Continental Congress in Washington, DC, a DAR chaplain, and Clearwater Chapter, Children of the American Revolution copresident.

She was a past member of the Clearwater/St. Petersburg Chapter, National Wild Turkey Federation, Ducks Unlimited, and Tampa Bay Area Safari Club.

Boykin was also a charter president of the ladies' group of Rotary International started in England and Ireland. International Inner Wheel, Melbourne, Florida. She is a Paul Harris Fellow of Rotary

International. She is a licensed real estate salesperson with the Florida Department of Business and Professional Regulation. Past Florida Real Estate holder of selling land and homes.

In Mobile, Alabama, she is a co-owner and vice president of Tensaw Land & Timber Company and a former board of director and served as a trustee.

Boykin has traveled to all the states, including Hawaii and Alaska, and twenty-five countries and many more than once. She has published works of poetry and editor of other books as well as the fiction book *The Southern Hunt,* which is based on the story of the life of Frank W. Boykin. Also, an autobiography called *South of the Hill,* which is copyrighted but unpublished, about political years of Frank W. Boykin as a US Congressman for twenty-eight years, 1930s–1960s.

The self-help book and autobiography of Grace Boykin is called *A Turbulent Life ? ? ?.*

Grace Boykin is a resident of Milton, Florida.